Just Cause Just Facts

To order additional copies, please contact us.
BookSurge, LLC
www.booksurge.com
1-866-308-6235
orders@booksurge.com

Just Cause Just Facts

Stephen A. Miller

Booksurge.com
2005

Just Cause Just Facts

TABLE OF CONTENTS

PREFACE / PROLOGUE

The Enron story explodes, the Worldcom story explodes, there have been a volcanic flow of corporate related Wall Street crimes careening at the American voting and nonvoting public. Jobs have been lost, pensions have been lost, corporate crooks and the accounting firms who are supposed to oversee and certify the financial statements have crushed many people. The bean counters were happy to collect their fat fees while they looked the other way. The accountants like to term their criminal acts as creative accounting.

The lame excuses I keep hearing by government officials and media reporters should insult our intelligence by their consistency of falsely claiming to get tough with the crooks that ride to their offices in limousines. The workers lose their jobs and the stockholders pay fines after the management is caught. The news media spews out baloney about get tough laws and the regulators claim to be restoring faith in the American capital markets.

This story features criminal acts including jury tampering and falsifying the transcript of a criminal trial by a federal district court judge. It also will expose the criminal act of obstruction of justice by 19 other federal judges including all nine Supreme Court Justices. Do American citizens want a remedy for these problems?

The government prosecutors and regulators have been protecting the perpetrators of these crimes and there is no end in sight. The years just keep passing by while more fraud is uncovered and then white washed. The really big crooks are protected while the corporations are fined. The fines get paid by the shareholders allowing the executives to go unpunished. Can that be why campaign contributions, $2,000 plate dinners, fund our political representatives? These must be wonderful gatherings to attend. A group of criminals able to write laws that sanctify their crimes while socializing and enjoying the finest dining and entertainment available.

When I began to write this story, it was years before Enron, Worldcom, and the rest. I was confident that my story was so spectacular that it would produce a scandal so controversial that a new era would be born. Now I can plainly see that no matter how flagrant the crimes keep getting nothing is about to make any difference.

The politicians go through the motions. There have been hearings resulting in proposals. A new law was written following the Enron bankruptcy and the downfall of its accountants, Arthur Anderson. This law was created because Senator Sarbanes and Congressman Oxley wanted the public to believe that the current laws were insufficient to deal with Enron. That claim is a pure hoax and both Sarbanes and Oxley know it. To know that the Sarbanes-Oxley Act was necessary you would need to believe that laws against corporate fraud did not exist.

The story I have written seems so farfetched that it appears to be fiction. My imagination could never dream up the verbatim statements contained in this story. The story is a real criminal case of which I am the defendant. It's a case that the government wanted to keep from a trial, and because I was innocent of committing the crime, I needed a trial to clear my name.

There have been many stories written about trials both criminal and civil. These stories have been written in narrative form with a few quotes of important statements. Because I feel that a huge portion of the dialogue transcribed during hearings and during the trial of this case are not only remarkable but also very entertaining I have decided to use much of the real dialogue as the main portion of this story.

JUST CAUSE / JUST FACTS is a story charged with powerful decisions by senior government and media officials which are contrary to both laws and common sense. JUST CAUSE / JUST FACTS is a story which provides evidence of a massive criminal conspiracy joined by more than 20 federal judges including all nine United States Supreme Court Justices.

This story began in 1987, when I became a victim of a fraud to manipulate the global price of copper by the officials of COMEX, The New York Commodities Exchange where the world's prices of copper, silver, and gold are traded. This fraud jacked the price of copper from the $.65 per pound to a range from $1.15 to $1.60 per pound until 1997. The officials of COMEX generated about $9,000,000,000 in illegally controlled profits yearly for the worldwide producers of copper who mine and refine more than 18,000,000,000 pounds of copper annually. This is in addition to the illegal trading profits being generated to the

COMEX officials who manipulated and controlled the futures contract prices daily for ten years until 1997.

This story is bizarre and seems to be preposterous. The old adage, truth is stranger than fiction clearly applies to this story. More than half the story are real quotes contained in the court record of hearings, the trial, and the pleadings before and during the appellate phase of the case. I tried to make it as easy to read and entertaining as possible. Therefore, I have omitted the use of quotation marks and just used the speaker i.e. Judge Nevas, AUSA Appleton, Defense Attorney Reeve, Defendant Miller, etc., etc.

It was hard for me to believe that federal judges would resort to obvious and ludicrous lies. A fiction writer would never expect his audience to believe the real life behavior of the federal judges involved in this case. The exaggerations used by fiction writers are used to try to make their stories more entertaining but they could not dream of the thoughts by federal judges to be so inane as were exhibited in this case. It is easy to see why federal judges prohibit Court TV from broadcasting federal trials. Throughout my vast experience within the federal judicial system I read many truly bizarre cases contained within the legal briefs I read personally.

It is my hope to be able to expose to American citizens and voters the true nature of the deep seated corruption masked by massive doses of hypocrisy spewed out as propaganda to brain wash us. I never recognized the fact that I had been brain washed until 1998, when my petition for a writ of mandamus to the Supreme Court of the United States was denied. It is important to consider that when people have been brainwashed they are not aware of it. It is also considered insulting to be accused of having been brainwashed, so it is a very delicate subject to discuss. But the American government is a master of mind control which is a deliberate action exercised on a daily basis by the media, the hidden arm of our government. This is a radical conclusion only attained after my personal experiences contained in this story.

I had meetings with CBS 60 Minutes, The Wall Street Journal, The Washington Post, and many others to expose the fraud and the government regulators who protected this fraud. The reason I was told by the reporters was that the story was too complicated for them to publish. One of the first writers I met was Michael Lewis who wrote a story he titled Copper: up to a point, published by the British magazine BUSINESS. From that point in time forward Michael Lewis or his editors refused to follow up the story I provided to him.

America seems to suffer from an increasing preference for fantasy over reality, and to be losing the ability to tell which is which.

CHAPTER 1
"The truth is not a defense?"

On December 7th, Pearl Harbor Day, 1994, at shortly after 2:00 in the afternoon there were six F.B.I. agents standing on the steps outside my apartment with their guns drawn preparing to arrest me for an extortion charge after I opened my door to let them into my apartment.

I was expecting a call from Richard Jossen at 2:00 so when the phone rang and I heard Richard say hello and began speaking I was a little surprised to hear the female voice of F.B.I. Special Agent Lisa Skelly break into the conversation to ask me to open the front door. When I opened the door to my apartment at 284 Carlton Avenue in the Fort Green Section of Brooklyn, N.Y. I was surprised to see a bunch of guns pointing at me. The agents rushed into the apartment and asked where my weapons were hidden. I was immediately handcuffed and I responded by saying there weren't any weapons and there is only the cat who calmly sat on the floor as the agents were scurrying around looking for weapons. After the agents decided to believe that there were no weapons and were preparing to bring me to their headquarters for processing, I asked them not to lock my cat, Knucklehead, in the apartment because he might starve and to please bring him and the boxes of cat food upstairs to my neighbor for his new home. The agents pleasantly carried Knucklehead and his food upstairs.

I believed in the American judicial system. I had confidence that federal judges were carefully chosen, and I expected that when they took their oath to protect and uphold the Constitution, it was a solemn oath. I didn't have a clue that I had been brainwashed throughout my life by my family's values, and the greatest propaganda machine ever devised. I had just turned 52 years old on October 1st, 1994.

Being arrested is a very disarming experience in spite of what I had been doing during the past few weeks. I knew that being arrested was a possibility but I had expected other things to happen. The F.B.I. brought me to their headquarters in Manhattan and asked me to agree to being extradited to Bridgeport, Ct. I saw no reason to question or to fight extradition so I agreed on the spot. I had no idea of the government's motive at the time to want this case to be in Connecticut rather than the correct venue, which was the Eastern District of New York. I was not a fugitive from Connecticut and there was no legal basis not to bring this case in the correct venue.

After the paper work was finalized I was brought to the Brooklyn Metropolitan Detention Center to await the U.S. Marshals from Connecticut to transport me there. My first stop was New Haven where I met the attorney assigned by the court, United States District Judge Alan H. Nevas. The attorney's name was Richard Reeve and he impressed me as a very conscientious person who claimed that he hated the government and wanted to end his legal career after working on a high profile case. Dick wanted to return to teaching he was telling me because he was appalled by the constant, endless corruption that impacted the criminal justice system. I was thinking that I had really gotten lucky because I was sure that I would be the high profile case Dick was looking to represent and my case would expose the government he despised.

About a week later I met Dick again in the Bridgeport, North Avenue jail which would be where I lived until Judge Nevas decided to prevent me from my right to trial protected by the Fifth, Sixth, and Fourteenth Amendments. The most important revelation this story was written to expose is the failure by the Judicial Branch of our government to honor its oath to uphold and protect the Constitution of the United States of America.

I know that readers of this story will find it impossible to believe the incidents revealed on the official record by the Federal Judges in this case. Readers are going to suspect that I created false statements because some statements will sound bizarre and even dumb. It is farfetched to me that educated judges would make statements on the record or write an order or disposition that is an obvious blatant lie. But in this context, keep in mind that in this context President Clinton claimed he didn't inhale his marijuana, and he didn't know that oral sex was sex too.

American society has been dumbed down to hear its officials make ridiculous statements to us and we dismiss them. Our society fails to get angry. It has failed to get angry at a rash of corporate and Wall Street scandals and rip offs that began with Enron, Worldcom, Tyco, etc., etc.

and our society has failed to get angry at our government that protects the perpetrators of these frauds.

I didn't just get angry at the perpetrators of the fraud that victimized me, I decided to do something about it. I kept pushing government officials to do their job. I kept creating very clever traps that would force the perpetrators of the crime before a jury in a Federal Court.

I remember Dick's beginning because he abruptly explained to me that he had conferred with four other attorneys about my case. Dick claimed that they all had agreed that I had no way to win and should therefore plead guilty and try to get the most lenient sentence possible from Judge Nevas. I immediately responded to Dick that he had very little knowledge of my case having spent no time with me, and that I didn't care if 4,000 attorneys thought I should plead guilty; I intended to go to trial. This meeting changed my opinion of Dick Reeve. I would later learn after a series of events that Reeve was working for the government and with the government to wreck any chance I had to receive a fair trial.

I began to contact a few attorneys in Bridgeport who I knew personally to represent me. None of them asked me for any retainer and they all said that they were too busy to represent me. I knew Gary Mastronardi very well. We played golf, we dined, and we socialized at local night clubs back around 1989. Gary and I tried to encourage the company I had worked for to hire him for a civil suit to recover more than $50,000,000 they had over paid for copper used in their manufacturing process. This company, Echlin, made after market repair parts using millions of pounds of copper each year. Gary wanted a $250,000 retainer to initiate a law suit but for reasons Echlin refused to give, Echlin management was not the least bit interested in the welfare of the shareholders for whom they worked. Interestingly, Gary's main criminal client in Bridgeport, Gino Cappozziello was serving weekends on a one year sentence. I met with Gino by going to Catholic Mass because Gino was segregated in the jail's hospital each weekend. I asked him to ask Gary to represent me but Gary declined with no explanation. Gary would be one of my witnesses I called for my defense when I eventually went to trial.

In late November '94, before my arrest I had given a package of documents to Bobby DiNicola, which contained the critical evidence I would need in the event I was arrested. I called Bobby to drop off the package to Dick Reeve's office. Shortly thereafter Dick brought the package to me at the Bridgeport Correctional Center so we could begin preparing for my trial. Dick and I spent two intensive days focusing and discussing the evidence, which I had prepared during the prior seven years concerning the rigging of global copper prices by the manipulation of copper futures contracts by the senior officials of COMEX. John Moore, Chairman of COMEX, and Richard Jossen, Vice Chairman, would be put on the witness stand by the government during my trial. John and Richard were the perpetrators of the manipulation of the copper futures contract prices.

Dick asked me many questions to explain parts of the evidence to learn whether or not there might be a doubt as to my allegations that the five member "Quotations Committee" team at COMEX was in fact violating the written rules which had been approved by the C.F.T.C. (Commodities Futures Trading Commission) established to create settlement prices on all of the contract months.

This story is about money and a massive criminal conspiracy. The technicalities about copper futures contracts are a very minor part of this story, but I want the reader to have some idea of basic facts relative to this fraud.

After the close of the market on each commodity the prices of deferred months that trade infrequently must be brought into line with the active month contract. The primary and only reason to adjust these prices are for margin calls. Margin calls are made to the losing side in order to make sure that sufficient funds are there to pay the winning side. The two sides are a) long, meaning the buy side of the contract, and b) short, meaning the sell side of the contract. So if the market price increases the long side is gaining value making the short side send money into the clearinghouse. And the reverse is true if the market price decreases, then the short side is gaining value making the long side send money into the clearinghouse. The clearinghouse is there to protect the winners' equity so they will get paid by the losers. The settlement price rules are very simple so the quotation committee members are there to follow simple rules, not to make complex judgments only capable by highly sophisticated traders.

I answered Dick's questions directly and clearly for two solid days. His questions were very insightful indicating that Dick had a very good grasp of the issues involved. At the end of the second day, Dick said, "I think you're right."

I replied, "Do you think I'm sitting here?"

He looked at me for a minute with a question on his face and I replied, "You don't think I'm sitting here, you know I'm sitting here. You don't think I'm right, you know I'm right. We aren't talking about beyond a reasonable doubt, we are talking about black and white conclusive facts which leave no doubt whatsoever." I think lawyers are trained to believe that there is always some doubt, even when the facts are simple and the evidence is unequivocal.

The crime that made me a victim was very simple and very

unsophisticated. During the trial these facts will all be brought out by the testimony from the principle perpetrator, John Moore and me. John Moore elevated himself from the Chairman of the Quotations Committee when this fraud began, to the Chairman of COMEX itself. I reported this crime to the government in October 1987, because I was a victim, not as a whistle blower. I believe that there is a distinct difference between a victim and a whistle blower. A whistle blower is an associate of the perpetrators who decides that his associates are committing a crime, which he or she does not approve of committing. A whistle blower is never the victim of the crime he is reporting. To be more clear, a rat or snitch is a perpetrator of the crime who decides to help the prosecutor against his fellow conspirators in order to have his sentence reduced for the crimes he has committed. A victim who reports a crime is not a rat or a whistle blower.

To this point in time I had been arraigned and had been given a bond hearing. AUSA Appleton and Judge Nevas decided to deny me any bail regardless of the fact that no injuries to anyone had occurred and that no weapons had been brandished by anyone or found in my apartment. Judge Nevas claimed that I was a danger to the community and should be held without even a high bond. The basis for bond in our system is to not punish defendants until they have been found guilty. Defendants are presumed innocent until found guilty, right?

Ironically, Judge Nevas, AUSA Robert Appleton, and defense counsel Reeve were all fully aware that I am fighting to have a trial. If they release me on my own recognizance there is no chance that I will fail to appear for my trial, and they know that. To deny bail in this case is going to be step one of many other steps to prevent any remedy provided and guaranteed by our Constitution.

During one of our meetings Dick told me that Judge Nevas would hold a hearing to order a psychological evaluation to decide if I was competent for trial. I asked Dick why my competency is an issue in the first place and Dick replied that Judge Nevas wanted to make sure that I couldn't use competency as an issue for an appeal. I then explained to Dick that I had no intention of using an insanity defense for any reason and that I wanted him to write an affidavit to waive any use of an insanity defense for any purpose whatsoever. I was contending to be an expert. Any use of an insanity defense would diminish my contention for being an expert. Experts deemed officially crazy have slightly less impact with the jury.

On the other hand the government wanted to prevent me from going to trial by claiming that I was incompetent for trial. In line with Dick's warning (AUSA) Assistant United States Attorney Appleton filed a Motion for a hearing on competency. I literally had to force Dick to mention to the court that I had requested him to write and file an affidavit to waive any use of an insanity defense. The court responded, "I don't care what he wants to waive, I'm going to order an evaluation."

Dr. Paul Amble was hired to come to the Bridgeport jail to interview me for the court. We spent about three hours, which began with the basic three tests all psychologists use to decide competency. The first question is to have the defendant subtract by sevens from 100, (93,86,79, etc.). The next question is to remember an article of clothing such as a tie or collar of the shirt worn by the psychologist which he intends to ask about five minutes later. The last question is to identify the time drawn by the hands of a clock drawn by the psychologist. Dr. Amble asked me to discuss my marriage and other personal issues of my life along with discussing the factors involved in my case. I was very open and expansive with Dr. Amble throughout this evaluation because I had nothing to hide.

Dr. Amble reported back to the court that I was competent for trial. A follow up hearing was then convened for Judge Nevas to set dates for choosing a jury and then to proceed to trial. Jury selection was scheduled for April 11, 1995, to be followed by a trial scheduled for April 18th.

On April 11th, the U.S. Marshals transported me to court for the voir dire and my jury was selected. On April 13th I was brought back into court for a surprise hearing on AUSA Appleton's <u>MOTION IN LIMINE TO EXCLUDE EVIDENCE</u>. The proceeding began at 10: 00 A.M. His Honor, United States District Judge Alan H. Nevas seated himself on the bench and began.

Nevas: All right. This is the government's motion in limine to exclude evidence, Mr. Appleton.

Appleton: Thank you your honor. As your honor's aware the government has filed a motion to exclude evidence in this case that is scheduled to commence next Tuesday. The court is aware the defendant is charged in a two-count indictment, count one charging the defendant with Hobbs Act conspiracy; count two charging the defendant with use of an interstate facility to commit extortion. The government has demonstrated in its memorandum that the defendant entered into an agreement with more than one person to attempt to obtain money by the threat of force, violence, or actual force. The elements of that would be the agreement that the defendant intentionally joined that conspiracy.

Your honor, as the court is obviously aware and is anticipated by the government, the defendant is anticipated to offer evidence that the reasons for his actions were such to bring attention to a perceived fraud and price fixing conspiracy to rig the global price of copper by manipulating copper futures contract prices traded on the COMEX Exchange in New York. Your honor the government is moving to exclude evidence on that issue, as it is not probative or relevant in this case. Whether or not this fraud existed, or whether this defendant is even right about his theories, does not have any relevant bearing on any issue in this case. The government cites in its memorandum that even if the defendant's contentions were true, assuming they are, and just for purposes of argument **the truth is not a defense.**

Does Mr. Appleton have a rational understanding of the proceedings? The prosecutor just told the court that, "The truth is not a defense." Is it possible in any federal district court in America that the court will agree with a prosecutor that the truth is not a defense? Would any fiction writer consider writing such an inane statement by a federal prosecutor made on the record?

Appleton: The issue of whether or not this defendant committed those acts for the purpose of drawing attention to this fraud does not bear on those issues. So I think there are a couple of areas that the defendant is likely to pursue if this case were to proceed on Tuesday.

When Appleton states, "if this case were to proceed on Tuesday", is the first indication that this case is not going to proceed because we all understand that this case is only intended to expose senior officials of our government in their part to allow and condone a massive fraud. The jury has been sworn in by the court, which means that the only legitimate reason to prevent my trial would occur if I waive my right to trial by pleading guilty.

Nevas: You say that the defendant would seek to admit evidence that the fraud theory is valid, you mean through his own testimony?

Appleton: Well I think there are a few ways it's going to be attempted. It's anticipated that he would call affirmative witnesses. People from the commodities exchange is one way, or he could cross-examine the government witnesses, the victims in this case. And I would submit in the latter that that is going to be beyond the scope of direct examination, because I'm certainly not going to ask them about any perceived fraud on the market which began in 1987. The questions by the government will only be concerning the relevant time period in connection with the threats that were articulated. Any affirmative efforts to subpoena witnesses to prove that this theory is valid would be something that the government would submit is completely irrelevant, because again, the validity of the theory has no bearing on the case.

The last way is for the defendant to testify about the theory and about the reasons for why he acted.

The government is not going to say that it does not have to prove that this defendant attempted to obtain property through the threat of violence. The government has to prove that. If the defendant's defense is, I didn't intend to obtain property through violence but I intended to draw attention to the fraud, the government is not going to object to him testifying as to that, but it seems to me that anything beyond that is not relevant because all that is relevant is what he intended at the time. His efforts to report criminal allegations to the C.F.T.C. and to the Justice Department, and to elected officials, and to the media for the past seven years has no relevance. This case is about extortion and not about copper fixing frauds or other theories that occurred or may have occurred.

Nevas: Mr. Reeve?

Reeve: Yes your honor. I'd like to address two things, the facts and then secondly the relevant statutes. Because much of the factual matter in this case is not disputed, Mr. Miller's defense is not that he did not write these letters. Its not that they weren't communicated to the individuals involved. Mr. Miller is a whistle blower who has tried for many years to convince various government agencies, I think the court is aware that he has gone to the F.B.I. and to the U.S. Attorney's office…

Nevas: Mr. Reeve I'm really not interested.

Reeve: Your honor, let me address these documents because I think it's important to start with respect to the offenses that are charged and to look at what's not charged. What's not charged is 875I, which in my view is a lesser-included offense of 875(b). The element that's missing from 875(c), which is contained in 875(b), is the intent to extort. (c) requires a general intent, an intent to communicate the threat. The communication of the threat has to be done intentionally. It can't be done by mistake, inadvertence, etc.

Nevas: So what you are suggesting Mr. Reeve is if the government had charged him with 875(c) he would have pled guilty?

Reeve: I'm not suggesting that your honor because that's a hypothetical situation. If the person in fact did not intend to take money from someone, but intended to make the threat for another goal, I think that is the question in this situation. If there is no intent to extort, if the threat is communicated for some other reason, those are the issues that the court has to decide. The court could rule that Mr. Miller's beliefs are all irrelevant, that's one possibility. Another possibility is to allow evidence about his belief, but not the validity about those beliefs. And the third option for the court to allow the defendant to stand up and say that's what I intended to do without providing the jury with the background so they can assess whether or not that really was his belief. So the jury can say maybe that really was his intent.

Nevas: So the jury ends up determining whether or not there was a fraud, is that what the jury is going to decide?

Reeve: Well your honor I think there is a middle ground and you don't get into the validity of the theories. Now Mr. Miller I have to say would like this to be a trial about the validity about the approach and his beliefs, but then the court is going to have to draw some lines about what's admissible and what's not. There is no dispute that there were previous extortionate letters which went unanswered and when brought to the attention of the government by Mr. Miller himself, the government took no action in any way. From Mr. Miller's perspective, that shows he continued to make efforts and that this is part of an ongoing continuous series of efforts to expose what he believes is a fraud. I understand the court's concerns about that.

It was at this point in the hearing which involved factors that Dick had learned during our intensive two day meeting which should have given him an opportunity to motion the court to dismiss the charges against me. The court would then have been forced to hear decisive information, which it clearly didn't want exposed to a jury.

Appleton: Your honor I think that what I'm hearing is that even if there was an 875(c) charge there would still be an attempt to justify it.

Nevas: Yes but the court would be able to limit the attempt at justification considerably greater than under (b) where as Mr. Reeve points out, you have to prove an intent to extort.

Appleton: I think that's right your honor. I think a charge under 875(c) that this defendant would have no defense.

Nevas: Wouldn't it make more sense to proceed under (c) than (b)? I would say if the charge was 875(c) there would be absolutely no defense even assuming what Mr. Miller is saying is true. All right let me go off the record for a minute and ask counsel to come to the bench. We'll take a short recess.

After the bench conference Dick came back to the defense table and began telling me that I had no chance to win my trial without any witnesses allowed to corroborate my testimony. The best recommendation was to plead guilty to 875(c) and serve five years.

I told him that if I was denied any witnesses regardless of the merits pertaining to any specific witness concerning my defense, that maybe the jury would recognize the obvious injustice, unless they were all in a coma, and they might acquit me. This is precisely the reason that the

Bill of Rights provided our jury system. If that failed, I would have a good chance that the Second Circuit would reverse the judgment on appeal. I told Reeve that I wouldn't plead guilty even if Judge Nevas sentenced me to five minutes. Furthermore after this charade I'd be crazy to trust Judge Nevas about anything. I explained to him that it was very unlikely that the government or the judge would chance having any trial because they both knew that I was capable of exposing their conspiracy with their own evidence written by me.

Then Dick began to agree with me that there wouldn't be a trial because Judge Nevas is going to claim that you are incompetent for trial. He is going to order a competency evaluation again by a B.O.P. (Bureau of Prisons) psychologist. At that point I was locked up until the recess ended.

Before court reconvened I asked the marshal to ask Dick to visit me again. I decided to tell Dick that I changed my mind and was ready to plead guilty. If Judge Nevas decided to accept my guilty plea on the record then he had to decide that I was competent; at that time I would make that argument on the record.

I also urged Dick to file a motion to dismiss my charges so he could argue that he knew about factors I had told him when we had had that intense two day session. Dick refused to motion to dismiss my charges. The letters I had written to Richard Jossen and to John Moore contained language, which allowed him to cross-examine them about the fraud they had been rigging since 1987, which Dick was afraid to use or more likely was happy not to use. Dick was free to stop practicing criminal law at any time he wished so I believe it's foolish to consider that the apparent intimidation from Judge Nevas bothered him at all. It was Dick's free choice to represent the government. After all it was Dick's choice to volunteer to the court and the government to change its charge to 875(c) to eliminate the burden of proving that my intent was to extort money and not to use the court as a forum to expose senior government officials who had conspired to allow the fraud to continue.

I was allowed back into the courtroom and Judge Nevas began the hearing again.

Nevas: Before we proceed any further, I think it's appropriate that the court place on the record certain conversation and discussions that have taken place off the record at the bench and also in chambers. Essentially the court made the suggestion to counsel after listening to argument that if the government would agree to charge Mr. Miller under 875(c) rather than under 875 (b), would he agree to plead guilty to that charge? That would cap his exposure at five years. It would lower his guidelines of course. It would give the court an opportunity to frame a sentence that the court believes would be helpful to him in the sense that the court would recommend a medical facility for whatever period of incarceration the court would impose. The court could put him on some form of supervised release following his release from incarceration with conditions for treatment and mental health counseling. It seemed to the court that that was a reasonable proposal that was fair to the government in the sense that he would be pleading to what the court considers to be a serious offense. But from Mr. Miller's point of view, he would be limiting his exposure. The court asked the government what it thought his guideline range would be if he was convicted of the charges and the government suggested his range would be 87 to 108 months. Mr. Reeve thinks that maybe high, and I don't know. No one knows. But in any event it's a significant exposure on his part.

Mr. Reeve indicated in chambers that his client was not interested in that proposal and Mr. Appleton indicated that the government would agree provided that he be sentenced at the maximum five years. Mr. Reeve indicated even if his client was willing to consider the proposal he wouldn't accept it with the condition that he be incarcerated at a medical facility.

That means a psychiatric institution for the criminally insane to brand me as crazy making any contention that I am an expert in anything, ridiculous.

Nevas: The court finds itself in a real dilemma because the court believes that the proposal is very fair and reasonable. By rejecting the proposal and electing to go to trial and exposing himself, if convicted of course, to a very significant sentence.

The court now calls into question his competence and whether or not he has the ability to assist his lawyer in the defense of his case. Title 18 U.S.C. section 4241 says that on the issue of competency to stand trial, if there is reasonable cause to believe that the defendant may presently be suffering from a mental disease, rendering him mentally incompetent to the extent that he is unable to understand the nature and consequences of the proceedings against him, his insistence that he go to trial on the indictment, and his insistence that he be permitted to go into his whole theory, that his defense is that he is right about this massive conspiracy and fraud going on. His insistence on doing that is now causing the court to begin to think that perhaps there may be a problem with his ability to assist properly in his defense. Essentially what the court is considering at this moment is to vacate the trial and remand him to Butner for an evaluation. Mr. Reeve?

Reeve: Your honor Mr. Miller has indicated to me he would like to address the court and I think he should be permitted to do that.

Nevas: Mr. Appleton?

Appleton: I have no objection your honor.

Nevas: All right Mr. Miller I'll hear from you.

Miller: Thank you your honor. There has been a miscommunication completely. The miscommunication is very simple and that is this. I did agree to plead guilty in the discussion with Mr. Reeve if there was any chance at all I would avoid a psychiatric facility. He and I went down the three options here and I said my first choice is to just get a fair trial without any limitations, which I think is a very normal, common sense desire. If in fact there are limitations put on the trial which has been the subject of the government's motion for this hearing we are all in now, I was considering taking a chance that the jury might see that there is something being hidden and evaluate my defense appropriately in that light, and acquit me of the charges.

During the recess in our discussion, Mr. Reeve brought up this issue by saying, 'If you're willing to take this tremendous sentence instead of just a five year max, with an investigation into your allegations by the F.B.I., a legitimate investigation, your mental health is questionable.' I then made this emphatic to him, and now I want to emphasize to the court that your characterization of my choice is not accurate. Maybe you heard it inaccurately from Mr. Reeve. I don't know where the discrepancy lies between myself and you your honor, but no defendant can be competent to plead guilty, and incompetent to exercise his constitutional right to trial guaranteed by the Sixth Amendment of the Bill of Rights; simultaneously.

Innocent defendants have been found guilty in the past and if the court and the defense counsel are both helping to prosecute the defendant during trial, the risk of conviction is raised dramatically. This is the purpose for the higher courts to decide. If the lower court always conducted fair trials there would be no need for any oversight by a higher court. I have sat before this court silently from the time I was arrested and arraigned. This court has no basis whatsoever to suggest that I maybe incompetent for trial, and it's conclusion that if I refuse to plead guilty, and refuse to waive my right, the same right as any criminal defendant is guaranteed under the Sixth Amendment, this court can rest assured that I will file an interlocutory appeal on your order.

If my judgment on this matter seems contrary to yours, or to what you think would be a normal, guilty defendant's way of approaching the situation, it is because I am not guilty. It isn't true for you or accurate for you to decide I am incompetent for trial because I perceive risk differently than you do your honor especially since your honor has no idea of what the testimony and evidence will eventually be during trial. I intend to expose senior government officials who deliberately decided to allow a massive and simple criminal fraud to continue since 1987, and that is the only reason given today in open court by Mr. Appleton himself, to falsely claim me to be incompetent for trial and for you to stigmatize me by recommending that I be held at a psychiatric facility.

I spoke to Mr. Reeve in the lock up and he hasn't been out of my sight, so I know he hasn't conveyed this to you, I reevaluated where I am as of right now based on the proceedings here. I'll plead guilty under 875(c) which was the offer you just in fact made.

Nevas: Well it wasn't an offer by the government; it was a proposal by the court.

Miller: All right the proposal. If I termed it offer instead of proposal, I can just say I'm sorry. I'm not an attorney. I'm just trying to communicate as effectively as possible. I asked him if he would request that I be transported out of the Bridgeport Correctional Center and put into a federal facility right away. And that whenever your honor schedules the sentence under that guilty plea, that I be brought back here for that purpose. That's what I just asked for. So I absolutely did not come anywhere near anything that you put on the record.

Nevas: I want to make something very clear.

Miller: Could I say one more thing?

Nevas: Let me just interrupt you Mr. Miller, and tell you something because I don't want there to be any misunderstanding about this. Whether you plead guilty and I sentence you, or whether you go to trial and you're convicted and I sentence you, whichever way I sentence you, you can be certain that I am going to recommend that you go to a medical facility during the period of your incarceration. And any term of supervised release that I impose is going to carry with it a condition, which will require you to continue mental health treatment.

Miller: Now may I speak please?

Nevas: Yes.

Miller: Since you're going to recommend that I go to a psychiatric facility...

Nevas: I didn't say psychiatric, I said medical facility.

Miller: Well medical, I don't have physical problems which concern this court, is that true your honor?

Nevas: I think you do have a mental health problem, yes.

Miller: Okay, I'm saying I'm not going to a medical facility for a physical problem, which concerns this court.

Nevas: I am unaware of any physical problem.

Miller: That's why I say psychiatric facility. I think we are communicating here. Then obviously my only hope to avoid a psychiatric facility, is to be acquitted. You put me into a corner. You say if you want a trial you've got to be incompetent so I am going to have you evaluated and then we'll commit you by falsely claiming you're dangerous. I am going to keep you in prison regardless. I got more than I bargained for, I can tell you that. A jury was chosen two days ago to conduct a legitimate trial. My attorney coached you and Mr. Appleton to change the charge to 875(c) which he claims changes intent to general intent, whatever that may mean.

Nevas: Your attorney did what he should do.

Miller: Well I directed him to motion this court to dismiss my case because my right to trial is being violated to protect corrupt government officials who are up to their ears in a massive criminal conspiracy with the Wall Street crooks who will have to testify in order to prosecute me.

Nevas: Your attorney is representing you and what he considers your best interests.

Miller: My attorney is helping you to get me locked up without any trial into a psychiatric facility in order to ruin my credibility because he told me after a two day session studying the evidence I compiled for seven years that he knows I'm right. He knows I can win my trial unless you have fake jurors who are really government law enforcement agents or federal judges.

Reeve: Judge I'd like to put some things on the record if I can because of the comments that the court and Mr. Miller have argued. I think it should be clear as to what's going on here. Immediately after we met at side bar off the record I think your honor accurately summarized that conversation. I met with Mr. Miller after the side bar at counsel table for about 15 minutes. That's the 15-minute meeting that Mr. Miller referred to. I told him that I thought that there were a number of different options. One was going to trial on the indictment. One was to plead to the 875(c), and I told him that I thought based on our conversation off the record at side bar with respect to the 875(c) that the court would rule that he has no defense of any kind to that charge and therefore perhaps that was something that he should very carefully consider. He indicated to me that he wanted to go to trial unless his decision not to go to trial, excuse me, unless his decision to go to trial was going to result in a reversal in the court's competency decision. I told Mr. Miller that I had no information that that decision was going to be reversed, but nor would I bring that up with the court at any time because I didn't think that was an appropriate factor to bring up. We then met in chambers. I then met with Mr. Miller and told him in general terms the discussion that we had had in chambers, including the court's indication that if convicted there would be a recommendation by the court to a medical facility for mental related evaluation and treatment. Because when we were in chambers I had gotten the message from the marshal to come up because Mr. Miller had something important to say, which was that he had changed his position and that he wanted to plead guilty to 875(c) if the marshals would agree to move him out of the Bridgeport jail and the government agreed to a good faith investigation of his allegations about the copper market. When I told him that any sentence that the court would impose would include a recommendation of mental health treatment and evaluation at a federal medical center, which was unacceptable to Mr. Miller. And he then said, 'I want to go to trial because my only alternative to avoid psychiatric treatment at a federal medical facility and the possibility of forced medications and other problems meant to discredit me, would become a reality.' And so that's where we are right now and I don't think it's as much of a miscommunication as it is that I didn't communicate to the court in chambers that Mr. Miller's biggest fear was going to a federal medical center and he would do anything to avoid that, including pleading guilty.

I don't know that I explicitly indicated that in chambers because I didn't feel it was appropriate. We normally would not have these kinds of discussions but this is an unusual case and I think given the fact that Mr. Miller has indicated that there was a miscommunication; I don't think there is a miscommunication. I think we all agree now and I make those comments to make sure that the record is clear as to where we are right now.

Nevas: All right I think Mr. Miller's had his opportunity to speak and Mr. Reeve has too. And I think that's all very good. I don't know if there's anything you want to add Mr. Appleton?

Appleton: No your honor.

Nevas: Well I want to be candid about this. The court is now even more troubled than it was because of Mr. Miller's apparent inability to recognize that he does need some form of therapy. He just said on the record, to avoid a medical facility he will not plead guilty; he will go to trial hoping for an acquittal, risking a substantial period of incarceration. I think that's unrealistic and in my own amateurish way, it's delusional. Mr. Miller is deluding himself if he thinks he doesn't require treatment for what I think is a psychiatric problem. His inability to understand that he has a problem gives the court serious concern. His refusal to consider anything other than a trial and hope for an acquittal so he can avoid being treated is exceedingly unrealistic and causes the court to question his competence to assist properly in his defense. The court is going to order a competency examination at a federal facility; the court will then hold another hearing after that report is received.

Therefore the jury that was selected will be discharged, the trial will not begin next week, and we'll await the findings of the mental health professionals. Anything else Mr. Appleton?

Appleton: Nothing from the government your honor.

Nevas: Mr. Reeve?

Reeve: No your honor.

Whereupon the matter was adjourned at 12:20 P.M. This specific time is going to become very important for what is going to happen during the next two hours in the chambers of Judge Nevas.

The jurors are now going to have to be contacted so they don't take time off from their work to come to court on the following Tuesday, April 18th. Two days later on April 15th, I read a short article published in the CONNECTICUT POST which reported as follows:

COMEX threat suspect committed

Bridgeport — A man who allegedly threatened to kill a current and former official of the New York Commodities Exchange unless they paid him $6 million has been committed to a federal prison in North Carolina for a psychological exam.

U.S. District Judge Alan H. Nevas issued the order for Stephen A. Miller, 52, of Brooklyn, N.Y. following a hearing on whether he could make an opening statement during his trial. During the proceeding Miller offered to plead guilty in exchange for not being sent to a psychological hospital.

As a result of the judge's order, Miller will be committed to the prison for the next thirty days. If he is found incompetent to stand trial, authorities could keep him for four months before seeking a renewal.

Meanwhile Nevas discharged the jury, which was to begin hearing evidence Tuesday. Should Miller be found competent to stand trial, a new jury would have to be picked.

The F.B.I. arrested Miller in December after he allegedly had a threatening letter delivered to the Westport home of Richard Jossen, a former Vice Chairman of COMEX.

A similar letter followed up by a telephone call was sent to the New Jersey home of John Moore, who is a current COMEX official.

The extortion charge carries a maximum sentence of 20 years in prison and a $250,000 fine.

MICHAEL P. MAYKO

After I read this article, the phrase, "following a hearing on whether he could make an opening statement during his trial" became astounding to me since nothing of the sort had occurred.

The next time I spoke with Dick Reeve was in June while I was being held at MCC (Metropolitan Correctional Center) the federal prison in lower Manhattan where all the pre-trial inmates are held for the Southern District of New York. I had been taken there instead of Butner, North Carolina for my competency evaluation.

I asked Dick why the court published a story about a hearing concerning the false assertion that I wanted to make an opening statement during the government's hearing which had nothing whatsoever pertaining to any opening statement issue.

Dick replied, "Didn't you see the motion I filed for an opening statement?"

I said, "No, please send me a copy."

When the mail arrived I noticed that the <u>DEFENDANT'S MOTION FOR OPENING STATEMENT</u> had been dated April 11, 1995, but it was time stamped, filed in the court on April 13, 1995 at 2:19 P.M., two full hours after the hearing had been adjourned and an hour and 17 minutes after the court had filed it's own order for the competency evaluation. Not to mention the fact that Dick knew that there wasn't going to be a trial well before the hearing was adjourned. The only reason Dick filed that motion was to try his lame attempt to legitimize the lie Judge Nevas decided to publish in the CONNECTICUT POST. Judge Nevas, Bob Appleton, and Dick Reeve weren't going to publish the truth of what had happened during the hearing. They obviously had not planned that I wasn't going to plead guilty because I knew that their scheme was a bluff to avoid conducting my trial. When I had told the court I would plead guilty Nevas guessed right that I intended to trap him if he claimed I was competent to plead guilty.

Now the next time I spoke with Dick about the time stamps, which proved he had acted in bad faith, Dick decided to file a motion to withdraw from the case. Nevas not only decided to deny Dick's motion to withdraw, but Nevas himself decided to withdraw and turn my case over to Judge T.F. Gilroy Daly in Waterbury, Ct.

CHAPTER 2
THE OPENING STATEMENT

When the jury is brought into the court room the first event for it to hear are the opening statements from both sides. Different lawyers have their own styles but it is fairly standard that they try to appear likeable to the jurors. The old saw, a first impression is a lasting impression is the cornerstone of the opening statement. It should set the stage for the jury to hear the testimony by witnesses and observe the exhibits that will be presented.

Quite naturally the prosecutor will try to suggest that the government is august, fair, and is there to protect the citizens from criminals such as the one they are about to prosecute for that particular criminal's behavior. The government doesn't want jurors to suspect that it might be heavy handed even to criminal rogues that have performed vicious acts against American citizens. The government wants to claim that defendants are considered innocent until proven guilty.

The reverse will be true for the defense. The defense is there to protect the rights of the unfortunately accused and wrongly accused defendant who has committed no crime and is being falsely accused. The false accusation may be due to an honest mistake of misinterpreted evidence, or malicious witnesses and a malicious government prepared to falsely accuse this particular defendant.

The opening statement can and should be a very powerful portion of the trial when it is performed effectively. In the context of this case and this story, the opening statement will play a key role even throughout the appellate phase of the case. Because Judge Nevas decided to publish his false story in THE CONNECTICUT POST concerning an opening statement issue that Nevas claimed aborted the trial from April 1995, until September 1996, it will be beneficial to expand on the opening statement phase of the case. According to the article Stephen Miller wanted to deliver his own opening statement instead of having defense counsel do it. In addition Dick Reeve had submitted a motion for an opening statement even though he knew Judge Nevas prevented the trial by ordering a competency evaluation.

Suppose a defendant wanted to deliver his own opening statement, would that decision make the defendant incompetent for trial? It would be very unlikely that any Federal judge would allow a defendant to deliver his own opening statement but that decision wouldn't indicate that the defendant was incompetent for trial. It would only indicate that the defendant lacked a realistic background for how trials are conducted in Federal court. Incompetence for trial is determined when the defendant is incapable of assisting counsel and fails to have a rational concept of the proceedings. A rational concept and a realistic concept are not the same.

When this trial finally proceeded 17 months later the government was allowed to make its opening statement but the defense wasn't. It is the court's primary job and purpose in accordance with the Fifth, Sixth, and Fourteenth Amendments of the Bill of Rights to provide both sides a fair trial. Preventing the defense an opportunity to make its opening statement is so unfair that appellate oversight would naturally reverse a conviction. In order to prevent a reversal of the conviction in this case, Judge Nevas decided to have his court reporter, Susan Catucci, delete Robert Appleton's opening statement from the transcript, making it appear that neither side had made an opening statement apparently seeming to make it fair.

Appleton had filed his opening statement with the court and decided to call it the GOVERNMENT'S PROPOSED REQUEST TO CHARGE. When the jury was seated by Judge Nevas the judge then directed Appleton to begin by reading this document. I had been given a copy of the document and I followed along while it was being read to the jury. This is the verbatim opening statement as written in the aforementioned document:

"The United States of America, by and through the undersigned Assistant United States Attorney, Robert M. Appleton hereby respectfully submits the following proposed jury instructions in the captioned matter.

Count one charges the defendant with conspiring to obtain and attempt to obtain the property of Richard Jossen and John Moore, with their consent, induced by the wrongful use of threatened force, violence and actual fear.

The first element which the government must prove beyond a

reasonable doubt to establish the offense of conspiracy is that two or more persons entered the unlawful agreement charged in the indictment.

In order for the government to satisfy this element, you need not find that the alleged members of the conspiracy met together and entered into any express or formal agreement. Similarly you need not find that the alleged conspirators stated in words or writing what the scheme was, its object or purpose, or every precise detail of the scheme or the means by which its object or purpose was to be accomplished. What the government must prove is that there was a mutual understanding, either spoken or unspoken, between two or more people to cooperate with each other to accomplish an unlawful act.

You may of course find that the existence of an agreement to disobey or disregard the law has been established by direct proof. However, since conspiracy is by its very nature characterized by secrecy, you may also infer its existence from the circumstances of this case and the conduct of the parties involved.

In a very real sense then, in the context of conspiracy cases, actions often speak louder than words. In this regard you may in determining whether an agreement existed here, consider the actions and statements of all of those you find to be participants as proof that a common design existed on the part of the persons charged to act together to accomplish an unlawful purpose.

The second element which the government must prove beyond a reasonable doubt in order to establish the offense of conspiracy is that the defendant knowingly, willfully, and voluntarily became a participant in, or member of the conspiracy.

If you are satisfied that the conspiracy charged in count one existed, you must next ask yourselves who the members of the conspiracy were. In deciding whether the defendant was a member of the conspiracy you should consider whether, based upon all the evidence, the defendant knowingly and willfully joined in the conspiracy. You should ask, did he participate in the conspiracy with knowledge of its unlawful purpose and with the specific intention of furthering its objectives?

You are instructed that, while proof of a financial interest in the outcome of a scheme is not essential, if you find that a defendant had such an interest, that is a factor which you may properly consider in determining whether or not the defendant was a member of the conspiracy charged in the indictment.

As I mentioned a moment ago, before the defendant can be found to have been a conspirator, you must first find that he knowingly joined in the unlawful agreement or plan. The key question is therefore whether the defendant joined the conspiracy with an awareness of at least some of the basic aims and purposes of the unlawful agreement.

The defendant's participation in the conspiracy must be established by the independent evidence of his own acts or statements as well as those of the other coconspirators.

A defendant's knowledge is a matter of inference from the facts proved. In that connection, I instruct you that a defendant need not have been fully informed as to all of the details or the scope of the conspiracy in order to justify an inference of knowledge of his part. Furthermore a defendant need not have joined in all of the conspiracy's unlawful objectives.

The extent of a defendant's participation has no bearing on the issue of a defendant's guilt. A conspirator's liability is not measured by the extent or duration of his participation. Indeed each member may perform separate and distinct acts and may perform them at different times. Some conspirators play major roles, while others play minor roles in the scheme. An equal role is not what the law requires. In fact even a single act may be sufficient to draw a defendant within the gambit of the conspiracy.

I want to caution you however, that a defendant's mere presence at the scene of the alleged crime does not by itself make him a member of the conspiracy. Similarly mere association with another member of the conspiracy does not automatically make the defendant a member. A person may know or be friendly with a criminal without being a criminal himself. Mere similarity of conduct or the fact that they have met together and discussed common aims and interests does not necessarily establish proof of the existence of a conspiracy.

I also want to caution you that mere knowledge or acquiescence, without participation, in the unlawful plan is not sufficient. Moreover the fact that the acts of the defendant without knowledge, merely happen to further the purpose or objectives of the conspiracy, does not make that defendant a member. More is required under the law. What is necessary is that the defendant must have participated with knowledge of at least some of the purposes or objectives of the conspiracy and with the intention in the accomplishment of those unlawful ends.

Extortion is the taking of another person's property or money with his consent. The consent is induced by the use, or threatened use of force, violence or fear.

In considering whether the defendant used, or threatened to use force, violence, or fear, you should give those words their common and ordinary meaning, and understand them as you normally would. The violence does not have to be directed at the person whose property was sought to be taken. The use or threat of force or violence might be aimed at a third person, or at causing economic rather than physical injury.

Lastly the government must prove that the defendant acted with the specific intention of extorting money or property."

This last sentence should have become the heart of the opening statement delivered by counsel, Richard Reeve. As it turned out that day September 11, 1996, Judge Nevas would prevent Dick Reeve from delivering any opening statement. However, let's suppose Dick had been given the opportunity to deliver his opening statement to the jury. Let's try to examine what it could have been like.

First of all Appleton was very impersonal with the jury. He came on as their instructor, dictating what they were required to do. He never tried to present himself as doing his job by being concerned with victims. He almost ignored extortion and focused upon conspiracy. Conspiracy was never charged in this case and at no time during the trial was conspiracy ever being proven or disproven.

The key element of the defense had to address the last sentence by Appleton. The government could never prove, "That the defendant acted with the specific intention of extorting money or property." This was the reason that Dick Reeve emphasized that the charge be changed from 875(b) to (c). The language in (c) failed to require that the government prove intent.

If I had been able to create Dick's opening statement it would have sounded friendly and gone something like this.

Good morning ladies and gentlemen, my name is Richard Reeve and I represent the defendant, Stephen Miller in this case. I first met Steve in December 1994, when he was brought to New Haven by the United States Marshals from Brooklyn, New York because he was extradited from the Eastern District of New York to the District of Connecticut when he was arrested in this case at his home in Brooklyn. Steve never fought his extradition to Connecticut because he believed he would get a fair trial in any district in the United States.

As Steve and I have grown to know each other during the past 17 months since December 1994, we have become friends. I have grown to like Steve as a person of principle, a person of dedication, an expert in his chosen profession, and a person who tells the truth who you will hear testify on the witness stand in his own defense. It is most often in criminal trials that the defendant does not testify in his own defense. But as you are going to learn, Steve has nothing to hide, he is not a criminal, and he wants you to hear him answer the cross examination by Assistant United States Attorney Robert Appleton.

The most critical factor in this case for you to decide is did the government prove the point that Mr. Appleton finally stated in his opening statement, "Did Mr. Miller intend to extort money or property from the alleged victims in this case." The reason that Mr. Miller has had to wait for 21 months since his arrest for this trial is because the government, Assistant United States Attorney Robert Appleton, has tried to prevent any trial from being held in this case. Instead of a trial Mr. Appleton has attempted to incarcerate Steve by falsely claiming that Steve is incompetent for trial, that he is also dangerous, and that Steve should be committed indefinitely on the grounds of insanity. If Judge Nevas had allowed the commitment of Steve Miller to a Federal Bureau of Prisons prison for the criminally insane Steve's credibility would have been destroyed and it is very likely that his mind would have been destroyed with psychotropic medications that generated severe side effects.

When a healthy mind is subjected to psychotropic drugs severe damage to that healthy mind is sure to occur.

Ladies and gentlemen of the jury I want you to know that under the American Bill of Rights only the defendant in a criminal proceeding has the right to use an insanity defense. Unless the defendant invokes the use of an insanity defense, neither the government represented by Mr. Appleton, nor the Judicial Branch, Judge Nevas in this case, has the power or the right to force Steve Miller to use an insanity defense.

The reason that this trial has been delayed since April 1995, when another jury had been chosen to hear this case on April 18, 1995, 17 months ago, is because the court ordered Steve held for a competency evaluation, a competency hearing in October 1995, and finally ordered Steve shipped to FCI Butner's psychiatric prison facility to be restored to competency. Steve then filed an interlocutory appeal to the 2nd Circuit Court of Appeals to appeal that order, and Judge Nevas then decided to reverse his own order and allow Steve his constitutional right to trial.

During this process Steve was evaluated by a Bureau of Prisons psychologist, Dr. Thomas Kucharski who testified under oath and wrote an affidavit asserting that Steve Miller did not intend to perform the criminal act of extortion. The defense intends to call Dr. Kucharski here to testify in lieu of his finding.

The defense intends to prove in this courtroom that Steve was the victim of a fraud in October 1987, that Steve reported that fraud to law enforcement, the government, and unfortunately the government decided to condone, allow, and protect the perpetrators of this fraud, the alleged victims mentioned by Mr. Appleton, a Mr. John Moore, and a Mr. Richard Jossen. During the years from 1987, until Steve's arrest in 1994, Steve has created some fascinating traps to end this fraud. The fraud still continues at this present time, almost 10 years since 1987.

You will learn that the government had decided to ignore those traps created by Steve until he was finally arrested in 1994.

Since Steve's arrest in 1994, the government has tried to cover up, not only the fraud to rig global copper prices on a daily basis by John Moore and his associates who officiate The New York Commodities Exchange commonly referred to as COMEX, but also Steve's intention to expose the government's role. During this trial ladies and gentlemen you will learn that Steve staged the extortion of John Moore and Richard Jossen in order to draw them before you into this Federal courtroom.

After you have heard all the testimony from all the witnesses and observed and read carefully all of the exhibits presented as the complete package of evidence in this trial it will be your job to deliberate and conclude whether Steve intended to extort money from Mr. Moore and Mr. Jossen or whether Steve intended to force Mr. Moore and Mr. Jossen into this Federal courtroom because Mr. Moore and his criminal conspirators victimized Mr. Miller while Federal law enforcement protected Mr. Moore.

There were a series of events when Mr. Moore and Mr. Jossen refused to contact law enforcement. You will need to decide what was in their minds at those times when they decided not to contact law enforcement. Were Mr. Moore and Mr. Jossen paranoid because they were perpetrating criminal fraud by rigging global copper prices and thereby afraid to disturb law enforcement? In particular the testimony of Richard Jossen's father Walter Jossen should give you distinct enlightenment upon the state of Mr. Moore and Mr. Jossen's minds.

There were also a series of events when Steve spent years contacting law enforcement and senior media officials trying to report the daily fraud that victimized Steve, other copper traders, and industrial consumers of copper. I don't think the conclusions you will find will be difficult and you will then acquit my friend and my client Steve Miller.

When it was finally time to help prepare Dick Reeve to develop his opening statement Dick told me that Judge Nevas would not allow him to make an opening statement. It was then that I told Dick that I wanted him to file a motion for an opening statement by defense counsel so Judge Nevas would be forced to deny the motion on the record. I needed to preserve the record for appellate purposes while I still believed that my right to have counsel make an opening statement would reverse a guilty verdict.

At that point in time I had no way to suspect that my appeal would be stayed. I had no way to suspect there would be no due process by the higher courts including The United States Supreme Court.

During the winter of 2003, Bridgeport's Mayor Joseph Ganim went on trial in Federal court in New Haven. I decided to watch this trial which happened to be well covered by the media. When Assistant United States Attorney Ron Apter made his opening statement to the jury, he detailed the names of witnesses who were Ganim's codefendants and claimed that they were prepared to testify about the conspiracy they had with Ganim to extort a number of companies that made kick backs to them that they had shared with Mayor Ganim. This was also an extortion case that was based upon kick back agreements necessary to business with the city of Bridgeport.

When defense counsel Richard Meehan made his opening statement he claimed that there would be no proof that any money had ever been paid to Mayor Ganim. That the extortion had been committed by two associates of Mayor Ganim who pled guilty but that they had never shared their money with Ganim.

Both attorneys had prepared the jury for the upcoming testimony and the exhibits used as evidence for both sides. Both of Ganim's codefendants, Len Grimaldi and Frank Pinto swore up and down that they had shared their payments of hundreds of thousands of dollars with Mayor Ganim. This was exactly what Ron Apter had prepared the jury for during his opening statement.

By the same token at no time did either side present the bank statements of the defendants that would prove that the money received by Grimaldi and Pinto was shared with Mayor Ganim. There was a massive amount of evidence that Grimaldi, Pinto, and Ganim shared fabulous dinners, bought some nice clothes and expensive wine but if in fact there were payments split with Grimaldi, Pinto, and Ganim, attorney Meehan was right, no proof was ever presented.

One thing is certain, after the corporate checks had been deposited in Grimaldi and Pinto's accounts if they had split it with Ganim there would have had to have been a withdrawal. Why didn't the prosecution use Grimaldi's and Pinto's bank account statements to show the withdrawal they had to make to share the money with Mayor Ganim? Also when the FBI came to Mayor Ganim's home with the search warrant they opened the safe to see if there was money in it. There wasn't.

In the final analysis Mayor Ganim was deceived by his attorneys. His attorneys had to know that there was no chance to win an acquittal. They charged Joe Ganim a lot more money to go to trial than they would have charged for a plea bargain. In addition Joe Ganim was sentenced to 9 years because he denied guilt instead of about 3 years if he had admitted guilt. His lawyers had to know that Ganim would be sentenced to a much greater sentenced for his refusal to admit guilt.

I discussed these points with Ray Ganim, Joe's brother who became angry at my point of view.

It is important for people to understand that well paid lawyers regularly screw their clients and rarely do their clients win acquittals unless they are very well connected. Let's agree to save the OJ Simpson case for another time and another book. There are two possibilities that are very difficult to evaluate, most of the time impossible to evaluate. The first possibility is that the client/defendant is truly innocent of all charges. The second possibility is that the defendant is guilty of some or all charges but no evidence was left to prove guilt. Barry Scheck has had more than 70 completely innocent convicts released from death row. Scheck won't take a Federal case because he says in his book that the Feds will only pay $5,000 to an innocent convict for his time spent. Scheck is interested in earning part of the money paid to innocent convicts for the time they wrongly spent on death row. He focuses on death row cases because they all are acquitted because DNA tests proved conclusively that the sperm, blood, or other physical evidence is available to exonerate the convict.

There are surely some other innocent convicts that have been accused of cases where no violence was involved and therefore no DNA to test.

When counsel makes his opening statement and mentions evidence he intends to use to win his case it is wise to keep in mind the summation. Before the judge charges the jury both sides have a chance to argue their summation. It is wise to reflect back to his own opening statement and the opening statement for the other side to point out the evidence he had originally cited during both opening statements. Often their will be claims made that were never fulfilled.

In the Ganim case for example, counsel claimed that there will be no money that ever was collected by Ganim that was the essence of the case. Pinto and Grimaldi both testified that they had given Ganim his share and that Ganim wanted even more than his share. To me that claim was extremely powerful and I watched intently for the proof of that claim. Counsel had access to the banking accounts of both Pinto and Grimaldi. Surely those accounts would have shown the deposits of the large checks they collected. Then they also had to show the disbursement of the payments. When Grimaldi deposited the check and withdrew payment for Pinto, if the withdrawal was only half or one third, then Ganim never collected his one third.

For some reason AUSA Ron Apter also never used the bank accounts either to prove that Ganim had collected his third. When the FBI came to Ganim's home with their search warrant they opened the safe and found no money. The deduction that the FBI was looking for Ganim's share indicated to me that they had no proof that Ganim collected his third from a withdrawal by either Grimaldi or Pinto. Neither side addressed the evidence that had to exist.

During the summation counsel never solidified the premise he had made during his opening statement. In the end Apter never argued that he had provided evidence that Ganim had collected his share of the money. What Apter did that I believe convinced the jury that Ganim was guilty was that he reminded the jury that P.T. Barnum lived in Bridgeport and Barnum was credited with a famous saying, "Suckers are born every minute." The jury would need to be suckers if they acquitted Mayor Ganim.

CHAPTER 3
CONSIDER THE INSANITY DEFENSE

To consider the use and the misuse of the insanity defense takes deep thought. The Bill of Rights, in particular the Sixth Amendment, is very clear. It only gives the right to waive the privilege of a criminal trial to the defendant. No judge, no defense counsel, and no prosecutor have the right to force any criminal defendant to waive his or her right to trial. The statutes pertaining to the court's decision to order any psychological evaluation, including a competency evaluation, can not be used to waive the right of any criminal defendant for a jury trial to determine either the guilt or the innocence of the defendant. Those statutes violate the Sixth Amendment right, the Fifth Amendment right, and the Fourteenth Amendment right.

There is the presumption that counsel has the interest of the defendant because of the mandate by the Sixth Amendment. Not only can there be no guarantee that counsel will always act in the interest of the defendant, but in my case, as you will continue to learn, the courts prevented justice throughout the entire proceedings by forcing counsel to sabotage my defense. You will be seeing this on a continuous basis as this story progresses. The term created by our courts to soften an act of sabotage by the defense is "ineffective assistance of counsel". To me, the terminology ineffective assistance of counsel sounds like the attorney made an honest mistake by being negligent. What I am writing about is a dishonest, insidious attempt to sabotage my defense because the presiding judge is ordering counsel to sabotage my defense. Under the Sixth Amendment of our Bill of Rights, this is clearly prohibited and is grounds for impeachment of the judge. Judges under our system have complete power to make mistakes, but they don't have the power to obstruct justice and conspire with criminals by protecting them, even if they include the Attorney General of the United States.

American justice is a myth. I have formulated a theory about why corruption is rampant by the criminal justice system. My theory is based upon my firsthand experience from having observed a pattern of behavior and a pattern of facts. My case is not typical; it is contrary to the norm. But while I was inside the system fighting my case, I was privy to many other cases. I watched how the system used the insanity plea option.

Suppose the defendant is truly incompetent for trial and is also truly innocent of the charges imposed? An insanity defense would then presume guilt and therefore would be dead wrong and completely unjust. Within this context through my experience I have learned that the vast majority of criminals are afflicted from mental illness too. Paranoia is extremely prevalent throughout the inmate population, and delusions and hallucinations are also fairly common. It is for these related reasons that either a trial or a guilty verdict should determine guilt first, before the issue of mental health is addressed. There have been cases when defendants have pleaded guilty and later have been found innocent.

More than 70 capital cases have been overturned by using DNA. Interestingly none of these cases were in the federal system. You will never guess the reason that Attorney Barry Sheck never takes a federal case. The federal system will not pay for false imprisonment. The inmates released from state prisons are given money to compensate them for their inconvenience on death row. Barry Sheck states in his book that the federal courts will only pay $5,000 for false imprisonment.

I found a state case in New York where a severely mentally retarded man was locked up by mistake. He shared the same name as the guilty suspect. The federal court awarded a payment from New York State of $3,200,000 for his 2 year inconvenience. If the same case had been federal the innocent inmate would have only been awarded $5,000 according to Barry Sheck.

A high profile criminal defendant who was prevented by the court for his right to invoke an insanity defense was Vincent "The Chin" Gigante, the boss of the Genovese crime family. Because Gigante had explicitly wanted to use the insanity defense, the court could have spared its own time by committing Gigante because he was dangerous. This commitment would have been indefinite, lasting until the court deemed Gigante was cured of his mental illness and was therefore no longer dangerous.

It is extremely important to recognize that any criminal defendant who invokes the insanity defense is also admitting guilt. It is a claim that the defendant is not guilty by reason of insanity, but it also is an admission that the specific crime alleged in the indictment was in fact committed by this defendant. In Gigante's case the strategy he attempted to use was that because he was afflicted with a mental disease, that disease rendered him incapable for having committed criminal acts as a crime boss. But if Gigante was innocent of being the boss of the Genovese crime family he was trying to prevent the government's ability to produce its evidence that he was guilty. The issue always revolved around the question that Gigante was feigning his mental disease. The government failed to simply go along with Gigante's claim and could have legally committed Gigante without the burden of a trial. It made no sense for the government not to simply use Gigante's own strategy to commit him indefinitely. And it made no sense for highly paid defense counsel to subject Gigante to the indefinite term a commitment might have initiated. In the end, Gigante was sentenced to twelve years but is now facing additional charges for continuing to run the Genovese crime family from prison.

The reverse of that high profile case was the case of the "Unabomber". The "Unabomber's" defense team decided to team up with the government and claim that he was a schizophrenic, and therefore not guilty by reason of insanity. This strategy was clearly a violation of the defendant's right to trial. Ted Kuzcynski was known to have been a highly educated and a brilliant man. He had eluded detection for about 18 years. He was charged for having sent bombs to a variety of corporate executives, some of who were killed or hurt, by his bombs. He had a right to trial to prove that there was no evidence that connected him to the crimes alleged. He objected strenuously to his counsel's unauthorized use of the insanity defense recognizing that their strategy undermined his right for a fair trial. At the last minute and after his jury had been selected, the court ordered Dr. Sally Johnson, the chief psychologist and Associate Warden of F.C.I. Butner, to fly out to California to evaluate him for competency. In a four-day time frame she claimed that the "Unabomber" was competent for trial or to plead guilty.

It is also important to know that no court can accept a guilty plea from a defendant who has been ruled to be incompetent.

After the court had held its competency hearing and heard Dr. Johnson's evaluation that he was competent, Kuzcynski tried to fire his lawyers and invoke his Sixth Amendment right to be pro se, that is to represent himself. The court then ruled to deny the defendant's right to be pro se. All criminal defendants have a right to counsel. It is the defendant's right and it is also the defendant's right to represent himself. At that point Kuzcynski had a right to motion the court by filing a notice of appeal so he could file an interlocutory appeal to overturn the court's ruling which had denied his right to proceed pro se. As we now know, Kuzcynski buckled under the threat of a death sentence and pleaded guilty to life imprison. It is very likely that he didn't know that he could have filed an interlocutory appeal and then defy the court to proceed. Also he was very lucky that his case was a major news story, which would have given him a terrific advantage if he had delayed the trial with an appeal.

In my case I used my right for an interlocutory appeal after Judge Daly ruled me incompetent. I told Dick Reeve to file a NOTICE OF APPEAL right away because there is a 10 day deadline to file the notice. Dick told me that I couldn't appeal. I told him that I could and that I would write the NOTICE OF APPEAL if he refused. Dick then filed it for me. Most defendants would have accepted their attorney's claim and not filed. Then once the 10-day deadline passes, to try to overturn that problem is a nightmare. You are going to learn that my interlocutory appeal of the competence ruling was the most critical legal strategy I employed throughout my case.

The One Flew over The Cuckoo's Nest ruse when Jack Nicholson portrays a convicted criminal who tries a ruse for an insanity defense is used fairly often by real criminals. In my real life experience during my nine years of incarceration, I have never seen this strategy work to any convict's advantage. In fact these people wind up with far more time than if they had been sentenced for the crime.

With these points in mind, let's get back to what happened after Judge Nevas ruled that I needed to be evaluated for competence. A few weeks later the Marshals drove me to M.C.C., New York. I was assigned to a Dr. Kucharski for the evaluation. I was housed on 11 North where I began to meet a number of New York mobsters. At that point in time a very weird plan by the government began to be hatched which would involve two mob rats, positioned there to try to get into the witness protection program.

I met with Dr. Kucharski a total of three times. During our first meeting Dr. Kucharski told me to take the Minnesota Multiphasic Exam which comprised more than 500 questions. When Dr. Kucharski finally allowed us to converse I tried to explain to him the very simple factors involved in the **COMEX** manipulation of copper futures contract prices which rigged the global price of copper. This was the entire purpose of my decision to force this case into a federal court. This was the key element and only element brought up by AUSA Appleton during the hearing that had aborted my right to trial. But Dr. Kucharski refused to let me explain anything about the COMEX manipulation.

Dr. Kucharski knew what he was expected to do. He was there to write a report to the court to claim that I was incompetent for trial. The Minnesota Multiphasic Test did not matter, and nothing I said mattered. The court wanted its PhD. Psychologist to find me incompetent and that was what would happen. This is a very dangerous position created by powerful, deceitful authorities. There is no check and balance available in a sea of corruption covered up by waves of hypocrisy. A legitimate psychologist would have laughed at the Court's order and found me competent to stand trial. However, it is important for readers to know that the Court has the ultimate power and does not have to agree with any psychologist's recommendation. Regardless of that, under the Bill of Rights, the Court does not have the power to waive the defendant's right to trial. My story would eventually prove to me that the Court, including the entire 2nd Circuit and the entire Supreme Court has no regard for the Bill of Rights and their own oath to uphold and protect the Constitution. (Eventually I will file a petition to the United States Supreme Court that will shock me into reality.)

Who would imagine a respected judge and a respected doctor to deliberately ignore the constitution to prevent a trial guaranteed by America's Bill Of Rights? Don't Americans believe that the insanity defense was created by liberal legislators to protect the rights of the mentally impaired? Should fake mental disorders be used to protect criminals?

Appleton never claimed that **COMEX** had not rigged copper futures contract prices. He repeatedly stated that it was my perception. The fact that the crime was so simple and unsophisticated was critical to my defense. The simple fact that I had worked with U.S. Congressman Christopher Shays and staff people he had assigned to me from late 1987 until Shays wrote his letter in March 1989, to Attorney General Richard Thornburgh was critical for my defense. Even though this letter was an exhibit for my trial, Judge Nevas prevented me from reading the letter to the jury. Nevas knew how powerful Shays letter was. Shays claimed this fraud had existed and should have been very critical to this evaluation by Dr. Kucharski. I had a copy of Shays' letter for Kucharski's evaluation, but Kucharski was adamantly opposed to learning about this issue too. He constantly refused to read Shays' letters or discuss any part of the facts I had learned when I had investigated this fraud. My claims to Kucharski that the fraud was so simple that any person could understand it failed to force or induce him to learn the facts. Does that mean he was a willing conspirator to cover up the fraud? Dr. Kucharski will make that claim under oath on the witness stand.

When Dr. Kucharski is called to testify, is there any chance that he will state, your honor my job was at stake to find Mr. Miller incompetent? For him to believe that I am part of the conspiracy to protect the Attorney General who decided to allow the COMEX people to rig copper prices proves he is delusional and therefore incompetent for trial. Mr. Miller wanted to explain the fraud and I refused to let him do that because I wanted to be sure that he could not convince me that this fraud continues and it is plain to see by anyone.

When Shays wrote his letter to A.G. Thornburgh, Shays dropped this crime into the lap of the Attorney General of the United States. And the fact is that Thornburgh had clearly decided to allow this crime to continue since 1987, and pass it along to his successors, William Barr under President George Herbert Walker Bush, and then Janet Reno under President Bill Clinton. Shays letter refuted any notion that I was delusional, paranoid, or had grandiose ideation. The story of why these letters were written by Shays in 1989, is also quite interesting.

Before I leave the mentioning of Attorney General William Barr I later learned from a very interesting expose entitled **COMPROMISED** that Mr. Barr had been a very high level official with the C.I.A. His code name was Robert Johnson and he was Ollie North's boss in the Iran/Contra scandal. The author of **COMPROMISED** , Terry Reed had been employed by the C.I.A. and worked to train pilots at the Mena, Arkansas airport which also involved Governor Clinton. It is fascinating to me that William Barr and William Jefferson Clinton were never featured in their important roles during the Iran/Contra hearings. **COMPROMISED** is a fascinating story I would recommend all citizens and especially voters to read. It is one of many stories that put our elected officials and there surrogates into proper perspective. My being locked up gave me both much more time, and much more drive to learn as much about the frequent crimes by government officials, which take place with regularity.

If you're thinking, man this guy is obsessed with scandals, please keep in mind that I didn't write these stories, I read them. Also I was in a game and I intended to study as much information as possible so I could play this game to the best of my ability. I needed to learn as much about the behavior of the government officials who were willing to be involved in criminal and unethical behavior to be able to fight my own case. I hoped that there might be limits that judges might not cross and I wanted to try to find those limits. My search concluded that no limits exist. **This is a study far more important to me than all the college courses I failed to take.**

Let me revert back to the story in <u>COMPROMISED</u> when Terry Reed's C.I.A. associate Barry Seal who made the fatal mistake of trying to blackmail George Bush for the cocaine Barry Seal was flying into the United States for Bush's sons to sell. United States District Judge Frank Palazola sentenced Seal to a halfway house in Louisiana. Two days later Seal was riddled with bullets by Columbians. Did Judge Palazola purposely make Seal an easy target? Would I be a conspiracy nut to question a possible conspiracy by Judge Palazola to have Seal murdered? Anyone who believes that a Federal Court would sentence a cocaine dealer capable of flying mega kilo shipments into America to a halfway house and not a prison would be a fool.

The common phrase "conspiracy nuts" is applied to the huge number of people who studied the conspiracy to assassinate JFK, as an example of the many conspiracy stories that grew out of a long list of government conspiracies. The nuts are those who always believe the government's version of the huge number of events that become public knowledge when they are caught creating conspiracies.

I made it very clear to Dr. Kucharski that if he continued to refuse to address the very simple evidence contained within the Shays letter to Attorney General Thornburgh, and another letter Shays had written to the Controller General of the G.A.O. concerning Shays' dismay at the G.A.O. investigation of the COMEX fraud, that this evaluation had to be prejudicial.

It would not be wise for me to dismiss the actions of Judge Nevas at the hearing that resulted in his order to prevent a legitimate trial in his court. This is also coupled with Reeve's suggestion to have the charge changed to one Reeve claimed I couldn't defend because it removed the element of intent.

It was very obvious that Judge Nevas expected Dr. Kucharski to find me incompetent for trial and Kucharski had to know that. The essence of this case and the essence of my defense was my desire to expose the **COMEX** fraud. Whether or not I intended to extort money from the perpetrators of the fraud was the issue of my intent. I had created safe guards, which would clearly protect me from any criminal conviction. One of those safe guards was a letter I had written in November 1994, before I sent the two messengers to Richard Jossen's home in Westport, Ct. This letter was written to Howard Heiss, the Chief of Securities and Commodities Fraud Unit for the Southern District of New York. The letter explained to Mr. Heiss that in case the money I demanded from Richard Jossen and John Moore, the Chairman of COMEX, was wired to my bank account that I intended to send this money on to him. That would prove that my intent was not to extort. It would establish evidence that Moore and Jossen had wired their money because they were more afraid to go to prison for their crimes than they were afraid to pay a small portion of their monster rip off to me and my mob associates.

Dr. Kucharski was adamant about refusing to learn anything about the fraud, the essence of what he will later testify about concerning the competency issue. The issue becomes an assertion that I claim that many senior government officials have been made aware of the fraud, including and especially three consecutive Attorney Generals. Regardless of the facts supported by the Shays letters and others, Dr. Kucharski contends that I must be afflicted with a delusional belief that these pristine, puritanical government officials are automatically above being part of any crime.

It will not be until September 21st, 1995, four months after this phony evaluation that the competency hearing will be held. A huge departure from the four day Kuzcynski competency evaluation and hearing by Dr. Sally Johnson, the Associate Warden of F.C.I. Butner where I will be sent, twice.

During the weeks I lived on 11 North at M.C.C. (Metropolitan Correction Center) I began speaking with Anthony "Tony Limo" Saravola, and Bobby Montano. I explained to them that the government had no intention of putting me on trial because they knew I intended to expose senior officials including Attorney Generals Thornburgh, Barr, and Reno. I also suggested that if powerful mob bosses were inclined to use my ability to pressure the Justice Department because of its decision to allow this fraud to continue, that they would benefit too.

While at the same time I was talking to Tony and Bobby, I was attempting to talk to other mob guys in the unit. It was obvious that Tony and Bobby had no contact with Mateo Romano, Handsome Johnny Lester, and the rest of the mob guys. I never asked any of them why they remained aloof because I decided to avoid any suspicion that I wanted to know their business. At that time in my experience as a prisoner I was too uninformed to know that there were rats all over the place. I suspected that all the known rats were in protective custody for their own safety. This turned out to be far from the truth. Although some rats are housed in secure units, many if not most are not. I have no way to know the reasoning behind the decision making of the B.O.P. on this issue.

When I am finally brought to my competency hearing you will learn the details of why I was locked up in the hole for about a month before I was sent to F.C.I. Otisville. Otisville was the best prison experience I had during my whole nine-year incarceration. During that summer the weather was beautiful and we were allowed excellent rec (recreation) and pretty good food. I met all the mob guys and had a lot of laughs with them. I had some very memorable experiences.

Throughout my life I have been fascinated by the mob. I read most of the books written about them, and considered myself a mobologist. I was about to learn first hand that these people are outright fakes compared to the image they portray.

I believed I had captured Tony Saravola and Bobby Montano's

interest for using the power I had developed against our common enemy, The Justice Department. One day Tony told me to go up to the roof for rec at M.C.C. so we could discuss his plan to use my power. Tony claimed that his top contacts had decided to **kidnap** Judge Nevas, Richard Jossen, and John Moore.

I was amazed. I told him that this was crazy. I told him that if these people believed that kidnapping judges could help them, that there was a whole court house full of judges for them to kidnap. I told him that I had no intention of committing any crime and that my power to expose the senior officials involved in the protection of the COMEX price rigging fraud was not understood by his mob friends. I suspected that John Gambino, a very powerful Sicilian and a Gambino capo had contacts in Sicily who could expose my story from Sicilian media companies, in a similar way that the Iran/Contra story was published by a Lebanese media company. I believed that John Gambino was sophisticated and even brilliant. I had gotten that impression from reading a book called **OCTAPUS** that exposed the Sicilian LCN with elaborate detail and mentioned John Gambino.

I learned first hand from living amongst many made mob members that they are way overrated by the authors of these books, and that they are very unsophisticated, unreliable, uneducated people who are convinced that they know everything. They are all very provincial gossipers and only think about crime and time. Most of them are degenerate gamblers and quite a few are dope addicts. When I was in F.C.I. McKean I learned that Joe Gambino, John's brother, was claiming that he was guilty of racketeering instead of heroin dealing. I had watched the complete trial of Joe and John Gambino in 1993, in Judge Leisure's court in the Southern District of New York. That trial ended in a hung jury. Mateo Romano and Lorenzo Manino were also codefendants with John and Joe Gambino. I went to that trial to learn if I could explain to a trusted member of John's crew that I possessed powerful evidence that his prosecutor, United States Attorney Mary Jo White was presently allowing a major Wall Street fraud to continue.

On one occasion I spoke with Mateo Romano. I also spoke with an associate of John's crew. They wanted me to speak with their lawyers. These mob people have complete confidence in their lawyers. I distrust lawyers in general and I had specific knowledge that Joe Gambino's lawyer worked to help the prosecutors.

While on the roof with Tony Sarivola he threatened that I would be murdered if I didn't cooperate with their plan to kidnap these people. He also explained that they had no intention of hurting their captors and that while they were captives that they would be video taped explaining their own roles in the COMEX fraud. Also as part of the kidnapping plan I would need to write a letter to United States Attorney, Mary Jo White explaining my role in the kidnapping plan. Tony suggested that the first step to recovering the hostages would be to have me released. When I was released I would go to Staten Island and call Tony's home to tell Tony's wife where I could be picked up so I could be brought to the hostages and help in the production of the video tape.

I completely believed that Tony had mob connections and that this kidnapping plan was real. In prison people rat on other inmates for things like gambling, narcotics, and extortion, but kidnapping a Federal Judge is far beyond the norm. The only other alternative had to be that Tony was a rat trying to help Mary Jo White to charge me with a crime having nothing to do with the COMEX fraud. I also thought that the plan to video tape Judge Nevas, John Moore, and Richard Jossen was very clever.

I told Tony that I would give careful thought to this plan but that it seemed to be a very bad idea. I began to consider the murder threat very carefully and all of the other points he made. It seemed far more likely to me that I could be murdered in prison than being able to kidnap three people simultaneously. I recognized that if I agreed to their plan to kidnap a Federal Judge that that would expose the complete package. I knew that this plan would be beyond sensational. Of course I considered the possibility that Tony and Bobby were rats who were threatening me for the benefit of and under the authorization by the United States Attorney but this plan seemed too weird for the government to be involved.

I went back to Tony and agreed to write my letter after the kidnapping had been accomplished. He then claimed that the plan would be put into action and that a lawyer would visit him to pass my letter onto Mary Jo White. A few days later Tony claimed the kidnapping had been accomplished and I wrote my handwritten letter to Mary Jo White. I then began to await a call to speak with the F.B.I. or United States Attorney.

Bingo, at about 3:30 P.M. that afternoon, a C.O. (corrections officer) came to my room and asked me to step outside so he could hand cuff me. I was then taken to the hole. My cellmate in the hole had a radio so I asked him if I could listen to the news. When I heard nothing on the news about the kidnapping I decided, of course they weren't going to put this on the news because that would expose the whole problem. I waited and expected that my cell door would open any minute for me to be debriefed. Nothing happened for two days. I was absolutely mystified that there was no communication. A Lieutenant delivered a shot (an incident report) which claimed that I was under investigation for illicit activity.

Two days later I decided to do something no criminal would ever consider. I wrote another letter to Mary Jo White. I mentioned my concern about the welfare of the people who had been kidnapped and I waited for someone to speak with me about it. I was absolutely convinced that I would get a response. Still nothing happened. Also for a week I was not allowed out of my cell for rec or to make a call to anyone. On a daily basis I continued to write letters to Mary Jo White in care of Dr. Kucharski. I wrote a total of 12 letters during a period of three weeks. I then wrote a letter to Dick Reeve to ask him to confirm if Judge Nevas had been kidnapped. Finally I was allowed to call Dick and he told me that no one had been kidnapped.

I then explained to Dick that he had lied to me many times in the past and that his credibility was now nil. I said, "Let's start with the story published in THE CONNECTICUT POST which claimed that I had wanted to make an opening statement. This never occurred and you know that." He then asked me if I had received the <u>MOTION FOR DEFENDANT'S OPENING STATEMENT.</u> I said, "No why don't you send it to me." At that point Dick said that he needed to withdraw from this case. I replied, "That's the best news I've heard in a month."

When I returned to my cell and considered that it was so unlikely that Tony Sarivola and Bobby Montano had pulled a prank involving such a serious matter as a kidnapping, I still was convinced that the kidnapping was true. This led to my next move which I believed would clear the matter up completely. I wrote another letter to Mary Jo White, c/o Dr, Kucharski, stating that if they would order the marshals to drive me to Bridgeport on the following day to see if Judge Nevas was on the bench, that I would plead guilty on the spot if he was there. Furthermore, that I would reveal all the details involving those who had conveyed my letter based upon the hoax that there had been any kidnapping. My letter given to Tony Saravola had to have been delivered directly to Mary Jo White by hand, because if it had been dropped into the mail box in the morning, it would not have been read before 3:30 P.M. that afternoon when I was locked up. The coincidence that I had handed the letter to Tony at 10:00 AM and that I was locked up at 3:30 PM that afternoon left no doubt that Tony had direct contact with the Justice Department.

This was a very important fact because it proved to me that Tony and Bobby Montano really had a close connection to the Justice Department that was supposed to be Tony's lawyer. I never considered that they might be rats because how could I imagine that United States

Attorney, Mary Jo White would be a party to threatening to murder an inmate? Now that is a really crazy supposition.

To my amazement, my offer to plead guilty was ignored. That reinforced my belief that there had truly been a kidnapping. But about a week later I was released from the hole and transported directly to F.C.I. Otisville where I lived with the general population.

Looking back on these events seems to be a strange behavior pattern. On the other hand being in prison is an experience that puts unusual pressure on any person. In hindsight I am sure that Tony Sarivola and Bobby Montano had deep connections in the mob. It is not impossible for the mob to kidnap three people simultaneously including a federal judge, but it is very improbable that the mob would entertain a crime of this magnitude. The mob truly fears federal law enforcement. I use the murder of Gus Farace by Mario Gallo as a frame of reference.

Farace had murdered a DEA Agent and the Feds let the mob's bosses know that Farace had to pay or their heat would be unbearable against all mob operations.

My competency hearing was finally held four months later after my fake evaluation by Dr. Kucharski. The following is the verbatim record of my hearing on September 21st, 1995. I was transported to the court in Waterbury, Ct. of The Honorable T.F. Gilroy Daly. When Dick Reeve filed his __MOTION TO WITHDRAW__ Judge Nevas denied Reeve's motion but decided to withdraw from this case himself and be replaced by Judge Daly.

To make reading this hearing more enjoyable, I have removed the boring and unimportant parts of it.

THE COURT: Good morning.

MR. APPLETON: Good morning your honor. Bob Appleton on behalf of the government. We're here pursuant to 4241 of Title 18 for purposes of a hearing under the competency of this defendant to proceed to trial in United States v. Miller. With me at counsel table is Dr. Kucharski employed by the Federal Bureau of Prisons at the Metropolitan Correction Center in New York."

THE COURT: Thank you. How are you Mr. Reeve?

MR. REEVE: I'm fine your honor. If it please the court it's my understanding through contact with your Honor's clerk as well as with chambers of Judge Nevas, that there are now three separate issues that are pending before this court on transfer by Judge Nevas. One is the renewed motion to withdraw that I filed. The other is a motion that I filed on behalf of Mr. Miller to permit him to proceed pro se. And the third is the competency issue.

The reader needs to recognize that every defendant is deemed competent for trial unless and until the court has heard the issues and then ruled. This hearing was held on September 21st, 1995, and this court would not finally rule on the competency issue until March 1996. Until that ruling was made I was deemed competent for trial.

THE COURT: Until I determine his competency I can't grant either motion unless the finding is that Mr. Miller is competent.

MR. REEVE: Your honor I agree I am in a bind, but I think I need to put on the record Mr. Miller's desires. I've had a number of phone conversations with Mr. Miller. Mr. Miller wants the court to know what the present status is so I will do that. He feels that I have misrepresented him which includes a failure to file a waiver of his appellate right to claim incompetence in the event he is convicted. I did not do that.

I think as your honor is probably aware we picked a jury in this matter. Then at the time of the motion in limine, Judge Nevas had determined that Mr. Miller was incompetent to proceed to trial. He believes that I set him up. At that hearing Mr. Miller believes I raised the issue to charge him under 875(c) to prevent him from using his intent, that Mr. Miller could properly raise in a trial of section 875(b). Mr. Miller believes that I raised that issue in order to coerce a guilty plea out of him, and that I did something that was not in his interest. And it is true that I did not consult with him.

Also Mr. Miller believes that I filed <u>DEFENDANT'S MOTION FOR OPENING STATEMENT</u> after Judge Nevas ordered this competency evaluation to conspire with Judge Nevas on a false story published by THE CONNECTICUT POST which stated he was committed because he wanted to make an opening statement, **which in fact never occurred during the hearing on the government's motion in limine.** He has expressed to me that he believes I am conspiring with the government, and that I have lied to him during a number of phone conversations over the course of the last two months. He has told me that I am surreptitious, that I am underhanded, that I am a liar, and that he refuses to allow me to represent him. And frankly your honor, I don't believe that in the context of that situation that it is appropriate to proceed with a competency hearing at this time.

THE COURT: Thank you, does the government wish to respond?

MR. APPLETON: Your honor I would simply state Mr. Reeve, as the court is well aware, is going to zealously and effectively represent the interest of his client. It appears that this is somewhat of a tactic to delay the inevitable. As the case law is clear, Mr. Miller does not have the right to any counsel, but to counsel. I don't believe there's anything that has just been cited that leads to the conclusion it should be unreasonable for Mr. Reeve to represent Mr. Miller, at least as far as these proceedings are concerned.

THE COURT: I understand Mr. Reeve's concern about his professional position in this case. For example, the item you raised of concern to your client was your refusal to draft an affidavit giving him the right to waive the issue of competency. I wouldn't accept that waiver without a hearing on the issue of competency. So there's always a little bit of the issue of which comes first, the chicken or the egg. And I don't know how to resolve that. But we are going to start today with a competency hearing. I think I see Dr. Amble in the court.

The question of competency is one where the burden lies with the government. The government here is claiming incompetence. I'm going to put the burden on the government to start off, let's go.

I should say with regard to the motion to go pro se, a competency hearing is needed before I could consider that motion. That's another reason why I'm going forward with the competency hearing.

MR. REEVE: Your honor before we proceed, Mr. Miller would like to address the court on the issue of counsel.

THE COURT: He's got a lawyer. I don't need to hear from him, thank you.

DIRECT EXAMINATION BY MR. APPLETON

Q. Dr. Kucharski, how are you permanently employed sir?

A. I'm a forensic psychologist for the Bureau of Prisons stationed at the Metropolitan Correction Center in New York.

Q. Now Dr. Kucharski, do you know the defendant in this case, Stephen Miller?

A. I know Mr. Miller from my personal interviews with him in May 1995, for approximately five hours. I was ordered by Judge Nevas to conduct an evaluation regarding his competency to stand trial. Beside the normal process used to conduct a competency evaluation I have been the recipient of a number of letters from Mr. Miller that were addressed to me to be delivered to the United States Attorney, Mary Jo White. Those letters came subsequent to the filing of my report. I should comment that I also had meetings subsequent the receipt of those letters with the Deputy Assistant United States Attorney for the Southern District of New York who is responsible for prosecution of organized crime.

Q. We'll get into that later. Dr. Kucharski did you formulate a diagnosis in connection with your evaluation of Mr. Miller?

A. Yes I did. Given that competence is predicated on the existence of mental illness, it was my opinion that Mr. Miller currently or at the time suffered from a mental illness, that his illness was longstanding. It's my belief that Mr. Miller suffers from a delusional disorder. His delusional disorder has both grandiose and paranoid features. He has a very elaborate rather circumcised, non-bizarre delusional belief of a conspiracy on the part of the commodities market to have fixed prices. Mr. Miller has a fixed, longstanding belief system that the governors of the commodities market and individuals including former attorney general, former judges, and former attorneys have been orchestrating a great, white-collar crime. So there's a conspiratorial, paranoid quality to his belief system. There's also a grandiose quality in that he believes that he has a special insight regarding this conspiracy. **Its quite possible that the commodities market is rigged and I wouldn't have any way of knowing whether it was, or whether it wasn't.**

Q. Then why do you say it's delusional if that's the case?

A. It is a very powerful central belief of Mr. Miller that he's not mentally ill. It's what we sometimes refer to as delusional denial.

Q. Doctor, assume Mr. Miller is right, that the fraud does exist, would your opinion be the same?

A. Yes it would.

Q. And why is that?

A. Because of the expanding nature to include individuals who are highly unlikely to have been involved in this commodities scandal, including the Attorney General of the United States. I know personally that I'm not involved in this conspiracy. Even if it were true, Mr. Miller interprets the actions of many individuals as a product of that conspiracy, which would be a misrepresentation of reality on his part.

Q. What do you mean by a product of the conspiracy?

A. The fact that I would say to Mr. Miller, I think you have a mental illness must mean that I am trying to suppress information regarding this conspiracy. It's not possible that I could be partially accurate as a person who perceives him as mentally ill, making me part of the conspiracy, as well.

Q. On page six of your report you refer to the fact that Mr. Miller seeks venue into the federal courts by committing crimes for purposes of exposing the copper conspiracy. Perhaps you could explain a little more about that?

A. Without forming an opinion about criminal responsibility**, it's clear to me that Mr. Miller is not a typical individual in terms of his criminal acts. He does not appear to me to be a person who would engage in extortion for financial gain.** Mr. Miller's motivation, it appears to me, has not been for financial gain, but to draw attention to find a way to finally have someone attend to this perceived fraudulent conspiracy to rig copper prices.

Dr. Kucharski, made it clear to the court that my intent was not to extort. When I finally got to trial in 1996, I wanted to call him as my witness. **I can't lose my trial with Dr. Kucharski's professional, expert opinion.** But as you will learn Judge Nevas will decide to prevent me from any mention concerning this mental health episode.

Q.   What relevance, if any, does that have with respect to Mr. Miller's competence to stand trial?

A.   Its clear to me that Mr. Miller has a factual understanding of what goes on in the court. **He is a very bright, intelligent man, and he's very articulate.** It goes to the issue of the rational understanding of the proceedings.

Q.   Assume that he is unwilling to consider an insanity defense to the charges. What effect, if any, does that have on Mr. Miller's rational ability to understand the nature and consequences of the proceedings?

A.   A defendant's ability to consider an insanity defense and to waive an insanity defense must be rational. There are very good reasons often for a defendant to not want to pursue an insanity defense. That should be a choice that is made in the context of weighing the merits of all other possible options. When an individual is in marked denial of his psychiatric disorder, such that he can't perceive himself as mentally ill, he can't perceive that as a potential defense. And in fact, he sees that defense as potentially very harmful and damaging to him as opposed to one of the multiple options that he could pursue in any kind of court proceeding. Not only is his ability to weigh the merits of the insanity defense limited, but it impairs his ability to weigh the merits of the other defenses because they are in essence defenses that need to be rationally considered. The whole process of evaluating his legal strategy is impacted by his inability to rationally weigh the merits of the insanity defense.

Q.   Are you saying that it would be rational to reject the insanity defense if you consider it?

A.   I think the decision of which defense the defendant is going to pursue is the defendant's decision. And before that decision can be made there must be a rational consideration of all various options. It then places counsel in the position of explaining those various options, giving legal advice as to the merits and consequences. In this case the defendant has real problems in terms of his ability to rationally do so.

Q. In your opinion based on your interviews and what you know, has he rationally considered the insanity defense?

A. In this case I think that there are real problems in terms of his ability to rationally do so.

Q. How about with respect to the second prong of the competency issue, that is his ability to assist counsel? Have you come to an assessment on that issue?

A. Yes I have. Mr. Miller can speak in a quite articulate way. He's capable of communicating to others what he thinks. The ability to assist counsel involves a very interactive mode that involves a certain degree of intellectual sophistication and cognitive ability unencumbered by delusional ideas.

Q. How does that relate to this case with Mr. Miller?

A. I don't think that Mr. Miller can accept that mental illness has played a role in his defense. And given that, I think it has severely impaired his ability to interact and work with counsel. There maybe good reasons for wanting to represent yourself. I don't know of any, but nonetheless, there may be and they may be rational. But if that decision to waive the right to counsel and to go pro se is based on the belief that counsel is somehow perpetrating a hoax, somehow collaborating with the United States Attorney's office, he's a liar, he's deceitful, then another element of competency, which is the waiver of important constitutional rights, the right to counsel, and his right to go pro se is impaired. The difficulties he's having with Mr. Reeve, that is a thorny issue in terms of consultative abilities.

Q. In your opinion doctor, does Mr. Miller have the capability to rationally waive constitutional rights and assist in his defense?

A. In my opinion he does not. Because of his delusional disorder he's not able to weigh the merits of pro se representation versus representation by counsel.

Q. Please tell the court what is your conclusion concerning Mr. Miller's competence to stand trial in connection with this case?

A. That he does not have a rational understanding of the proceedings against him, and that he is mentally ill, that he suffers from a delusional disorder. He does not have the ability to assist counsel, he does not have the ability to make crucial constitutional waivers to enter a plea agreement, or to engage in many aspects of competence as I see them in terms of a trial.

Q. Now you've mentioned before that you received correspondence from Mr. Miller subsequent to your issuance of this report in this case. Could you relate to the court the substance of that correspondence?

A. They are difficult to relate in terms of a comprehensive picture, specifically in terms of the motivation. Those letters allege that Judge Nevas has been abducted along with two of the governors of the commodities market. Mr. Miller believes that these individuals have been abducted by people who he refers to as the bosses, which I interpret to mean organized crime figures. There's a history of him speaking to John Gotti's attorney for example. There's other information that relates to ideas or thoughts or statements he's made about John Gotti, So I infer from this, what he means by the bosses is that he believes that Judge Nevas has been abducted and is being held somewhere. He goes on to speak at great length about the incompetence of Ms. White and others in her office for failing to free Judge Nevas from this abduction, and that her failure to do so is evidence of the government's involvement in this commodities conspiracy. There's a tremendous amount of information which to me brings his delusion more to the foreground in terms of the court actually involved. Somehow this belief in this commodities conspiracy has led to Mr. Miller making allegations that Judge Nevas and the other individuals have been abducted together, and that the government has done nothing about this. He doesn't go as far as to say Judge Nevas is involved in the conspiracy, but it certainly is a very unusual twist to have the judge that's presiding over his case be alleged to have been abducted.

Somehow I don't know how this fits in terms of his motivation and what's going on in his head regarding this. But it certainly is troubling in terms of his understanding the proceedings and how he would be able to proceed under those conditions.

Q. In connection with your assessment regarding competence, what relevance if any do those letters hold?

A. I think they are further evidence of the expanding nature of the conspiracy. So those letters I think are confirmatory of some of my earlier views and opinions of Mr. Miller.

MR. APPLETON: No further questions your honor.

THE COURT: Thank you, Mr. Reeve.

CROSS EXAMINATION BY MR. REEVE

Q. Dr. Kucharski, your position is not that a criminal defendant is competent only if he makes correct decisions in his case, right?

A. That's correct.

Q. In other words, competent people can make very bad decisions in this process?

A. I assume so, yes.

Q. And they may decide to go to trial when in hindsight or maybe in foresight that's a bad decision, right?

A. Yes, that's correct.

Q. Doesn't that make them incompetent?

A. That's correct.

Q. As I understand what you're saying, an individual must look at the potential consequences of what options are open to him as he sits charged with a crime in the criminal justice system, correct?

A. That's an element of competency, yes.

Q. And in fact if he is found incompetent, he is looking at an intermediate period of time in the custody of the Bureau of Prisons, correct?

A. That's not exactly correct. If he's found incompetent, he would be hospitalized for a period not to exceed four months to determine whether he could be restored. There's a possibility that that process would result in restoration and he would return and go to trial.

Q. But your view on that issue is that it's unlikely that he's going to be restored to competency, right?

A. No, that's not my view.

Q. You believe there is a likelihood that he will be restored to competency?

A. Yes.

Q. If he pursued an insanity defense, then he could be incarcerated for an indefinite period of time, correct?

A. Subsequent to a finding of dangerous, yes.

Q. And as long as psychiatrists in the employ of the Bureau of Prisons made a determination that he was dangerous to himself or to others, his incarceration could go on in perpetuity, correct?

A. No, that again is slightly off. It would be a judge's decision as to whether or not he was dangerous and would continue to be incarcerated.

Q. But if the judge found he was dangerous he could be looking at a totally indefinite period of incarceration, is that right?

A. That's possible, yes.

Q. **Wouldn't you say that a rational person would take a look at that and assess the potential consequences which may lie down the road in assessing whether to insert an insanity defense?**

A. Yes, that's my point.

Q. **And wouldn't you agree that Mr. Miller has examined those issues in detail?**

A.   No, I do not agree with that at all.

Q.   Did you ever discuss the possible consequences with him if he asserted an insanity defense?

A.   Yes.

Q.   And didn't he talk to you about his fears of continued indefinite incarceration?

A.   Certainly he did, yes.

Q.   So he has thought about these consequences, right?

A.   I think your question was did he think about it rationally.

Q.   By the way, do you believe that Mr. Miller is presently a danger to himself or others?

A.   I have no opinion, I have not assessed that.

Q.   Now you indicate that you don't know whether there was or was not fraud in the copper market, right?

A.   I presume there probably is some minor fraud, but I don't know of any fraud of the magnitude that Mr. Miller is talking about.

Q.   You presume during the course of your evaluation of him that the major fraud that Mr. Miller described is not real, right?

A.   I presume that, yes.

Q.   And you don't know that?

A.   No, I don't.

Q.   You indicated to this court that one of the bases for your opinion that Mr. Miller is delusional is because this fraud is not real, he rejected your opinion, correct?

A.   No, I don't believe that was the substance of my testimony. The substance of my testimony was that it is conceivable that there is a fraud in the commodities market, and that that belief in and of itself was not the basis of my opinion that he was mentally ill. But the expanding nature of how other individuals become incorporated into this conspiratorial notion forms the basis of my belief that he's mentally ill.

Q.   Correct me if I'm wrong, I understood your testimony provided your opinion to him that his beliefs are delusional, right?

A.   Yes.

Q.   But you don't know in fact that they are delusional?

A.   No it's my opinion.

Q.   And you don't really have a basis for knowing if they're delusional?

A.   Yes I do. I believe I do.

Q.   In terms of the facts as relate to the copper market?

A.   Well, I believe that I'm not part of that conspiracy. When I get brought into it, I think I have a basis for saying whether or not I am personally part of that.

Dr. Kucharski knows a number of undisputed facts important to this case. He knows that Congressman Shays wrote a letter to Attorney General Thornburgh that stated Shays' concern that the CFTC exhibited systemic regulatory weakness regarding fraudulent price setting by COMEX. I tried to get Dick Reeve to force Dr. Kucharski to answer the following direct question. **If you are in fact a knowing part of this conspiracy right now as you testify, you are not about to admit your guilt to this court, right? His only possible answer would be, of course I'm not about to admit that on this witness stand.**

Could Dr. Kucharski state that he would admit his own guilt if he was a knowing part of this conspiracy? If he decided to claim that he would admit guilt, that would be a lie on its face. When Shays wrote and sent his letter to Thornburgh he dropped the crime in Thornburgh's lap. Shays disputed the investigation by the GAO of the CFTC, which obligated the Justice Department to investigate Shays' allegations. After that point in time the reliance by the Attorney General upon the CFTC's investigation of COMEX was moot. Did Kucharski believe that Shays was delusional too?

Playing stupid is commonly accepted by our society. That is what is going on in this court room right now. I am considered impolite for pointing this out but I am being kept in prison without due process.

Finally, Kucharski knows I'm competent and not delusional, so he is conspiring with Nevas to keep me from going to trial. Nevas isn't keeping me from going to trial because he thinks I might be acquitted, he is keeping me from exposing Thornburgh, Barr, Reno and other senior officials who refused to investigate a large number of complaints from Shays and others.

Q.   Let's talk about that for a minute. When you say you're brought into the conspiracy, are you telling the court that Mr. Miller believes that you are an active participant in the copper fraud as he perceives it, or is what he is really saying, your failure to act makes you a conspirator, that is, your silence or acquiescence, which is it?

A.   I think there's a third, it's neither of those.

Q.   What's that?

A.   The third opinion is in essence, I'm involved in at least a cover up of that conspiracy.

Q.   Because your determination that he is incompetent, if relied on by the court, eliminates the possibility of the trial he needs to prove he is innocent of intending to extort money from Mr. Jossen and Mr. Moore, right?

A. I don't have anyway of knowing that. It's conceivable. I don't know if it's within the scope of an expert testimony. It's possible that that would happen, yes.

Q. And he does not want you to come in this court and say that he's incompetent, right?

A. I would presume that yes.

Q. He wants to be found competent, right?

A. That's correct.

Q. And he wants to proceed to trial, right?

A. Right.

Q. And he's told you that?

A. Yes.

Q. On repeated occasions?

A. Yes.

Q. And you indicated in your testimony that part of your basis for determining he does not have a rational understanding, is your view that the criminal justice system, I think these are your words, that a defendant should be focused solely on the issue of adjudicating his innocence or guilt on the underlying offense, in this case extortion. Is that right?

A. Correct.

Q. I take it then that from your prospective, people who commit acts of civil disobedience intentionally are incompetent?

A. No. Because civil disobedience is not the product of a delusion. To be incompetent one has to be mentally ill first. If I'm acting in some very bizarre manner as a product of a mental illness that would get me arrested for civil disobedience, which I don't believe is against the law, we're talking in circles. The difference and distinction here is that the basis for the process of viewing the court as a forum, is the product of mental illness. Absent a mental illness, he can believe anything he wants and still be competent. It's no longer part of my expertise. The situation here is that his belief is the product of a mental illness.

Q. In order for Mr. Miller, in your view to be competent, he would have to divorce himself from his belief about the COMEX conspiracy?

A. No.

Q. What changes in Mr. Miller would render him competent?

A. If Mr. Miller was able to say, counsel, I don't believe I have a mental illness, nonetheless, everybody else does. I think that it may well be reasonable for us to talk about the basis of a legal strategy involving insanity. I've opined on many occasions that delusional people are able to go to trial because their delusion doesn't have anything to do with the trial. He may say I don't want the insanity defense for very rational reasons and at the same time retain his delusion. It's not mutually exclusive. He can be delusional and be competent. He can reject the insanity defense and be competent.

Q.   In your view for Mr. Miller to be competent he has to acknowledge that your opinion is correct and that he suffers from a mental illness?

A.   No, he does not.

Q.   So he can still be competent and believe he's not mentally ill, is that right?

A.   That's correct.

Q.   Do you agree that Mr. Miller's prior experiences within the federal criminal justice system can have a bearing in a rational way on his choices now?

A.   Certainly.

Q.   The only choice that Mr. Miller has for avoiding the Bureau of Prisons treating him for mental illness is if he's found not guilty, right?

A.   Right.

Q.   Your strong opinion is he understands the participants in this proceeding, right?

A.   He has a very strong factual understanding of the proceedings.

Q.   And your opinion is that he can communicate, he communicated with you?

A.   Definitely, yes.

MR. REEVE: Your honor, I would like to review the doctor's notes, and I'd also like to see the letters before I say I'm done with my cross examination. I think I have a right to do that.

THE COURT: Did you seek them before starting the examination?

MR. REEVE: I did not.

THE COURT: To the extent they're available, unless the government has objection, they'll be made available to counsel. We'll take a recess.

DIRECT EXAMINATION BY A.U.S.A. APPLETON

Q.   Good afternoon Dr. Amble. We met before, right?

A.   Yes.

Q.   Prior to your report of February 17, 1995 we discussed this case, right?

A.   Yes.

Q.   And prior to February 17th, you had the opportunity to interview and conduct an evaluation of Mr. Miller in connection with his pending case in federal court in the District of Connecticut, right?

A. Yes.

Q. Now Dr. Amble, in your report you conclude that Mr. Miller at the time was competent to stand trial?

A. Well I concluded that he understood the nature and consequences of the proceedings against him. And that he had the ability to properly assist counsel in his defense.

Q. Now you have learned by what was represented by Mr. Reeve at the beginning of this proceeding that the defendant is dissatisfied with his counsel because his counsel didn't file a waiver of appellate rights, and Mr. Miller claims Mr. Reeve set him up at the time of the hearing to exclude evidence because Mr. Reeve failed to consult with Mr. Miller concerning the use by the government of charging 875(c), do you remember that?

A. About the 875(c)?

Q. In any event, if you don't remember that, do you remember that Mr. Miller is dissatisfied with Mr. Reeve, correct?

A. Yes.

Q. He has moved to withdraw from the case?

A. Yes.

Q. In light of those facts, does your opinion change regarding Mr. Miller's competence to stand trial in this case?

A. The opinion I gave on February 17th does not change. I don't have sufficient basis to draw a new conclusion.

Q. Would you say then, that Mr. Miller is competent to stand trial as you sit here today with what you know?

A. No.

THE COURT: That answer no, didn't mean in your view, that he's incompetent. You just don't have an opinion?

THE WITNESS: I just don't have an opinion.

THE COURT: As of today?

THE WITNESS: Yes.

THE COURT: Thank you.

CROSS EXAMINATION BY MR. REEVE

Q. Dr. Amble, you're indicating you don't have a present opinion now. You did have an opinion in February that he was competent?

A. Yes.

Q. You indicated that Mr. Miller had in your view, some reasonable arguments not to pursue an insanity defense, right?

A. Yes I did state that in my report. Could you point to me where?

Q. It's the second full paragraph on page 12.

A. Yes.

Q. At that time you indicate you were of the opinion that he had a rational understanding of his options, and that his decisions with respect to his defense were reasonable, right?

A. Yes.

Q. I take it you mean he could have presented an insanity defense or he could have decided not to, and the decision that he made to not present an insanity defense was rational, right?

A. Yes it was based on rational reasoning, yes.

Q. It doesn't mean it was the correct decision, but it means that there was some reasoning underlying his decision making process, right?

A. Yes.

Q. And you reached that conclusion because you discussed the underlying reasons with him?

A. Yes.

Q. And you spent some time trying to understand what was motivating Mr. Miller in terms of reaching the decision not to pursue an insanity defense, correct?

A. Yes.

MR. REEVE: I have no further questions. Your honor, Mr. Miller would like to testify.

THE COURT: All right, he's entitled to. I take it you've advised him the testimony under certain circumstances may be used against him?

MR. REEVE: Yes your honor.

THE COURT: Do you understand that Mr. Miller?

THE DEFENDANT: Absolutely your honor.

DIRECT EXAMINATION BY MR. REEVE

Q. Mr. Miller how old are you?

A. 52.

Q. And you are presently incarcerated in Otisville?

A. Yes I am.

Q. For how long have you been at Otisville?

A. Since June 14, 1995.

Q. Can you tell the court what you have done for a living, your main source of livelihood?

A. Yes I can. I began working on Wall Street in 1966, and became a stock broker and commodities broker. I have worked as a broker, a consultant, and a money manager since that time.

Q. As a result of your employment experiences, do you have beliefs about fraud that has existed in the copper market?

A. Yes I do.

Q. And do you have beliefs about fraud, which has been ongoing in the copper market?

A. Yes I do.

Q. And have you made efforts to complain to both state and federal law enforcement authorities?

A. Only to federal law enforcement authorities.

Q. Have those efforts been successful in that they have ever led to an investigation?

A. The efforts of my complaints as I pursued them is a long story, can I expand on this please?

Q. Okay.

A. Initially I was told that a fraud was being perpetrated by a very unique individual named David Johnston. Mr. Johnston was the Director of the Commodities Department for E.F. Hutton while I had been a broker for Hutton. Mr. Johnston was also the largest commission producer for Hutton and was on the Board of Directors. He had huge accounts which traded copper in particular and he had also been a Governor on the COMEX Board. During a phone conversation with Mr. Johnston at his home in Southport, Ct. on October 17th, 1987, which I had initiated to discuss the opening by David of a potentially very large account to trade copper for a large end user of copper wire. We began discussing factors which were influencing the current price trend which had rallied copper prices from about $.65 per pound in May 1987 to the current price in October of $.87. My purpose for calling Dave was to use his influence and credentials to impress my client. My client was Echlin Inc. who I had worked for since 1979, managing their copper risk management effort. The last time I had dealings with Mr. Johnston had been five years earlier in 1982. I was feeling Mr. Johnston out about his view of the copper market, which he stated would continue moving higher. When I asked him why he felt copper prices would move higher, his reason was because the dollar was weak. I replied back that if copper prices were going higher because the dollar was weak, it would stand to reason that all other international commodities such as gold, oil, sugar, wheat, cotton, etc. would also be affected, but they hadn't been. I was being polite because his reason was foolish. He then made a statement I will never forget.

He said, "There's a game being played."

'There's a game being played," means the price is being rigged illegally.

Coincidentally, I had an appointment on October 20th, at Echlin to meet with Echlin's C.F.O., Dick Patterson, the Treasurer, Rich Wisot, and Bill Bowman, who was their consultant for pension investments and had been invited by Rich Wisot to consider my proposal concerning the price inversion of copper futures contracts, discounting the back contract prices. This had tipped me off to the fraud before I spoke with Dave Johnston. When price inversions occur in commodities which are both storageable and nonseasonal, they only invert after the price has risen substantially. This is always the case. Contracts don't begin to invert at historically low prices which is what began in copper during June 1987, when copper prices were trading for a long time at $.65 per pound. These are facts which knowledgeable investigators need to know.

If I had been given cooperation from the C.F.T.C. or the Chief of Commodities & Securities Fraud Division unit, I would have been able to show them historical price charts so they could have learned the important facts which related to many pieces of evidence which would convict the COMEX crooks. I can assure you that the bureaucrats working for the government who have no experience trading commodities as professionals don't know what I have learned during my many years of experience.

On the day before the Echlin meeting, October 19th, was the infamous "Black Monday Crash" of 508 points for the Dow Jones Industrial Average. My life was filled with memorable events on my Saturday conversation with Dave Johnston, the Monday stock market crash, the Tuesday meeting at Echlin, and the simultaneous crash of copper prices along with pandemonium and panic which clobbered all commodities futures contracts.

I was very focused on copper prices and considered the severe problem David Johnston and his colleagues had, concerning huge margin calls on their copper positions which had dropped from $.87 down to $.74 on the opening Tuesday morning. "The game being played", backfired.

David Johnston and his colleagues, the criminals rigging copper prices at COMEX went broke overnight. They became desperate. They had been caught with their pants down. They had to jack prices back up immediately because they had no money to finance their huge losses. There are technicalities involved in my explanation which I know this court will not understand. After the close of trading, there now became three and four cent changes to contract prices by the five man COMEX Quotations Committee. The evidence of this fraud now was staggering and very simple. No one with a copper position could miss the spectacular aberrations which changed the real price after trading ended. It was similar to the score of major league baseball games being changed half an hour after the games were completed and the phony scores were posted in the newspapers each day. Who could miss such an obvious fraud? No one having a position in the copper market could fail to see the fraud.

First I decided to go personally to COMEX at the World Trade Center to visit the Compliance Officer for COMEX to learn what he intended to do about the mind boggling fraud which had concocted prices back from $.74 to $.87, in only four trading days which followed the world wide panic. I found their compliance office on the third floor and entered to meet the compliance officer. I greeted a secretary and explained my purpose. First a Mr. Cohen, the market surveillance official invited me into his office. My first request was to see the written rules or by-laws concerning settlement prices. We chatted a bit and I asked Mr. Cohen if he had noticed the enormous disparity which changed contract prices after trading hours?

He seemed evasive and excused himself. A minute later Tom Cohen brought Jim Goodwin, Vice President of Compliance, to meet me. Mr. Goodwin invited us into his office where I began again to ask for the rules. Mr. Goodwin told Mr. Cohen to fetch the rules for me, and we continued our conversation in a pleasant manner. But Mr. Goodwin denied knowing or recognizing any type of fraud concerning the huge changes after the close.

It isn't polite in American culture to say, Mr. Goodwin either you are a liar who believes he is talking to a simpleton, or you are a simpleton who has no clue no idea what is happening. I decided to remain polite because I expected that Mr. Goodwin got my message and would take appropriate steps to stop this fraud in its tracks.

My final point was that I was there to recover my own personal loss or I intended to seek help from the C.F.T.C. When I left Mr. Goodwin's office, I expected the fraud would cease and the market would snap back on its own.

David Johnston and his group of crooks had an opportunity to cash out with the sizable gains they had at $.87, but they decided not to stop at that point. The price rocketed to $1.40 by year end.

My next visit two days later was to the C.F.T.C. office at the World Trade Center. First I spent three hours with a lady who patiently took voluminous notes.

The next Saturday, October 31st, I was invited by David Johnston to meet at his mansion on Sasco Hill Road to discuss the Echlin account. As we discussed the fraud and the profit potential for Echlin, I asked

Dave what we would do if the stock market took another dive. He laughed and said, "Pray a lot." He handed me an account form and expected I would set up the Echlin account, shortly.

The next Monday morning I was back to the C.F.T.C. office to explain my meeting with Dave Johnston at his home. It was then that I met the Regional Director, Herbert Sue. I suggested that he contact the F.B.I. for them to put a wire on me before I went back to David Johnston's office for the meeting Dave had expected. I would then be able to discuss the fraud with Dave again but this time it would be on tape. I was amazed when Mr. Sue refused to contact the F.B.I. Instead he asked me to return after lunch to speak with their economist, which I did. This encounter with the C.F.T.C. began their stonewalling operation which is now in this phase along with the Justice Department. Preventing me from trial is a stonewalling operation aided by the Court. Isn't the Judicial Branch of government supposed to be a check and balance to the Executive Branch?

When I tried to speak with someone in the U.S. Attorney's office in Bridgeport, they dragged their feet. I went to F.B.I. headquarters in Manhattan which became another waste of time.

Finally I went to a town hall meeting in Fairfield to meet Congressman Shays. I wanted to be in front of a group of citizens so I could put Shays on the spot. This tactic worked. Shays suggested a meeting in his Bridgeport office. Before my meeting to see Shays I spoke with Attorney Frank Riccio to ask him to accompany me to see Shays. This meeting with Shays led to a follow up meeting at Shays office in Washington. It was the meeting at Shays' Washington office that he decided to be diligent. Shays was on the Government Operations Committee which had oversight over the G.A.O. He decided to request an investigation by the G.A.O. into the way the C.F.T.C. had responded to my complaint. Shays tasked Chris Mathews a Minority Staff person working on the Government Operations Committee to work with me to compile critical evidence from the COMEX computer files for months of trading prices called the Time & Sales Register. This evidence gave me the critical data so I could generate an analysis to clarify the fraud on a daily basis.

The G.A.O. investigators never contacted me directly. I became concerned that its investigators would lack the knowledge and experience about the rules and the facts concerning this specific investigation. I was also concerned that the C.F.T.C. officials who had decided to allow this fraud to continue on a daily basis would intimidate the G.A.O. investigators who probably didn't hIvI any idea what this investigation was all about. I could only try to educate Chris Mathews and then hope that he could guide the G.A.O. investigators into recognizing the daily pattern which still continued as the months progressed from 1987, into the beginning of 1989.

At this point I want to thank this court for its indulgence of my long tale. I have skipped many important details which are intertwined involving many meetings with attorneys and corporate executives whose companies had been impacted by the copper fraud. I am trying to address enough key incidents to portray a comprehensive picture concerning my competency for trial by this court. I might add that Dr. Kucharski refused to allow me to explain the copper fraud and to analyze the letters written by Congressman Shays. I will soon conclude my testimony by explaining a fascinating encounter which led up to the Shays' letters I have just referred to.

Sometime in early 1989, and after more than a year had expired from the time Shays had initiated the G.A.O. investigation I received a most memorable phone call from Congressman Shays. I answered my phone and heard, "Steve, this is Chris." Shays has a very high pitched voice so I knew immediately it was him. He said, "They said you're full of shit."

I asked him, "Who said I was full of shit." I was dumbfounded by the way he put it.

He said, "The G.A.O. sees no problem with the C.F.T.C."

I said, "Okay, can I make a final request and I'll drop this issue. How about a meeting in your office with the C.F.T.C., the G.A.O., you, and me? Then you'll find out who's full of shit here."

He agreed. I went to his Washington office for the meeting about a week later. The following details of this meeting are crucial to my testimony concerning my competency for trial and the false testimony and false reports presented to this court by Dr. Kucharski, today. It is foolish to expect Dr. Kucharski to admit he is here to commit perjury in order to protect his job working for the Attorney General and working directly for the United States Attorney for the Southern District of New York. It is preposterous for Dr, Kucharski to fail to grasp the fact that when Attorney General Richard Thornburgh received the letter from United States Congressman Christopher Shays who addressed the COMEX fraud to rig global copper prices, that this crime was put directly into the lap of the Attorney General. Unless Mr. Thornburgh acted responsibly by responding to Congressman Shays the Attorney General automatically became a willing conspirator with the COMEX crooks. The Attorney General is obligated under the law to respond to Shays or he is obstructing justice.

I must also commend my counsel for his brilliant cross examination of Dr. Kucharski which left no doubt as to Kucharski's willingness to commit perjury and insult this court's intelligence. The strategy

Dr. Kucharski seems to believe will work is to expand the conspiracy to himself and then claim Miller is delusional when he claims the conspiracy is expanding. Why not fill this court with 50 more marshals and other government officials to expand the conspiracy faster and further?

I will rap up now with a brief description of our meeting in Congressman's Shays office which influenced him to write his letter to Controller General Charles Bowsher, and to Attorney General Thornburgh in February and March 1989, successively.

There were two C.F.T.C. officials and three G.A.O. officials there with Congressman Shays and myself. All three G.A.O. investigators sat on the couch throughout the meeting and never said a word. One C.F.T.C. official began speaking, using a lot of jargon and sounding very technical. But in essence it was mumbo jumbo. I had no idea what he was saying. It became obvious to me that this was a filibuster because he knew that my last meeting would be no more than an hour at best.

I decided to interrupt politely. I said directly that I had no idea what this man was talking about and that it was apparent that he intended to run out the clock and bury me. Shays then said, "We're not here to point our fingers at anyone."

I then replied that I am pointing my finger directly at this C.F.T.C. official who is covering up this fraud. I would like to put my evidence on this table so we can all see it and let it speak for itself. I then laid some documents on the conference table and pointed to the prices. I pointed to the last price of each day and showed the huge discrepancy of the settlement price chosen by the Quotations Committee members which simply falsified the price of copper on that same day. I said, "Any fool can see this simple, unsophisticated fraud, and now Congressman Shays can see who's full of shit here."

Nobody decided to argue my point because it was so simple. The COMEX by laws were very brief and very simple concerning the duties of the Quotations Committee. It was this meeting which led to the letters written by Congressman Shays to Thornburgh and Bowsher, and those letters gave Thornburgh unmitigated responsibility to stop this crime from continuing. May it please the court to allow me to read these letters into the court's record now.

Dear Mr. Attorney General:

This acknowledges Assistant Attorney General Thomas Boyd's letter of March 28, advising me the Justice Department is not willing to respond to my request to look into potentially illegal price setting on the New York Commodities Exchange (COMEX), specifically on the copper futures market. I find this particularly disappointing in light of the Justice Department's investigation of the Chicago Board of Trade and the Chicago Mercantile Exchange.

What I find most disturbing, however, is the referral of my concern to the Commodities Futures Trading Commission (CFTC), especially in light of current investigations into the ability of the CFTC to regulate and monitor commodities markets effectively. In previous correspondence, I have pointed out the CFTC has been unable to adequately address my concerns for more than one year.

I am specifically concerned that oversight of the COMEX by the CFTC has not been effective, and that illegal pricing, particularly in the copper market, may be occurring as a result.

I have pointed out to the General Accounting Office (GAO) that there maybe systemic weaknesses in the CFTC's market surveillance on the COMEX. It seems to me that sound regulatory mechanisms governing price setting on the COMEX by the CFTC, particularly on the copper futures market, do not exist. The checks and balances set up to ensure fair trading for all investors do not effectively guard against conflicts of interests for the Quotations Committees, whose members often trade on the same markets for which they set prices.

I am also concerned that a double standard exists between the penalties given prominent traders who have broken CFTC and COMEX regulations and those given less important investors. Specifically, just prior to his election as Chairman of the COMEX last year John Haneman paid $40,000 in fines for executing prearranged and non-competitive trades and for taking the other side of customer's orders, yet he continued to trade and was even elevated to a position of respect and responsibility. Conversely, I have a constituent who was fined $40,000 and given a five year trading ban in accordance with CFTC regulations for failing to report a large sugar position he held for a short period. A serious double standard appears to exist between this penalty Mr. Haneman received for a seemingly more heinous crime.

While I appreciate the Justice Department's need to allocate its limited resources in the most effective way it can, I am very concerned that Justice does not see the need to address my inquiry about potential pricing fraud on the New York copper market. These unusual pricing differentials do not seem in accordance with COMEX rules 4.25, 4.27, 4.38, 4.41, and Section 141b(2).

Please know I will continue to pursue this matter until I am satisfied allegations of fraud and abuse on the COMEX have been adequately addressed or disproved. It is my hope the Justice Department can be of assistance.

Thank you for your time and attention.

Sincerely, Christopher Shays, Member of Congress.

Your honor, please allow me one more paragraph that Congressman Shays wrote to Charles Bowsher, Controller General on February 9th.

In addition, other futures traders have confidentially expressed to my office their concerns about the way copper prices have been settled in recent months.

One thing that no exchange can control is the open interest, or the number of contracts that exist on a daily basis in each of the commodities traded on that exchange. The collapse of open interest of copper contracts from 85,000 contracts down to under 20,000 contracts while the price of copper skyrocketed from $.74 per pound to $1.40 is impossible without unambiguous fraud.

Q. Steve I'm going to interrupt you at this point. Its clear that you have a lot of knowledge about futures contract trading and the copper market, in addition to the fraud which has been occurring, right?

A. Yes. But if you don't mind I'd just like to stay on track here for another minute please. Thank you very much.

One of the points that Dr. Kucharski made to the court was that I won't consider other opinions. I don't know of another reasonable, and I **emphasize reasonable** opinion to consider. I would be happy to consider any opinion brought forward in good conscience, but the F.B.I.'s report failed to state there was not a fraud, but that they wanted more evidence. They failed to be clear about how much more evidence, or what type of evidence they wanted. Nobody refutes the facts and their meaning as I have presented them. The case here is just plain simple. The prices were changed on a daily basis after trading ended each and every day. The paper trail exhibits cold hard proof which Dr. Kucharski refused to examine. If the government hired 100 more psychologists to agree with Dr. Kucharski, it would just prove that they paid for more perjury than Dr. Kucharski offered to this court, to conspire with John Moore and the other COMEX crooks. I'm addressing this competency ruse now, not copper contracts. Dr. Kucharski has not presented my mental health truthfully to this court.

And lastly, I know Mr. Reeve is about the finest litigator I have ever watched in court, and I have told him that. When I have called him a liar and deceitful, it was based on very specific details in the record. Because I have pursued this fraud up the chain of command to the highest level, whoever my attorney might be will need to be concerned that his career is at risk to say the least.

My integrity is at stake, which I need this court to understand. I am not here to trick people by using a ruse insanity defense, incompetence, or a plea bargain. I am innocent of committing any crime. I have been the victim of the fraud we have been concerned with in this hearing.

The fraud is no more a perception of a crime than if Mr. Reeve was murdered here in this court room in front of all of us. **It's as obvious as when Jack Ruby shot Oswald on television in the police station.** This happens to be the reason that Congressman Shays wrote his letter to Attorney General Thornburgh. **Shays saw the evidence on the table in his conference room right in front of the two CFTC officials who claimed that I was full of shit. Shays saw that it was they who were full of shit.**

There is nothing new concerning our highest officials in America committing crimes and engaging in criminal conspiracies. We are all familiar with Richard Nixon and Watergate, the assassination of President Kennedy and the many murders of witnesses who wanted to spill the beans about their observations. The Iran/Contra conspiracy of Reagan, North, Poindexter, General Secord, and a long list of others. Let's not forget about the Keating "5" Senators who were brought up on ethics charges which swept their criminal charges under the rug. There is nothing new here. Our history is loaded with senior officials committing criminal conspiracies and people committing perjury to cover them up. Please ask me any question you like, I have nothing to hide.

Q.   You feel that Mr. Appleton, Judge Nevas, Dr. Kucharski, and I have a problem because our careers are at stake trying to protect the Attorney General. Tell Judge Daly what you mean by that.

A.   It is apparent to me that you four people believe that your careers would be protected by falsely claiming that I am incompetent, and mentally ill. I am positive that you people know that I am neither incompetent nor mentally ill. Your strategy for this court to commit me does two things. It discredits my claim that the conspiracy which allows COMEX to rig copper prices has been elevated to the most senior government officials now including the past three Attorney Generals, Thornburgh, Barr, and Reno. It also gets me locked up indefinitely without due process, which cripples my intentions to expose this massive conspiracy. I cannot agree more with Mr. Appleton's claim. I intend to use the court as a forum to expose the perpetrators of this crime, Mr. Moore and Mr. Jossen. Both of them will be forced to testify in order for the Justice Department to prosecute me. In fact Dr. Kucharski just testified that I did not intend to extort money or commit any criminal act. Dr. Kucharski will be my best witness in my trial.

Even though you just did a brilliant job today when you cross-examined Dr. Kucharski, you have been caught in the past trying to sabotage my case.

Q.   And do you mean and believe that Mr. Appleton, for example is actively involved in the conspiracy in the sense that he's meeting with Mr. Johnston or trading copper contracts?

A. I doubt that Mr. Appleton has ever traded futures contracts or has ever met with David Johnston. Mr. Appleton is trying to prevent me from my right to trial in front of a jury, which is precisely what he did during his hearing conducted on April 13th, on his MOTION IN LIMINE TO EXCLUDE EVIDENCE. Mr. Appleton is a bureaucrat, marching to the orders of his boss United States Attorney, Christopher Droney. They know they have the power and that they love to abuse their power. I suspect that they have never considered making money by protecting John Moore and Richard Jossen while they are ripping off lots of money illegally. They probably have never considered that John Moore and Richard Jossen would love to have them on their payroll. Mr. Appleton and his colleagues are illogical and truly don't have a rational understanding of these proceedings.

There is no way for me to know if Mr. Appleton is being directed or if he knows independently to protect the Attorney General. It's too bad we can't put him on the witness stand and ask him what is motivating him to prevent me from going to trial. I can only hope that my counsel might decide to convince Mr. Appleton that this case should be resolved by using a logical approach.

Q. All right, now is it correct that you do not want to assert an insanity defense in this case?

A. That's absolutely correct.

Q. And is it also correct that you would like to be found competent so that you can go to trial?

A. Absolutely.

Q. Can you explain to the court why it is that you wish not to pursue an insanity defense?

A. Sure. I am not guilty of extortion. I do not have any mental illness and I have never had one, nor has anyone ever claimed that I have ever had a mental illness. It would be stupid on my part for wanting to be committed. I am not going to lock myself up by asking this court to find me incompetent and then for this court to falsely claim that I am dangerous. The government has established on the record during its hearing on April 13th, that it won't risk putting me on trial in this case. Let's not forget that my jury had been chosen on April 11th. The hearing to exclude evidence was another dumb bluff by Mr. Appleton which failed and then led to the false statement by Judge Nevas published by THE CONNECTICUT POST.

The answer to your question is that for me to pursue an insanity

defense is an admission of guilt and would result in having myself
locked up. Now, that would be crazy. Aren't these wonderful reasons to
not use an insanity defense?

I need this court to know that you have never suggested to me to use
an insanity defense. I want you to tell this court, now, on the record,
what benefit you would recommend for me to use an insanity defense.
If you can define a benefit to me and to this court for me to use an
insanity defense, please put it on the record right now.

Q.   Now you and I have our differences in this case, is that fair to say?
A.   I didn't hear your recommendation to this court as to why an
     insanity defense would benefit me Mr. Reeve. Please don't avoid
     this issue.
Q.   Are you willing to consult with a lawyer?
A.   I just consulted with you now in this court room. You have failed to
     advise me why it is in my interest to use an insanity defense. I am
     trying to assist you in my defense and you are dodging my question
     in front of this court on the record.
Q.   Do you have any problem with evaluating the different options
     that are before you with respect to how to confront the charge in
     the indictment?
A.   I am trying to assist you now in my defense. I'm open to suggestion.
     I'm willing to change direction if you have a strategy which makes
     sense. I have already addressed the options which have been put
     on the table by the government. Do you want to counsel me to
     agree to the defense strategy which the government prefers?
Q.   Are you willing to consider raising an insanity defense?
A.   I have no intention of destroying my own credibility by making
     false claims. And again you have not told this court on the record,
     why it would be wise for me to raise In insanity defense.
Q.   Now you are aware of the ruling that was entered in this case by
     Judge Nevas as a result of the government's motion in limine,
     which was filed shortly before we were scheduled to begin trial,
     right?
A.   Pertaining to what?
Q.   Pertaining to the ability to present witnesses and your ability to call
     witnesses to establish the validity of your beliefs about the copper
     market and the fraud therein?
A.   Sure.
Q.   And I take it you disagree with that ruling?
A.   Of course.
Q.   And you understand that if you continue to pursue going to trial,
     you might not be able to present evidence of the fraud during the

criminal trial of the extortion charges that have been filed against you?

A.   The fraud by Moore and Jossen was written into my letters which must be offered by the government. The bluff by Mr. Appleton and Judge Nevas disregards evidence which they can't exclude or suppress. The COMEX fraud comes into evidence from my letters to Moore and to Jossen. Moore and Jossen are automatic government witnesses in my case who will become marvelous witnesses for me. Does the government want a jury to believe that I chose Moore and Jossen to randomly extort money which has no connection to the copper fraud by COMEX? The government keeps trapping itself in its attempt to ignore trying to help COMEX officials Moore and Jossen rig copper prices. The government is afraid to validate the copper fraud because the government is protecting this fraud. My defense gets better all the time unless the government can seat juror imbeciles or fake jurors who are federal judges and prosecutors.

Q.   Would it be your intention to make any outbursts in the courtroom if you didn't like any rulings?

A.   I have never done that yet and I have no intentions of doing that in the future.

Q.   And you understand that the judge sitting on the trial in your case makes decisions. You might not agree with some of them, but you must abide by his decisions during the trial.

A.   Definitely, and I also realize that improper decisions by the court can be appealed to the higher courts if they result in a guilty verdict too.

Q.   Now, there have been references by Dr. Kucharski about letters you addressed to the United States Attorney in the Southern District of New York. He indicated that that supported his conclusion that you were incompetent. Can you explain that situation?

A.   Yes. I need to have this court fully understand all the issues in their entirety. When I arrived at M.C.C. New York, I began having conversations with Anthony Sarivola and Bobby Montano. They both made it clear to me that they were mobbed up in one of the New York crime families. People in prison are naturally curious about why others are there. It was in my interest to convey my situation as it then stood. I explained to them that I was charged with extortion involving the top people who ran COMEX and who had been rigging copper prices with the blessing of the most senior government officials including Attorney General Janet Reno, William Barr, and Thornburgh. I also explained my professional experience as a broker with the prestigious firms of E.F. Hutton,

Reynolds, and Smith Barney. It was vital to explain that the government had just refused to allow me to proceed to trial and had sent me here to be evaluated by Dr. Kucharski for competency. I explained that my jury had been chosen and my trial was on the docket, but that the government had backed away from the trial which was evidence that it was trying to protect Thornburgh, Barr, and Reno because they knew my plan was to expose them.

I had no way to know that Sarivola and Montano were both government rats. Later while I was in Otisville I was told by other mob guys that Sarivola had been in the witness protection program before this, and was trying to get back out of prison by earning his way back into the witness protection program.

I had been trying to make my point to as many organized crime people who I was meeting at M.C.C. and at Otisville that I had created powerful evidence which I was willing to share with the right people about the massive corruption by very senior government officials who had encouraged the COMEX staff to continue rigging copper prices. It was in my interest that organized crime understood that I had created a potential scandal which I was willing to share with them. We all had a common enemy who was trying to punish us even though this common enemy were criminals themselves. I believed that these mobsters were spending a lot of their money on lawyers who they believed were trying to beat the government. I wanted these mobsters to know that I had created a powerful negotiating platform by amassing evidence proving that senior government people were guilty of allowing a massive Wall Street fraud. I wanted them to know that the U.S. Attorney in my case had used unethical tactics to prevent me from my right to trial because the senior officials controlling the Justice Department needed to prevent me from exposing the conspiracy by my going to trial. I needed them to know that I welcomed a chance to retaliate against the government and could in turn benefit them too.

Tony Sarivola appeared to be well educated and claimed he had close ties to John Gotti. Tony told me that John Gotti was the Godfather of his daughter. Also my cellie was calling Tony's daughter and claimed that she had visited him here at M.C.C. I also began to play gin with Bobby Montano who also appeared to be a bright guy and who claimed he owned bars in Greenwich Village. Even though Sarivola and Montano never associated with the other mob guys on 11 North, the Unit we were on, I never suspected that they were both rats who were working with Mary Jo White the U.S. Attorney.

When I knew that a rat was in our midst, I would warn other inmates to be careful.

During our conversations I explained that I had read many books about the mob and knew many of the stories which included the story about J. Edgar Hoover who had been controlled by Frank Costello because they had pictures of Hoover involved in homosexual acts. The fact that during Hoover's reign, the Feds very seldom prosecuted the mob, corroborated the black mail story. Hoover was on record claiming that organized crime didn't exist, even though we all know that that was a silly lie. One of the most clever stories I heard was that Frank Costello arranged a vacation in Florida for Hoover and his boy friend. Hoover and Clyde were given free hotel accommodations along with the normal guaranteed horse tips that never lost. The free hotel room gave Costello the perfect opportunity to get pictures of Hoover dressed as a woman and performing homosexual acts with his lover.

I kept trying to explain the similarity of Costello's advantage with Hoover and my advantage with Attorney General Janet Reno and United States Attorney Mary Jo White to the current mob leaders. For some reason I'll never understand the Genovese, Gambino, and Columbo family leaders never understood the comparison. The people I spoke with seemed to tune out.

One day Tony Sarivola told me that he wanted to talk to me and suggested that we go up to the roof for recreation. Of course I was eager because I believed that he really had powerful contacts. When we were on the roof he began to explain his plan to use my power against the government. Tony claimed that the plan was to kidnap Judge Nevas, John Moore, and Richard Jossen. I immediately told him that that was a crazy idea, which I wanted no part of. I tried to explain very courteously that his friends had failed to understand my power and that I would have nothing to do with any crime, much less kidnapping a federal judge. I explained to him that if they believed that kidnapping judges was a good idea that there was a whole courthouse full of judges across the street.

Now, Tony threatened me. He told me, "You don't understand. We aren't asking you, we're telling you. We will have you murdered in prison if you don't do as you're told." Then he went on to explain all of the details. After the three people are kidnapped, they want me to write a letter to Mary Jo White to explain that the hostages will be freed after certain friends of the kidnappers are freed. I was to explain how I was connected to the kidnappers. Tony explained to me that the government would need to obey my orders because the kidnapping would expose the COMEX copper rigging fraud and the huge scandal would blow up. The government would have to release me first and then I would be taken to the safe house where the hostages were being held so we could make a video about the copper fraud and the decision by

Judge Nevas to prevent me from going to trial because my trial would expose Thornburgh, Barr, and Reno.

Judge Nevas would explain on video tape that Dr. Kucharski would falsely claim that I was delusional and incompetent for trial, which would prevent the scandal I would create if I was allowed to go to trial. After the video tapes were sent to their lawyers, their lawyers could negotiate the release of key mobsters including John Gotti.

After I wrote my letter to Mary Jo White, Tony's lawyer would visit him so my letter could be delivered to her.

When we left the roof I had plenty to think about. I was positive that they would find a way to murder me if I refused to write my letter to Mary Jo White. I knew that kidnapping a federal judge was a much more serious plan than having me murdered in prison. I truly believed that this plan was made by the mob and never considered that this plan might be one by Mary Jo White and mob rats trying to shorten their time in prison.

I continued to try explaining to Tony Sarivola that their plan was crazy and that the same objectives would occur if they understood that it made no sense to commit the kidnapping of Judge Nevas, Moore, and Jossen. But I also studied their idea very closely and began to realize that it was infallible if they could execute the kidnapping plan itself.

Finally I agreed to write the letter after the kidnapping was executed. Tony then told me that as soon as I was released from M.C.C. I should go to Staten Island and wait to be picked up at Joe & Pat's Pizzeria. I was given Tony's home number which I knew was accurate because I had copied down the number from a scrap of paper my cellie had written down because he was calling Tony's daughter. The fact that I knew the phone number was truly Tony's home phone made me more confident that this plan was for real.

We will never know what would have really happened if the kidnapping was actually committed. The question as to whether the government would have released me to prevent being exposed will never be known.

A few days later Tony came to me and claimed that the kidnapping had been executed. I began to write the letter and then handed it to Tony. I then expected to be ushered out of the unit sometime later that day. About five hours later an officer came to my room and asked me to step out to be hand cuffed. There was no question in my mind that the plan was in action.

It was just before the 4:00 P.M. count and I was brought to the hole. I expected to be questioned fairly soon. I listened to the news on the radio owned by my cellie in the hole. I expected to hear the story on the news. When the story never was broadcasted I began to believe, of course its not going to be broadcasted because that would expose exactly what the government didn't want exposed. A lieutenant came that evening with a shot which claimed that I was under investigation for illicit activities. A few weeks later I came to learn that none of the B.O.P. officials had any idea why I was in the hole. It was two days after no one questioned me that I began to write the first of my letters to Mary Jo White which I sent directly to Dr. Kucharski in order that he could monitor my letters. These are the letters Dr. Kucharski has mentioned to this court in his ridiculous attempt to claim that these letters added to his conclusion that I was incompetent for trial.

After two days from the time I was locked up, and nothing had happened, that is, I was not being questioned. I then decided to write my second letter to Mary Jo White. The letter speaks for itself. It describes my concern for all three hostages. It clarifies that I have no power to order anybody to commit a crime much less a kidnapping of a federal judge. It wonders why Mary Jo White is making no attempt to help Judge Nevas. And it explores the possibility that the kidnapping story is a hoax and if it is a hoax, that whoever is involved is really crazy. About a month later I am going to learn that it was Mary Jo White and her mob rats who were really crazy. For them to threaten to murder me in order to force me to write the first letter leaves no doubt that they were crazy for believing that this plan would involve me in a new and completely different charge.

MY TESTIMONY ENDS HERE AND THEN CONTINUES ON PAGE 76.

My letters were of course hand written while I was in the hole, but I am using the exact format and the precise words of the letters Dr. Kucharski is claiming to be evidence that I am incompetent for trial.

***

STEPHEN A. MILLER #12367-074
M.C.C. 9J
5/20/95
The Honorable Mary Jo White
United States Attorney
Southern District of New York
c/o L. Thomas Kucharski, Ph.D
Re: U.S. v. Stephen A. Miller
Crim. #3:94 CR 254 (AHN)
Dear Ms. White:

In the morning of May 18, 1995, I was informed that the abduction of:

A)   U.S. District Judge Alan H. Nevas
B)   John Moore, Chairman COMEX
C)   Richard Jossen, Ex COMEX Vice Chairman
had occurred.

I was instructed to write a letter to you pertaining to that incident. The coincidence later at about 1530 hours which placed me into Administrative Detention for "illicit activities" appears to confirm that the abduction actually happened. Proceeding from this premise, it appears to me that the failure to discuss this incident with me, is a very nonchalant response on your part.

You must know that I am totally powerless to order the manpower required to accomplish the abduction of anybody, much less a U.S. District Judge.

You must know that only the most powerful anti government **BOSSES** would be capable of an abduction of such magnitude. You must know that this abduction would be national news if it had really occurred (unless the government had to hide it to prevent a scandal).

If this abduction truly occurred it is my sincere hope that Nevas, Moore, and Jossen are returned safely to their homes. You must know by this time that I have the intelligence and knowledge to resolve this incident. You should know that if this incident is not resolved, that it will surely lead to more problems. You must know that eventually this story will surface and the scandal you want to avert will blow up right in your face. You should realize that this story will emerge in a foreign country at some point where the American government has no influence. You must know that it is in the interest of all concerned (to this point) to keep the story from the public. Therefore, I look forward to resolving this issue with you at your earliest convenience.

P.S.   If the abduction never happened, then the origin of that information must have some crazy motivation for involving me into it. The logic or benefit of their motivation completely escapes me. Why would these people want to involve me in some bogus threat?

Sincerely, Stephen A. Miller

***

To put this letter in its proper perspective, you must now read the letter which I had handed to Tony Sarivola after he had claimed that Nevas, Moore, and Jossen had all been kidnapped simultaneously. Also try to imagine believing that people able and willing to commit such a spectacular crime, wouldn't have much trouble being able to murder me in a prison.

As the years went by I finally realized that mob people are a bunch of doofusses who only murder their own friends by shooting them in the back of their heads. But at this time in my life I was controlled by the myths published in the movies and in books I had read about the mob. I wanted to believe the popular myths, that the mob bosses were criminal geniuses.

The following letter was hand written and handed to Tony Sarivola after he claimed that the kidnapping of all three people had been accomplished:

STEPHEN A. MILLER #12367-074
M.C.C. B1112
5/18/95

The Honorable Mary Jo White
United States Attorney
Southern District of New York
Re: U.S. v. Stephen A. Miller
Crim. #3:94 CR 254(AHN)

Dear Ms. White:

Judge Alan Nevas, John Moore, and Richard Jossen will be treated very courteously and returned home after my case has been dismissed and I am released by Friday 6:00 PM, May 19, 1995.

If I am not released at that time all three will be killed.

Their death will force national media coverage of the story which is centered upon the COMEX copper price rigging fraud which you are covering up by refusing me a fair trial for my extortion case. Judge Nevas has repeatedly violated his sworn oath to uphold and protect the Constitution by incarcerating me in a Federal Mental Health prison facility. I would rather have a death sentence than being tortured with psychotropic drugs for the rest of my life.

You will have three dead bodies if you fail to meet the Friday 6:00 PM deadline. After I have been released you will receive a list for President Clinton to pardon and release. When your part of the bargain is complete, all three men will be returned home safe and sound.

Sincerely, Stephen A. Miller

While I was sitting in the hole my mind was concentrating upon each possible factor involved in the events which had occurred and the many possibilities which might happen in the future. There were many times when I considered that Sarivola and Montano had duped me into this situation. To me then and to me now, it seemed inconceivable that anyone would be a part of even a fake kidnapping. I just never considered the possibility that the United States Attorney would be a part of such a scheme with mob rats. Only after I learned, without question, that it was a hoax, did I finally recognize that Mary Jo White had to be a partner in this scheme.

In addition, what Mary Jo White could have never contemplated was that any criminal would have written her the letters I wrote. A very important reason for her failure to expect me to write my barrage of letters concerning the kidnapping is because I'm not a criminal. There is a huge difference between the criminal mind and the healthy mind.

I also learned an important lesson from my wonderful and brilliant grandmother. Nana told me a story about a time when my father and she were driving back from a trip to Pennsylvania. Two women were hitch hiking a ride to New York who my Dad stopped to help. They said they were going to Brooklyn. When they got to Staten Island my father drove them to the ferry which went to Brooklyn, the women told my Dad and Nana that they wanted to be driven to Brooklyn or they would claim that my father had transported them for a prostitution ring, then called "white slavery". Nana said, "Dave, let's drive them to the police station and declare ourselves." The two women wanted nothing to do with law enforcement and decided to go on their way.

So my decision to contact Mary Jo White was simple, especially after I had written the original threatening kidnapping note in the first place. For Dr. Kucharski to attempt to use my letters to convince the court that I was incompetent was goofy at best. The letters were never submitted as evidence and they were never read to the court. It was only Dr. Kucharski's claim that my letters delivered by me through him to the United States Attorney was never offered to the court as evidence that I was incompetent for trial.

The following letters speak for themselves:
May 21, 1995
L. Thomas Kucharski, Ph.D
Psychology Department, 2nd Floor
Dear Dr. Kucharski:
The attached letter to U.S. Attorney White was just returned by Lt. Clayborn who refused to forward it to Ms. White. I am routing it through you in the hope that this problem will obtain serious consideration. It is highly probable that you have been informed that I was moved to segregation on May 18th at 1530 hours.

No M.C.C. staff claims to know why I was put into segregation. If the information I received was accurate during the morning on 5/18,

Nevas, Moore, and Jossen were abducted. The resources it would take to achieve a simultaneous abduction which included a District Court Judge are significant, if not spectacular.

The direction this is moving toward is not my choice. No one has questioned me about this yet which I find weird. If the abduction did not occur so that there is no urgency, I have no way of knowing. You of course realize that I have no power or ability to order the manpower required to render such a daring feat. The fact that Nevas, Moore, and Jossen are directly linked to my case, puts me into the thick of it. Assuming this is true, I find the callous, nonchalant response incredible by the government.

Isn't it time that you people quit making believe that you are not covering up the COMEX copper scam and remedy this catastrophe? If you all continue to think that you can hide this forever, you are just plain stupid and crazy. The resources available throughout the world to the perpetrators of this abduction appear to me to be substantial if not awesome. Please try to be sensible now.

Sincerely,
Stephen A. Miller

STEPHEN A. MILLER #12367-074
M.C.C. 9J
May 21, 1995

The Honorable Mary Jo White
United States Attorney
Southern District of New York
c/o L. Thomas Kucharski, Ph.D
Dear Ms. White:
My primary concern is the safe return of:
B)   U.S. District Judge Alan H. Nevas
C)   John Moore, Chairman COMEX
D)   Richard Jossen, Ex Vice Chairman COMEX
Please put yourself into their shoes at this moment. How would you want the government to handle your dangerous predicament? It appears to me that you are ignoring my ability to achieve the safety of these people. I am not going to put into writing certain facts. It is imperative that we approach this problem with dialogue. I can guarantee you that your hypothesis of my participation is plain wrong. I can prove that.

The criminal involvement of your office and of these men into the COMEX copper price rigging fraud must be a major factor for the necessity of sweeping this incident under the rug. Whether you admit it or not we are all guilty coconspirators of this mess without the knowledge of the public. You must be both stupid and crazy to believe that this incident will not surface in the news if it is not managed intelligently. It is my hunch that there will be more victims if a sensible conclusion is not arrived at soon. I can only hope that the 5/19/95, 6:00P.M. deadline was abandoned and that all three men have been better cared for than I have been. Time is only on the government's side when it is not guilty. The more time that expires now is going to work against the government.

Sincerely,

Stephen A. Miller

STEPHEN A. MILLER #12367-074

M.C.C. 9J

May 23, 1995 (6th day)

The Honorable Mary Jo White

United States Attorney

Southern District of New York

c/o L. Thomas Kucharski

Dear Ms. White:

I am trying to communicate with you on your level. The problem is I can't find your level because you are literally delusional. If you were only a liar there would be less of a problem. But you apparently have no sense of reality. Your willingness to commit crimes has put you into a desperate state of mind. Until you accept your position, as did J. Edgar Hoover—- the homosexual: no sensible conclusion of this mess can occur.

The crazy lie that I am incompetent for trial might be the lynchpin. Step one, stop the incompetence bullshit.

Sincerely,

Stephen A. Miller

At the three week mark I decided to write to Dick Reeve to ask him if Judge Nevas had been kidnapped on May 18th. On the next day I was allowed to call Dick Reeve who told me that no one had been kidnapped. As the days and weeks dragged by for me, locked up in isolation with only my thoughts to consider all of the possibilities, I continued to concentrate on the likelihood that it was a hoax. Of all the potential scenarios which might have been true I never considered that the United States Attorney would have Sarivola and Montano threaten to murder me if I refused to write my letter to her.

I decided to take a huge risk to try to learn the truth. My next letter explains my move that set me free.

STEPHEN A. MILLER #12367-074
M.C.C. 9J
June 7, 1995
The Honorable Mary Jo White
United States Attorney
Southern District of New York
c/o L. Thomas Kucharski
Dear Ms. White:

Bridgeport is only 70 miles away. Drive me to Bridgeport to show me this is a hoax. I have to go to the Nevas court anyway for my competency hearing. Let me see Alan Nevas sitting on his bench. If he is there now you can order the U.S. Marshals to bring me to the Bridgeport court tomorrow.

If he is there I will plead guilty to extortion on the spot and take the full twenty years. Plus I'll never say another word about the COMEX copper fraud.

However, if you do not transport me to Bridgeport tomorrow for me to see Judge Nevas in the flesh, then I will be positive that Slick Dick Reeve is a liar because Nevas, Moore, and Jossen were in fact abducted. The abduction was not a hoax and we are back where we began on 5/17/95.

Sincerely,
Stephen A. Miller

STEPHEN A. MILLER #12367-074
M.C.C. 9J
June 12, 1995
The Honorable Mary Jo White
United States Attorney
Southern District of New York
c/o L. Thomas Kucharski, Ph.D
Dear Ms. White:

Based upon the deduction that you failed to order me driven to the Bridgeport court to accept a guilty plea if Judge Nevas was on his bench last Friday, 6/9/95, it seems safe to conclude that:

18) Nevas, Moore, and Jossen were truly abducted.

19) Richard A. Reeve lied on 6/7/95 when he claimed Nevas was not a hostage.

20) You made another stupid mistake by trying to trick me.

21) You are allowing Judge Nevas to languish as a hostage rather than learn how I can help return Nevas to his comfortable office and home.

How stupid can you be?

Sincerely,
Stephen A. Miller

COMPETENCY HEARING ANSWER CONTINUED

A.   When I was transported from the hole at M.C.C. I was taken to Otisville by the marshals. There I met some Puerto Ricans who were going to trial in Nevas's court. One of their friends remained at Otisville and I asked him to contact his sister to learn if Judge Nevas was on the bench. After he confirmed that Nevas was on the bench I simply deduced that the hoax was a conspiracy with Sarivola, Montano, and Mary Jo White to threaten me to be murdered if I had refused to write my first letter to Mary Jo White on 5/17/95. If the court will review my letters mentioned by Dr. Kucharski, the court will know that Dr. Kucharski commits perjury with reckless abandon. His actions indicate that he doesn't have a rational understanding of these proceedings right now.

Q.   Do you have anything else that you feel is important to the issue of competency which is what Judge Daly is dealing with now?

A.   If the proper questions are now put to Dr. Kucharski the court would learn that his report is false from stem to stern. Nothing about his report is accurate except his conclusion that I am intelligent, articulate, and that I never committed a criminal act. He will be a great witness for my defense if this court permits me to go to trial.

Q.   Are there any specific points in Dr. Kucharski's report which you feel need to be considered?

A.   Dr. Kucharski writes at the top of page 10 in his report, "Mr. Miller, while logical and coherent will be unable to testify rationally in his own defense." That is an inane contradiction. My testimony right now is being transcribed. Why not have Dr. Kucharski address any part of my testimony which indicates to him that I am unable to testify rationally? The only expertise Dr. Kucharski has exhibited to this court is that he is expert at committing perjury without forethought.

MR. REEVE: Thank you Mr. Miller. I would ask to have Congressman Shays' letters read by Mr. Miller be made part of the record of this hearing your honor.

THE COURT: How long do you think you'll be on cross Mr. Appleton?

CROSS EXAMINATION

Q.   Good afternoon Mr. Miller.

A.   Good afternoon Mr. Appleton.

Q.   Is it fair to say that you are convinced that there is this fraud? You're sure of that, is that right?

A.   I'm as sure of that as I'm positive that you are standing in front of me right this minute.

Q.   There's no possibility that it did not happen?

A.   None. And it is still happening every day and even yesterday. Maybe it has stopped today, I won't know until I look at the Wall Street Journal prices in the morning tomorrow.

Q.   You voiced your concerns to many people, isn't that right?

A.   Right. I mentioned it to Thomas Cohen, Herbert Sue, Bruce Baird, Stanley Twarde, Congressman Shays, Chris Mathews, the two C.F.T.C. officials who were at the meeting in Congressman Shays office, Howard Heiss, Special Agent Ed Cugell, Fred Mancheski, Bill Bowman, Dick Patterson, Rich Wisot, all the people who attended the Echlin annual meetings in 1987, '88, '89, and 1990, the reporters I met with at the Wall Street Journal, Peter Angrist and John Valentine, Jerry Knight at The Washington Post, Philip Scheffler the producer for 60 Minutes and their investigator Errica Stewart, and plenty more. I can tell you of the details of all of these meetings in case you want the court to hear these details. I followed up each of these meeting with letters to confirm the gist of these conversations and none of these people ever disputed my claims to be false. I have been very careful Mr. Appleton which is the reason you don't want me on a witness stand before a jury in a federal court.

Q.   Let me show you what I'm going to mark as government's exhibit 3. Do you recognize this document?

A.   Yes I do.

Q.   Is that the letter you sent to Mr. Goodwin?

A.   Yes it is

Q.   In this letter to Mr. Goodwin you tell him to donate fifteen million dollars to the Miller Foundation For Homeless People, right?

A.   Yes.

Q.   At the bottom you say, "Make no mistake, this is an extortion threat," right?

A.   Right.

Q.   What was your motivation for writing that extortion demand to Mr. Goodwin?

A.   I was positive that my letter to Goodwin would produce unmistakable evidence by Mr. Goodwin himself which would confirm to law enforcement that COMEX had continuously been rigging copper prices. The letter also states that COMEX is rigging copper prices and I want part of that money or I intend to expose their crime. This letter confirms that Mr. Goodwin, Vice President of Compliance whose job it is, is to make sure that crimes are not committed by COMEX is afraid to contact law enforcement because he knows that COMEX is rigging copper prices. Mr. Goodwin did precisely that, he failed to report my extortion threat to law enforcement. About five or six weeks later I requested a meeting at my office with F.B.I. S/A Ed Cugell to show him this letter. Agent Cugell and the United States Attorney were then forced to make a choice. There were three options which I spelled out to Agent Cugell. The first and best option was to investigate Mr. Goodwin and the COMEX officials on the Quotations Committee who rigged copper settlement prices after trading closed each day. The second option was to arrest me for extortion which would force the government to expose its own cover up which followed the letters from Congressman Shays to Attorney General Thornburgh and other senior officials he had written to about his frustration from the willingness by regulators to allow this fraud to continue. The third option was to continue stonewalling and conspiring with COMEX which became the choice by Mr. Thornburgh.

Q.   So you sent that correspondence to Mr. Goodwin for the same purpose that you are asserting in this case?

A.   Exactly.

Q.   To bring this to the attention of the court, right?

A.   Yes and here we are. The court is looking at simple evidence which indicates that you Mr. Appleton are preventing me from the trial which would expose the past three Attorneys General, Thornburgh, Barr, and Reno for conspiring to allow COMEX to rig global copper prices. I am housed with inmates who are illiterate and retarded but none of their prosecutors are claiming they are incompetent even though most of them are paranoid and some are delusional. Most of these criminals plan to plead guilty which pleases the government. Doing time is part of their life of crime. My plan was to stage an extortion to force the COMEX officials into federal court, which is exactly where you and the Justice Department don't want them.

Q.   So you don't deny that you faxed letters you wrote dated November 30th, '94, and December 6th, '94 to Mr. Jossen and Mr. Moore, right?

A.   Well the November 30th letter was delivered to Mr. Jossen's home in Westport by two other men and then I faxed that letter to John

Moore's home in New Jersey after I was called by those men after they delivered the letter to Westport.

Q. In the November 30th letter to Jossen you said, "For your personal benefit and on behalf of the Board of Governors you need to make your first consulting fee payment of $6,000,000 by wire transfer into my account." And you give your account information to the Dime Bank.

A. Yes.

Q. And you say these payments will cement our business partnership in the copper price rigging fraud which you've had since 1987, right?

A. Yes.

MR. REEVE: Your honor, I do object to this whole line of questioning. I don't think it goes to the issue of competency. We're not conducting the trial now. I know that Mr. Miller does not contest these allegations, but frankly I just don't think it has anything to do with his competency unless there's another reason its being offered.

MR. APPLETON: It goes directly to his competency your honor. His belief in the purpose of this trial to use as a forum.

THE COURT: I may have misunderstood the doctor, but I don't think they find his belief in some conspiracy theory to be evidence in itself of competence. I'm not sure this is relevant. Mr. Reeve I agree with you on that.

MR. APPLETON: Respectfully your honor, it goes to the rational understanding of the nature of the proceedings that are in front of Judge Nevas.

THE COURT: I heard what the doctor said about that. Judge Nevas didn't hold a competency hearing, did he? Go ahead.

MR. APPLETON: No he did not.

Q. You indicated in your direct testimony that you think you can win the case, right?

A. Of course I did. If I didn't think I could win this case I would be incompetent. I wouldn't have a rational understanding of the proceedings if I wanted to go to trial believing I would be found guilty.

Q. Because you believe you can present your evidence that there is a fraud going on, right?

A. You just presented it yourself Mr. Appleton. The point is I wasn't saying secretly to pay me cash in a bag so no one can prove I am committing extortion. I'm saying when you wire me $6,000,000 I am going to send a personal check to Mr. Howard Heiss, the Chief of the Commodities and Securities fraud unit, to prove that COMEX wants to cut me into their fraud so I won't keep complaining to law enforcement or try to expose them in the media. It's really difficult for me to imagine that anyone could fail to understand the simplicity of the pattern of events and evidence we have discussed before this court. No one capable of earning a law degree such as you, could fail to grasp the sequence of events I have put in place.

Q.   You think the jury will acquit you because you're right?

A.   The jury will acquit me because I did not commit extortion. I staged four consecutive extortions and I notified Justice Department officials each time. The first time I invited Special Agent Ed Cugell of the F.B.I. to my office in Fairfield so he could examine the evidence of the fraud and the extortion letter I had faxed to the COMEX compliance office, directed specifically to Rich Goodwin the compliance Vice President. After Agent Cugell took a copy of my letter in 1989, I wasn't arrested. That simply means that the Justice Department decided to ignore two facts. The first fact was my admission of extortion and the second fact was the copper fraud which prevented COMEX officials from contacting the F.B.I. themselves. If COMEX was innocent, jurors are capable of understanding that COMEX would have contacted law enforcement themselves. Your motion in limine to exclude evidence was to prevent the jurors chosen to hear this trial from learning what I set in motion because you believe the jury will acquit me. What you are presenting to this court right now is the only way the Justice Department can avoid being exposed for conspiring to allow COMEX to keep rigging the copper prices.

MR. APPLETON: I have nothing further your honor.

THE COURT: I'm going to need proposed findings and conclusions here. I think it's clearly in the best interest of Mr. Miller that the provisions of the speedy trial act be waived. The defendant remains in the marshal's custody. Thank you.

On the trip back to F.C.I. Otisville with the marshals, deputy marshal Stretch (that was his nick name), told me three times that he was really impressed by my testimony. When I testify I am very deliberate and careful. Stretch kept complimenting me and told me he was convinced that Judge Daly was going to rule that I am competent. I kept thanking Stretch for his compliments but I also told him that he would be wrong because Judge Daly would rule me incompetent.

Not only is there danger from the misuse of the insanity defense there is no potential benefit to any of the parties involved. The parties involved encompass society, the government, the innocent defendant, or even the guilty defendant. From my experience of being incarcerated

I learned that the vast majority of criminals are inflicted with mental diseases. My suggestion to completely eliminate the insanity defense is based first on learning if the defendant is truly guilty or innocent of the criminal charges he or she faces. After establishing guilt or innocence, then a psychological examination should establish if the guilty convicted criminal has a mental disorder and if there is a treatment which might benefit the inmate while he or she is incarcerated. Some mental disorders can be benefited by treatment and others can't.

[82]   Stephen A. Miller

CHAPTER 4
THE JUDICIAL PROCESS

The next step was for Dick to write the <u>PROPOSED FINDINGS OF FACTS</u> under the court's order. Bob Appleton would also be writing his version of the <u>PROPOSED FINDINGS OF FACTS</u> for the government to submit to the court.

Dick did a brilliant job for me and I will list some of the points he made:

1)   Mr. Miller has had significant Wall Street experience beginning with E.F. Hutton in 1966. He has been employed as a stockbroker and commodities broker as well as a consultant and money manager with expertise in the commodities market in general and the copper market in specific.

2)   Nobody has ever refuted Mr. Miller's evidence of fraud, and it appears that no law enforcement official has ever evaluated the evidence in a thorough objective manner.

3)   Mr. Miller is an intelligent, articulate man who has not been disruptive in any court proceedings in this case.

4)   Mr. Miller has addressed the court on numerous occasions in this case, and testified under oath once (September 21, 1995). At all times he has been courteous, articulate, and precise, showing a command of the facts and law relating to his case, and an understanding of court room procedure generally.

5)   Mr. Miller has stated on numerous occasions his desire not to raise any issue regarding his competency or his mental status at the time of his alleged criminal offense. He has consistently stated his desire to proceed to trial and defend himself against these charges by utilization of a non-psychiatric defense, i.e. that he did

not intend to extort any money when he sent the letters or made phone calls to Jossen and /or Moore.

6) On October 10, 1995, Mr. Miller filed an affidavit with this court indicating his clear intent and desire to be found competent, and waiving any appellate right to assert error regarding any judicial determination of competency.

7) Mr. Miller believes that his lawyer is a good attorney, is willing to work with him, and believes he can and is capable of having effective communications with counsel.

There was much more contained in the 16 pages written to the court but this synopsis is the essential focus of the report. I was extremely satisfied with Dick's work ordered by the court, which gave the court solid grounds to rule me competent. Due to this bizarre experience I learned that the only official in position to make a finding of incompetence should only be defense counsel. Defense counsel is an officer of the court. In a case when the defendant is acutely retarded or clearly unable to assist counsel for some legitimate reason, counsel is the only official in a position to know this. Under our Bill of Rights, only the defendant has the power to waive his right to trial. In practice Federal judges very often abuse their power by preventing a defendant from trial even though no judge has the power to decide that any defendant is incompetent, thereby forcing defendants to use the insanity defense. This practice is used on suspects who either write or call a threat to kill the President. These defendants seldom if ever intend to execute their threat. They are never taken to trial or allowed to plead guilty. They are ruled incompetent and dangerous. I had close contact with these inmates when Judge Daly ordered me to the FCI Butner's psychiatric prison in April 1996.

The offenders who plan to assassinate the President don't make threats. They obtain weapons and try to position themselves to execute their plan. I have never met any of these lunatics because they are not held at BOP facilities. I don't know where these defendants are held.

When I stated that no judge can deny a defendant his Constitutional right to trial, I mean that it is a right that judges deny in spite of their sworn oath to uphold and protect the Constitution. In real life in America judges do whatever they wish. This is a topic for volumes of argument. Appellate cases published to make judges look bad are a façade to propagandize justice for the public. The really bad cases are unpublished and listed unpublished.

Judge Daly took an enormous length of time to make his decision. During this time I was enjoying my time at F.C.I. Otisville. The food was very good. The weather during the summer was ideal. The recreation was excellent including two tennis courts, bocci, weights, a heavy bag and speed bags, and a good library. The inmates there were fun to be around. I was friendly with most of the Italian mob guys who were always good for a laugh, and they always had access to the best food in the joint.

During this time I had another wild experience with a mob rat. Otisville was filled with pre-trial inmates and holdovers. The B.O.P. made a big issue of housing the pretrial inmates separately from inmates who had been sentenced who they choose to call holdover inmates. The first few days during my ten-month stay at Otisville, I was housed in a holdover unit. Then I was moved into a pretrial unit. But when I was in the holdover unit I couldn't help noticing an Italian guy who was constantly on the phone. All calls at that time had to be collect and that was very expensive. Whoever was footing the phone bill for this guy was spending around three to four thousand dollars each month.

I learned that this guy's real name was Rocky Balboa. About a month later Rocky was moved into my unit. This move came about in a bizarre way which looking back was done for a purpose. First, Rocky was sent to the hole for a few days. When he was released he was designated to my unit. On this day two of my friends, Sal Branco from Philadelphia and Joey Vararo from Brooklyn came to me and asked me to look out for Rocky. Rocky was very friendly with them, but I had never met Rocky because he stayed in the unit on the phone all day and night.

On the day Rocky came into my unit I made arrangements for him to move into my cell and have the Dominican who was in my cell move with someone he liked too. Rocky was a blast. He was very intelligent, he knew a huge number of people, and he knew an amazing amount of mob related stories. Amongst the mob, mob related stories are the main topic of conversation. The main areas of interests are funny or bizarre stories of themselves and other mob guys, food, and gambling. At this point in time nobody in Otisville knew that Rocky was a rat and probably had the F.B.I. paying his enormous phone bills.

Another guy in our unit we had a lot of fun with was Frankie DeFeo who came from Mt. Vernon, N.Y. Frankie got caught smuggling heroin with a stewardess on one of the airlines. Frank moved into my cell after I got rid of Rocky and Frank is one of the most fascinating and fun people I have ever met on this planet.

One night after our lights were out and we were falling asleep, Rocky said, "Steve, I need to talk to you." I came down off my top bunk and said, "Sure Rock, what's up." He proceeded to explain to me that he had a connection who worked at some big corporation. He said that his woman partner in crime was able to divert money out of corporate accounts and if I had a girl friend that I could trust we could all make a fortune.

First of all, I have an exceptional knowledge about money and banking. Remember I studied money and banking under Bernie Seligman when he taught this course at Hutton's training department. While I was listening to Rocky, I knew that what he was saying was preposterous. He might as well have told me that the cow was going to jump over the moon. But I went along with him because I wanted to see what he had in mind. So I explained that my good friend Sandra Saunders trusted me and I would tell her to open a bank account so his friend could divert money into it.

The next day I called Sandra. All the phones are monitored in the B.O.P. Anyone who decides to commit a crime using the phone in a Federal prison is asking for a charge he can't possibly deny. I explained to Sandra that the phone was monitored and I explained what Rocky had told me the night before. I wanted to create a record of this potential crime that was intended to charge me for a new crime having nothing to do with the COMEX copper fraud. I told Sandra to expect a call directing her to open a bank account and I told her to do whatever she was directed to do if it was legal. Opening a bank account is a legal transaction. I also told Sandra to tape the phone call on her phone message machine.

Sandra knows me well enough to know that I would never do anything, which would ever jeopardize her, and she said she would do as I had instructed her to do. Then I went back to Rocky and told him that Sandra was ready to set up the bank account for his plot. Later that day a woman called Sandra about this scheme. Sandra was very nervous and the woman told Rocky that he should tell me to find a different woman because Sandra was too nervous. Rocky then told me that I needed to find another woman, and he said it had to be a woman, not a man. I explained to him that I would call Sandra back and calm her down. As we discussed Rocky's plot he began telling me that after Sandra withdrew the money deposited into her account that the teller would be short this money but that it would disappear from the computer. Rocky also said that the teller would get into trouble and probably would get fired.

Then I called Sandra back to explain what Rocky had told me about her being nervous and that the teller would be in trouble after Sandra withdrew the funds diverted into her account. I explained that I did not want her to be involved in this scheme any longer. My purpose was to have this conversation taped so there was no question that neither Sandra nor I wanted anything to do with Rocky's crime.

I also knew that Rocky's scheme was a set up to trap me into another charge. I began to explain this story to "Big Sal" Branco and Joey V.

so they would learn that Rocky was an F.B.I. informant. They didn't believe me.

Later on a follow up incident finally made Sal and Joe recognize that Rocky was another rat. This story was really weird. Rocky was supposed to be in Otisville on another charge. That's why he was a holdover. For this charge he received a P.S.I. report. The P.S.I. report is a presentence investigation which every convicted felon gets to help the court decide the sentence it will impose. For some weird reason I will never understand, Rocky brought the report for Joey to read. In the report it mentioned specific incidents when Rocky had assisted law enforcement. Joey told Big Sal about the report and Big Sal came into our unit to speak with Rocky in our cell. No inmate is allowed in any other unit than the one he is housed. So Big Sal was taking a chance, which would get him locked up in the hole if he had been caught. Big Sal decided that his talk with Rocky was very important or he could have waited until Rocky met him in the rec yard. He sat there and questioned Rocky about the incidents in the report, which Rocky kept explaining away.

Because Big Sal and Joey V. had trusted Rocky, they just didn't want to believe he was a rat. I just watched in amazement while this conversation went on and Rocky could make Sal believe that he wasn't a rat. Rocky claimed that he was misleading law enforcement.

At this point I asked to be moved into a different cell to get away from Rocky and watch the rest of the Italians continue to deny that their friend Rocky was another mob rat.

When I hear people talk about street smarts, I only observed street stupid.

Big Sal had escaped from F.C.I. Danbury and was on the lamb for about nine years until he was recaptured. Because Danbury is in Connecticut, Sal now had this escape charge in a Connecticut Federal court and Richard Reeve had been appointed for his defense. There aren't any defense strategies for contesting an escape from a federal prison. But Sal had a very high regard for Dick which he explained to me. My answer to Sal was that I was happy for him that he liked Dick but I didn't share his view. As it turned out, Sal was right. When Sal got sentenced for his escape he received a five year sentence to run concurrent with his original 9 year sentence, effectively giving Sal no time for the escape.

Dick Reeve had no magic words to convince the court to not punish Sal for an escape. I doubt anyone has ever gotten a similar deal, and I have no knowledge to point to any assistance Sal has given to the government to offset his sweet deal. I suspect that Sal's high regard for Dick was supposed to convince me that I should trust Dick in spite of what had been done and what was to come in the future. As the story unfolds you will see obvious ploys that Dick used to make sure I was convicted when I finally went to trial in 1996.

In Otisville there were also many Columbian drug smugglers. Some of them were facing very long sentences and I also befriended some who I thought might want to try to help themselves by using my case to expose Attorney General Richard Thornburgh, William Barr, and now Janet Reno along with other senior officials who decided to allow the COMEX copper price rigging fraud to continue.

One day I called Dick to explain that one of my Columbian friends had been impressed by my recommendation of his superior legal talents and would consider hiring him for a large fee. I told Dick that if he agreed to interview the Columbian he would receive a $500,000 retainer. Dick declined the offer. Then I asked Dick how much he earned during the past year working for the Federal Public Defender's office. Dick stated that it was none of my business.

I sometimes had questioned Dick as to why he remained working for so long at the Public Pretender's office instead of earning much more in private practice. Dick didn't like that subject and never would give me an answer. (Dick is now in private practice in New Haven. I visited him at his nice office recently in 2003.)

In the mean time, one of the Columbians decided to pay his own lawyer to represent me. Three interviews were scheduled with his attorney who kept coming up with bogus excuses for failing to meet with me. I had written a few letters to this attorney about my case and I had one phone conversation with him. My reasoning for advancing this deal was that I believed that it might be used to help the Columbian to negotiate a better deal for himself. However, it was my impression that the Columbian who was very religious, believed that he was going to finance my legal expenses because it was the will of god. He believed that he was in god's hands and sincerely felt that he would get a sentence he deserved because of god's intervention.

On another occasion while I spoke with Dick he told me that he believed that Judge Daly was "a reasonable man" and that he might consider releasing me if I agreed to go into therapy. When I tried to pin Dick down as to whether or not this message had come from Judge Daly, Dick made it clear that it was his independent belief. Maybe I made a mistake by not confirming my willingness for therapy as a quid pro quo for being released. Instead, I asked Dick to explain to me what specific problem existed for me to agree to therapy. My strategy then was that I was convinced that Dick's hunch was not a hunch but a directive from the court.

There is no way to know the outcome if I had been receptive to therapy. I was in a game and tried to play it to my advantage. If the true outcome had been explained to me it was so farfetched that I could never have believed it. That's the point of writing this story, it's beyond belief. Its weirdness is its entertainment vIlue and hopefully it becomes informative.

I was convinced that this was a sign that indicated that the government would never put me on trial because they believed I could expose senior officials and would cause a scandal. I therefore believed that showing any weakness would undermine my final outcome. Now there is no way to speculate what might have happened if I went along with the therapy deal. The process evolved. It's clear that we all believed that it would be too risky for the government to take my case before a jury of regular citizens. But in the end it was done and no scandal ever developed.

People never like to admit a mistake. We don't want to say that we made a bad choice. No matter how much evidence is compiled to prove the corruption by our courts. Citizens will tune out because our precious system can't be flawed. Our brilliant Constitution can be trashed by the Supreme Court, but voters don't want to learn the truth. This is a cultural American flaw.

As it turned out, Judge Daly finally in late February ruled me incompetent and on April 1st, 1996, I was shipped on a Lear jet to begin a prescribed four month restoration phase at F.C.I. Butner.

As soon as Judge Daly's decision was final I told Dick I wanted him to file a NOTICE OF APPEAL. I had threatened to appeal an incompetence decision to Judge Nevas during the April 1995 hearing. When I told Dick to file my notice which must be done in ten days from the court's order, he told me that an appeal was not allowed. I told Dick that he was full of shit and that I would file the notice myself if he refused to do it. Then Dick stated that he would file it and he did so.

Subsequent to his filing my NOTICE OF APPEAL Dick told me that I would have to write the brief myself. I was opposed to writing this brief because I was concerned that the court might then claim that I was unable to assist counsel in my defense. After a few arguments with Dick on this subject he decided to withdraw for the third time which then forced the court to provide an attorney from the Public Pretenders office in Manhattan named Phil Weinstein to represent me. I had one 20 minute conversation with Phil right after I arrived at Butner, and he wrote my brief to the Second Circuit Court of Appeals.

Regardless of why any inmate is designated to the mental facility he is automatically confined in "seclusion". My cell-mate, John, was a bank robber who had been confined in seclusion because he believed that demons wanted him to pinch a nurse on the rear end. One morning his shrink was making the rounds and stopped to say good morning. John responded by saying that he was rebuking the demons. In return the shrink told him that when he quits rebuking the demons he would be released onto the compound. When the shrink left, I was curious and asked John why he was sure that there were demons. He replied that the Bible stated that there were demons. Then I asked John to show me the place in the Bible which confirmed that there were demons, and he did.

The B.O.P. is very conscientious about giving any inmate the Bible. Now we have poor John completely convinced in the demons and he is being kept in the hole until he quits saying he is rebuking the demons.

They released me to the compound in a few days and I began spending the next few months trying to maneuver my way out of the B.O.P. funny farm. My strategy now completely changed. I decided I would give no credence to this phony restoration process. I put my team, Dr. Bruce Berger and his associate on notice that I would have no communication with them for any reason. I explained this in writing because I wanted to eliminate any chance of being misquoted or misunderstood. I explained to them that I would be pleasant and courteous but I refused to acknowledge that there was any legitimacy to the court's ruling that I was incompetent. I would follow orders by going to any meeting but I refused to participate in any conversation. When I was asked to take a written test, I refused. When I was told by Dr. Berger that I was not cooperating, I responded by writing that that was correct. I had no intention of cooperating with their attempt to commit me into a psych ward indefinitely.

The strategy being used by the government was the old witch-hunt strategy. When people were accused of being witches they were offered remedies or opportunities to confess being a witch. Of course when they confessed they believed they would be forgiven or excused. Instead they were burned at the stake. Giving me tests and making me meet with other people using incompetence would make it appear that I was legitimately incompetent. One of these inmates sat there in a trance and claimed that he didn't know what his charge was. Another claimed that a taxi cab driver forced him to rob a bank. I don't know if they believed their claims or if they thought incompetence was their best legal strategy. I just observed the show without participating. I would be asked the same questions like, "Do you know what the judge does?"

About two months into this process, Dr. Berger asked me if I would speak to the B.O.P. attorney who worked for Warden Harley Lappin, the warden at F.C.I. Butner. I told him sure, I'll be happy to speak with their attorney. First of all I knew this procedure was something they would never suggest unless it was another trap, second of all I expected that the trap was that if I refused, they would claim that I was paranoid.

Then Dr. Berger asked me if I would contact Dick Reeve (who had officially withdrawn as my counsel) for his advice as to whether he would recommend my discussion with the B.O.P. attorney. I agreed. I was sure that this was their trap to try to get me to refuse to seek advice from Reeve and then claim that I was unable to assist in my defense. The following morning I was brought into an office to call Dick. We had a pleasant conversation, which I knew was being taped. When Dick advised me to speak to the B.O.P. attorney, I agreed immediately. Then Dr. Berger told me he would arrange for my meeting.

I was positive that this was a bluff. Around three that afternoon Dr. Berger told me that they decided not to have me speak with the B.O.P. attorney. I was right about the bluff.

About a week later Dr. Berger told me that if I agreed to withdraw my brief to the Second Circuit opposing Judge Daly's decision that I was incompetent that they would allow me to go to trial. This was a huge win. Dr. Berger then asked me to answer some questions for his final report. My reply was that I would be happy to answer any of his questions but that I preferred to have him write his questions and that I would write my answers in order to continue not having any verbal communication. He agreed to my request and I completed my time at Butner without any verbal communication with the psychiatric staff other than short pleasant greetings. This did not prevent Dr. Berger from creating another bogus report. As things turned out, my strategy worked by eliminating the competency issue and preventing the indefinite psychiatric commitment, which could likely have been a life term for me. It's important for readers to consider and hopefully recognize, that if the court was willing to impose its bogus insanity defense then it was also willing to bury me there for life and force me to be "medicated" into a zombie state. I watched them do this to Carl Zachowski and others.

When I met Carl I really enjoyed his company. He was a very witty guy from Jersey City who thought he could make fun of the medical staff. I tried to caution Carl not to play with these people but he wouldn't listen. His shrink was the Associate Warden, Dr. Sally Johnson. She paralyzed Carl's mind with psychotropic drugs for five years which made him psychotic. He finally hung himself. I felt very sad for Carl while I watched him being abused in the most vicious, sadistic manner. I had met Carl in 1991. I spent many worthwhile hours with him because he had a great mind and told me funny stories of the many pranks he had done before he came to prison. Carl had no mental health problems until his brain had been destroyed by huge doses of haldol.

In June 1996, I was shipped back for trial two and a half months into this four-month restoration process. Now I was quite certain that the government would find a way to dismiss my case because their whole process had backfired on them. I had Dr. Kucharski's sworn testimony that claimed my actions weren't criminal because I had no intent to extort.

My next prison (and worst location) was a private prison called the Wyatt Detention Center located near Providence, R.I. The Feds held pretrial inmates from Connecticut, Rhode Island, and Massachusetts in Wyatt. Here I spent July and August before my trial, which was docketed for September. While I was at Wyatt I had more encounters with mob guys as the months inched along while I waited for either a trial or some other method by the government to avoid putting me on trial.

Wyatt was also being used by the B.O.P. to house inmates after they had been sentenced in the Eastern District of New York and were awaiting their designation to a B.O.P. facility to serve their remaining time. The Eastern District of New York is where most of the mob guys are indicted and tried, so I got to meet many of them while they came through Wyatt.

We lived in a cell with four bunks but had five men in each cell. One man had a mattress in the middle of the floor. We were confined in these cells most of the day except for an hour and a half recreation period when we could come out to watch TV or go out to a small yard with a handball court and a basket for a basketball game. There were public phones, which were only used to make collect calls and were very expensive.

One of my cell mates who came from M.D.C. Brooklyn with an eleven year sentence was Mario Gallo whose girl friend was the niece of one of the most powerful capos in the Gambino crime family, Joe "Butch" Corrao. I had met Joe Butch on Mulberry Street. He had a restaurant named Toarmino's and a coffee shop named Café Biondi both located on Mulberry Street. Mario was very proud of his connection to Joe and was happy to let people know about his connection. Mobsters are huge name droppers. They want people to know that they are connected to powerful mobsters, while at the same time they appear to feign being in this secret life of crime. Because Mario and I had a lot of time to kill, I decided to explain in detail my efforts and experiences which included my analysis about Bruce Cutler who was loved and endeared by the entire mob. I explained to Mario all of the details which were being overlooked by the mob about Cutler's real deal which was to infiltrate the mob for the government. This began to make Mario very angry and he decided to challenge me to a fight outside during our recreation period. At my first chance, I went outside to await Mario. All he did was to give me a menacing look and then he wisely decided to forget about it. Mario had done a famous contract hit on Gus Farace. Farace had murdered a DEA agent. Law enforcement put heat on the mob to flush Gus out of hiding. When Mario was part of the team that took care of that problem, his stock went up.

There are many details, which took me a number of hours to explain to Mario about how I came to learn about Bruce Cutler and why I had drawn my conclusions. One conclusion I had omitted drawing in my analysis was that for the Gambino leadership to recognize that Bruce Cutler had duped them as their trusted lawyer and confidante, they would be signing their own death warrant. They had underwritten Bruce Cutler to many other LCN (La Cosa Nostra) families in America. This endorsement had to be punished by death to John Gotti and his closest people because they had underwritten Cutler.

I never considered this huge problem for myself until years later. I truly believed that I was helping them by cluing them in to this trap and they all knew that my intentions were genuine. Regardless, I still made them angry at me for my accurate conclusion which none of them wanted to hear.

Before you decide that I am wrong about Bruce Cutler please consider the following points. There is much more to my analysis than I will devote to this paragraph but the few contradictions I now mention are basic common sense. The published claim by the government for having Bruce Cutler removed from Gotti's defense was that Cutler was the "in-house counsel for the Gambino crime family". He wasn't just a lawyer like Shargel and the others. Bruce was considered as part of the mob. Then why didn't the government prosecute Bruce for being a criminal? If that was a valid reason, then why did the government allow Cutler to represent Joe Gambino and other defendants who the government alleged were made members of the Gambino crime family? These are simple contradictions.

Cutler promoted his ability to keep John Gotti the teflon don. Cutler influenced John Gotti to parade around bragging about being a criminal. It appears that the Gambino crime family learned its lesson because nobody knows who its boss is now. All there is now is speculation about who the real boss is.

Mario was taken back to M.D.C. for the new murder indictment. He decided to plead guilty and wound up with a total of seventeen years. He was sent to F.C.I. Loretto, a low security prison near Pittsburgh which is where I went for my last year ending in November 2002. Mario lucked out by getting into a fight at Loretto and was shipped to the medium security prison at F.C.I. Schuylkill, pronounced (skoolkill). Loretto was a sweet joint until it got very overcrowded. Mario was there before it got overcrowded, and I got there in July 2001 when it was terribly overcrowded. A medium security prison is far better than Loretto became before I arrived because almost everybody is assigned a two-man cell in a medium. Loretto was a sweet joint when it had about 600 inmates, but when I got there it was packed with over 1200 inmates.

Another inmate I met at Wyatt was Eddie Voccola. Eddie was in prison for the fifth time in his life for insurance fraud. He owned a large auto body shop and pleaded guilty for ripping off insurance companies. Eddie had accumulated millions of dollars, he had sugar diabetes and was 72 years old then in 1996. He had been sentenced to 3 years at the Skuylkill Camp, fined about $300,000 and agreed to restitution of about $200,000. His judge hit Eddie for contempt because he failed to make payments on the fine. His time didn't count at Wyatt, it was very uncomfortable, and his judge hit him for an additional $20,000.

Eddie told me a story that he had bought a building for $150,000 and he rented part of it to the Board of Education for $37,000 per month ($434,000 annually). While I was watching the Today Show in 2001, they were doing a story about Mayor Vincent "Buddy" Cianci and his codefendant Eddie Voccola. You guessed it, Mayor Cianci had arranged for the Board of Education to rent Eddie's building.

Eddie originally had been given the opportunity to self-surrender with his codefendant Frank Corrente in the insurance fraud case. When Eddie and Frank pulled up to the prison camp Frank decided he had better places to spend the next 18 months. Soon after Frank became disenchanted with being a fugitive so Frank decided to get in touch with the FBI and try to make a deal. Frank's offer included explaining the lucrative kick back scheme Eddie and the Mayor had arranged to split the rent from the Board of Education.

To my amazement United States District Judge Ernest C. Torres decided to dismiss charges against Eddie Voccola while his partner Mayor Cianci was convicted of the very same charges. Eddie had bribed the Federal Judge. He stepped up in class from bribing insurance adjusters to a Federal Judge.

Dick Reeve eventually came to visit me to prepare for my trial in September 1996. About a week before my trial Dick popped into Wyatt unexpectedly. He claimed he had to transport his kid to visit his grandfather and was in the area. He asked me what I would say when Bob Appleton cross examined me and asked me who the two men were who had gone to Richard Jossen's home to deliver my letters and appear to be mob extortionists. I told Dick that he would find out when I testified. Lawyers are trained not to ask questions unless they are reasonably sure of the answer. Dick's purpose for asking his question was to report the answer back to Bob Appleton. That important question was never asked when I was being cross examined by Mr. Appleton.

CHAPTER 5
THE TRIAL BEGINS

On September 4th, 1996, I was awakened at 3:30 A.M. for my trip to Bridgeport to choose my jury (for the second time). Another Wyatt inmate, Douglas McCarroll, was also brought to Bridgeport with me. McCarroll had already been sentenced to 15 years for growing marijuana and a gun charge. He claimed he had another case and planned to go on trial for that case too. McCarroll spent a lot of time in the law library and had amassed a huge file of papers for his appeal. What is going to happen on this day in Judge Nevas' court room is unprecedented, unique, and bizarre.

Nevas had brought up the question to me about whether I wanted him recused in light of the kidnapping incident. I refused to ask for his recusal and put that on the record. I really suspected that if I asked to recuse Nevas that he might claim that I was paranoid and send me back to Butner. It is very unlikely that Judge Nevas would bring this subject up for my benefit. Judge Nevas did nothing for my benefit, ever.

When court convened that morning both McCarroll and I were brought out to sit at the same defense table simultaneously. We had two separate cases and seating us at the same table with our lawyers and McCarroll's prosecutor was completely against protocol. McCarroll was pro se but he was given a standby lawyer, a Mr. Durham, who was provided to help McCarroll. The A.U.S.A. in his case was a Mr. Stapleton. Prosecutors don't sit with defendants in a court room.

If you watch Court TV, or any movie, or TV show about a trial you will never see any court ever seat two defendants in two separate cases at the same defense table, simultaneously. The obvious reason is that it would be a distraction to both defendants to have chatter interfere with the court's process. So it is important to keep this in mind for the last chapter of this story. Judge Nevas' purpose was to create a distraction for the court to be able to seat a juror who he knew would vote guilty, regardless of the evidence and proof which the jury was supposed to deliberate to decide a verdict.

I was seated with Dick at my side, facing the jury pool, our backs to Judge Nevas. To our right was the government's table where Bob Appleton was seated. And on the other side of my table were Mr. McCarroll, on his left was Mr. Durham, and on his right was A.U.S.A. Stapleton with their backs to the jury pool.

Judge Nevas began speaking to McCarroll about subpoenas for witnesses for his potential trial. But then out of the blue Mr. McCarroll began to claim that he might be interested in a plea bargain. Judge Nevas responded by saying, "Go ahead, sit down and talk." Nevas is directing them to discuss a plea agreement with their backs to the jury pool and facing Dick and me.

There are a lot of coincidences happening simultaneously. Here is a defendant who was sentenced to 15 years a very long time ago but who remained at Wyatt Detention Center instead of being shipped to his designated BOP institution. He lives in the law library every day working on his appeal. He talks a lot and never mentions that he has additional charges. Now he claims that he's going to trial for more charges but decides at the spur of the moment to plead guilty. Did Mr. McCarroll get some time cut off his 15-year sentence for his help? I don't know the answer to my own question.

Judge Nevas then directed the voir dire process to begin for my case. Each prospective juror is directed by the court to read off a short list of questions to be answered by each person in the pool. First they identified themselves by their juror number assigned to each person and gave their name. Then they would answer questions about the town they lived in, their employment, their family members, their hobbies, and their prior jury experience. There were 93 jurors in the pool and the complete process took 4 hours including a lot of rhetoric by Nevas and Appleton.

As the process continued I repeatedly asked Dick to request that Nevas move the McCarroll party elsewhere because I was being distracted. Dick refused to do this. This would be considered ineffective assistance of counsel if it was put on the record, but of course it wasn't on the record. Ordinarily I would have raised my hand to address the court because Dick was refusing to comply with my request. However, I was concerned that if I proceeded to speak to the court on my own that it would be characterized as an outburst and lead to a resumption of the incompetence issue. This was a huge risk I had no intention of taking. I had been asked repeatedly, what will you do in case you disagree with a proceeding in court? My answer was always that I would ask my attorney to question the problem. I was put into the proverbial "catch 22".

The noise was so loud that at one point Judge Nevas on the record said, "You want to keep your voice down Mr. McCarroll?" Keep in mind that if their negotiation disturbed Nevas who sat at least 25 feet behind me, it distracted me more. When I missed hearing something a potential juror was saying all I could do was to ask Dick if he heard it. But if I was speaking with Dick I was also missing other statements. My best guess is that I had asked Dick approximately 6, 7, or 8 times to put this problem on the record by requesting Nevas to move the McCarroll party.

When I read the transcript of the voir dire while I worked on my appeal, I saw exactly why Dick refused to ask Nevas to move the McCarroll party. There were a series of clues which all came together before I had read the following statement on the record.

JUROR: My name is Kent Moller, juror number seventy four. Reside in Newtown for the past ten years, married. I work as a union electrician out of Bridgeport. My wife works for the law firm of Cohen & Wolf also in Bridgeport. I work for Silverstone Electric, electrician for eleven years. Two children, two daughters, eighteen months and two and a half years at home. No experience as party in a law suit or as a witness in a law suit or as a juror in a law suit criminal or civil. Never rendered a verdict. Hobbies are my children and when I have a little time, do a little fishing.

My brother-in-law, Irving Kern, is a senior partner of Cohen & Wolf.

It is a fact that the court reporter heard Kent Moller state, "My wife works for the law firm of Cohen & Wolf also in Bridgeport." If I had heard this statement by Kent Moller, if I hadn't been distracted by the McCarroll commotion, I would have used one of my challenges to remove Kent Moller. As it turned out, Mr. Moller became the jury foreman in a jury which rendered a verdict in approximately 20 to 25 minutes.

Does any prosecutor or any judge want to have a juror in their case who has a financial interest from employment of his wife by the defendant's brother-in-law? Absolutely not, because if the defendant was found guilty, the appellate court would have to reverse the judgment and remand the case back for a new trial. The strategy by Nevas, Appleton, and Dick Reeve guaranteed a reversal by the Second Circuit Court of Appeals under law as set forth by the **FEDERAL RULES OF APPELLATE PROCEDURE** heretofore known as FRAP. This is not what happened.

Keep in mind that Nevas, Appleton, and Reeve all knew that I had a brother-in-law who was an attorney in a wealthy, powerful Bridgeport law firm who was not only not representing me but who had had a very nasty relationship with me since 1986 when he, and my sister Andrea refused to have any communication with me let alone inviting me to their home for any family functions on holidays as was our custom before 1986.

Unless the Second Circuit Court of Appeals decides to join the conspiracy to protect the COMEX copper price rigging conspiracy, I can't lose my appeal. I was positive that my conviction and my sentence would be thrown out on appeal after I had read the aforementioned paragraph in my transcript by Kent Moller, Juror #74.

Also try to keep in mind that if I had heard Moller's statement about his wife's employment and removed him from being seated on the jury, there is no way to know how Nevas would have proceeded. It is likely that he would have concocted another hearing to abort my trial and send me back to Butner for a commitment as dangerous. I can only thank God that I didn't hear the same statement that the court reporter heard, Nevas heard, and Appleton heard, because they were not being distracted by the McCarroll circus.

I would like to be able to question the other jurors in my case to learn what they thought my defense was all about. I had tried to keep the most intelligent jurors who also had the best jobs on my jury because I believed that they would understand my case better. If I could find a collaborator on this book, I would have him locate the other eleven jurors to ask them what they believed was going on in my trial and how they could find a verdict in such a short time. I am convinced that Kent Moller had the power to control them after they agreed to make Moller their jury foreman.

This is the list of individuals who were seated on my jury:
1)   Gina Cappiali works for the American Institute for Study.
2)   Stanley R. Daily is a product manager for Pitney Bowes.
3)   Lisa R. Ferrara is a human resource administrator for U.S. Surgical.
4)   Herbert Figueroa is a class "A" machinist for Rollerhand.
5)   Alan Gorkin owns a green house and nursery named Earth Garden in New Canaan.
6)   Norma Lamalfa is divorced and retired.
7)   Joanne Malaterra is the President of her own company, Professional Management Solutions.
8)   Kent Moller is a union electrician for Silverstone Electric.
9)   Sarah Murphy is an assistant for Home Health Care.

10) Pauline Oliver is the office manager in her husband's dental office.

11) Barbara Sawyer works for WPIX – TV in New York

12) Helen Seifert is a realtor for 28 years.

13) Gary Giannelli is the director of the Ferguson Library in Stamford.

About a month before my trial began I learned from Dick that the plan would be to drive me back and forth from Wyatt Detention Center each day. This meant that I would be awakened at 4:00 A.M. and by the time I returned to Wyatt for dinner it would be after the other inmates had been fed. When you come in and out of any prison, it can take hours each time for the staff to process the inmate. This would have been an exhausting process and put me at a terrible disadvantage. Therefore I wrote to the U.S. Marshals and the court to be allowed to stay in Bridgeport's North Avenue jail throughout my trial or I would appeal to the Second Circuit. I won this argument.

Before my trial began I brought up the opening statement issue with Dick based upon the phony motion he had filed on April 13th, 1995, after my hearing on Appleton's MOTION IN LIMINE TO EXCLUDE EVIDENCE. Dick told me that Nevas would prevent his making any opening statement. I told Dick that he had to file a RENEWED MOTION FOR THE DEFENDANT'S OPENING STATEMENT to create a record for appeal in case I lost my trial. I needed to preserve this issue for appeal in case I lost my trial. On the morning of September 11th, 1996, my first day of trial, Nevas denied this motion on the record. This is going to play a very important part of my appellate process. I was sure that Nevas' decision to deny this motion would completely eliminate my risk of trial. I believed that the appellate court would protect my right for a fair trial. I was betting on the justice, which our media always portrays in our free press. I had no way to know that this propaganda had programmed my mind.

In the mean time Appleton wrote a document he titled the GOVERNMENT'S PROPOSED REQUEST TO CHARGE, filed September 9th, 1996. After the jury had been seated on the morning of the 11th, and Nevas addressed them, this document was read to the jury. This statement being read to the jury was the prosecution's **opening statement**. I sat at my defense table and read my copy of the GOVERNMENT'S PROPOSED REQUEST TO CHARGE while the jury was listening to it. Right after the jury heard this statement read to them, the first witness was put on the stand for direct examination by Appleton.

Not only was Nevas preventing Dick from making an opening statement but he was allowing Appleton to make the government's opening statement, disguised by the title GOVERNMENT'S PROPOSED REQUEST TO CHARGE. Thank you Judge Nevas for an issue, which was even more unfair. It was a double guarantee for a reversal on appeal.

When I began to study the transcript for my appeal the first thing I looked for was the Government's opening statement. There were only twenty pages of the transcript before the first witness took the stand and this statement Appleton had read to the jury of six pages which I had a copy had been deleted from the transcript to make it appear that neither side had made an opening statement. Now it could be argued by the government that the trial was fair because neither side had made an opening statement. That is unless I could prove to the Second Circuit Court of Appeals that this written statement, read to the jury, had been deleted by the Court Reporter from the official Court Record.

The transcript is certified by the court reporter to be complete and accurate and is therefore considered to be prima facie evidence. This is going to lead to a battle to be decided by the United States Supreme Court. The court reporter, Susan Catucci, works for the judge and is deemed to be under the Court Reporter Act. When I learned that the transcript had been deleted it was automatic to realize that Susan Catucci had not decided on her own to delete the government's opening statement. First of all she wouldn't know to delete the opening statement on her own. Only Judge Nevas would be in position to direct Susan Catucci to violate the Court Reporter Act.

There is plenty of evidence including an electronic tape recording, which recorded the entire proceeding including the Government's Opening Statement. Not only is Judge Nevas violating my due process guaranteed by the Bill of Rights, he is committing crimes for which he needs to be impeached. All of these principles sound good but in America I am going to learn the hard way that my concept of justice is completely farfetched because I have been brainwashed by an avalanche of propaganda. As my years in prison continue I am going to learn that the judicial branch of our government is corrupt beyond imagination.

For my trial I was dressed in prison clothes. The court refused to provide street clothes. Dick came into the courtroom on the first day with a white dress shirt of his own. It had yellow stains and would fit him. Dick is about 130 pounds, I am 195 pounds with an eighteen inch neck. Finally Nevas decided to allow Dick to purchase three shirts for me to wear. Dick went out and bought XXXX Large shirts even though I told him I wear an X Large size. Did Dick want me to look ridiculous? If I hadn't been in such a dangerous position I would have requested that Dick exchange the shirts for the correct size.

Now here we go with verbatim trial statements:

THE COURT: I note again, as I did at jury selection, Mr. Miller is dressed in prison clothing, I raised this issue, I raise it again for the record.

MR. REEVE: Your honor, Mr. Miller would like to address the court.

DEFENDANT: Your honor, I think there was a misunderstanding about the street clothes. I believe I told you that Mr. Reeve had asked me for my measurements for street clothing which I gave him. Then the Marshal brought in a dirty white shirt which I decided not to use. But I would be happy to use street clothing if I had street clothing to wear.

THE COURT: All right we are going to proceed.

MR. REEVE: Your honor, Mr. Miller would like to make an oral argument on the motion I filed for him to be co-counsel.

THE COURT: Go ahead Mr. Miller.

DEFENDANT: Thank you very much your honor. As you're aware there is an issue that will arise when the government calls John Moore to the stand and it will concern technicalities inherent to rules and facts pertaining to copper futures contract trading at COMEX and the fraud John Moore has been perpetrating ongoing from 1987. There is no question that Mr. Reeve lacks the knowledge to deal with basic simple evidence pertaining to Mr. Moore's involvement as Chairman of the Quotations Committee and Chairman of the COMEX. Mr. Reeve has substantiated that premise for the past 21 months. He has had a problem understanding what long and short is. Both are basic simple terms meaning buy and sell. Consequently, I would be at a severe disadvantage because Mr. Reeve will not know how to respond to testimony given by Mr. Moore during cross examination. Mr. Reeve will not be able to address certain issues that may arise during direct examination. I am sure that if the court would allow me to cross examine John Moore it will become clear to the jury, the court, and to Mr. Appleton that Mr. Moore is truly the key operator of the fraud that is the essence for my defense concerning the indictment of crimes rendered by the Grand Jury against me. Now, if in fact it becomes very clear to the government after all this time, that John Moore is a criminal, and I believe its adequately clear because of the government's reactions to the complaints from not only myself, but from other people Congressman Shays mentioned in his letter to Controller General Charles Bowsher....

THE COURT: I don't want any speeches. I don't want any speeches Mr. Miller.

DEFENDANT: It will be completely unfair to try this case without proper counsel to handle technicalities that most likely will pop into the testimony....

THE COURT: I have every confidence in Mr. Reeve's ability and skill as a trial attorney. Mr. Reeve has appeared before me on countless occasions. He also enjoys an outstanding reputation in this district as a very able and skilled criminal defense attorney. He's tried dozens and dozens of cases and he enjoys the respect of the bench in this district as well as the U.S. Attorney's office and I'm sure the criminal defense bar in this district. I have every confidence that Mr. Reeve will be able to more than completely represent you in this matter, so the motion is denied.

DEFENDANT: May I just make one quick comment sir, your honor?

THE COURT: All right.

DEFENDANT: I want to make it very clear that in my opinion Mr. Reeve is an outstanding attorney who I have tremendous confidence in. That is not the question. Evidently the court completely misunderstood my point.

THE COURT: No I didn't misunderstand. I understood you completely.

DEFENDANT: Thank you your honor.

REEVE: Your honor I would move for witness sequestration in this case.

THE COURT: All right except for the case agent. There will be an order of sequestration except for the case agent.

REEVE: In order to preserve the record it's incumbent upon me under Second Circuit case law to establish a record during the course of the trial. I can make an order of proof as to what we would attempt to elicit from given witnesses outside the presence of the jury. It's incumbent upon me to preserve Mr. Miller's evidentiary claims in this case and I think that is going to require that the jury be excused at some point. I raise these issues now so we don't get into problems once the jury is here.

THE COURT: Well with respect to which witnesses?

REEVE: It would be primarily with respect to Mr. Moore. As your honor is aware and so that the record is clear, it is Mr. Miller's position there has been an ongoing fraud to rig the copper market since around May or June of 1987, a few months before the stock market crash of October 19th, 1987. The parties agree and the testimony will establish persistent, diligent efforts to uncover this fraud and to get the appropriate government agency to do an honest, thorough investigation of the data that he has compiled as a part of the efforts that he has made. The defense as your honor knows in this case is that Mr. Miller did not intend to extort $6,000,000 from anyone, and that Mr. Miller acted in this case just as he has acted for the past nine years in full view of the F.B.I. and the most senior officials of the Justice

Department. Everything he has done has been an effort to bring this matter to a head, and at every step he has been blocked by the highest officials of the Justice Department.

Mr. John Moore has been Chairman of the COMEX Quotations Committee that set the prices which are at the heart of the fraud, and I think it is appropriate to allow us to go in on cross examination to those issues with Mr. Moore.

THE COURT: What issues?

REEVE: The issue of whether or not there is a fraud in the copper market, because I think the jury is going to have to look at this and assess that Mr. Miller is not crazy, which has been suggested. The reality is it's entirely possible for the twelve people who are listening to evidence in this case to hear what is the substance of Mr. Miller's claims from someone other than Mr. Miller. Let Mr. Moore defend what's happened to copper prices if he can.

The questions and the offer of proof would be, first of all, that copper prices, until May 1987, behaved in a very consistent manner. And that manner was that the difference in each contract price moved up and down exactly in sync, measured by a constant premium for every successive month in the future, because that premium resulted from the carry charge, or cost of money i.e. interest costs on the money required to finance holding the value of copper for the period of time in question. During the years and decades prior to May 1987, the only variable which effected change in the premiums was a change in interest rates. When rates rose like they did in the early 1980's the premiums widened to reflect the higher cost. When rates declined like they did during the middle 1980's, the premiums on deferred contracts narrowed. As a matter of fact, the same conditions hold true for silver futures contracts and for gold futures contracts, all of which trade on COMEX.

THE COURT: What does all of this have to do as to whether or not Mr. Miller is in violation of the Hobbs Act?

REEVE: Because it has a great deal to do with the legitimacy of his beliefs and the nature of his intent when he acted as he did in this case. Without that framework, I don't believe that the jury is going to be able to legitimately assess what his intent actually was at that time. If the jury thinks he's some wild guy who doesn't know what he's talking about, then that's going to impact their assessment of his intent.

Mr. Reeve just gave a terrific opening statement if this statement had been allowed to be heard by the jury. That is why Nevas refused to allow him to make an opening statement for my defense.

THE COURT: Mr. Appleton?

APPLETON: Well your honor I would respectively submit as a factual matter there was an investigation. However, as we discussed, **whether or not copper prices were rigged is an irrelevant issue**. If Mr. Reeve wants to question Mr. Moore on whether or not he participated or committed some illegal act, I think Mr. Moore is more than able to answer those questions, and the government has no objection to that. If we start getting into substantive claims of fraud, the government would object as it is beyond the scope of this trial.

THE COURT: All right.

REEVE: Your honor, just so that it is very clear, it sounded like what the government is not going to object to is that I can cross examine Mr. Moore and say, Mr. Moore, is it true that you've been involved for the past nine years in a fraud, rigging copper prices. When he says "No" I'm stuck with that answer. That's worse than nothing at all. Either I can question him or I can't. I want the record to be very clear. I don't know what the court's position is.

THE COURT: Well I suppose Mr. Reeve if you asked him that question and he answered, "No", and you had evidence that in fact he had, you could pursue that line of cross examination.

REEVE: That's fine your honor. And that's what I'm asking for.

THE COURT: Well we'll see where it goes. Call the jury please.

The jury is then brought into the jury box, sworn in, seated, and the proceedings continue.

THE COURT: Nothing that the court may say or do during the course of the trial is intended to indicate, nor should be taken by you as indicating what your verdict should be. It will be your duty to find from the evidence what the facts are. The evidence from which you will find the facts will consist of the testimony from the witnesses, documents, and other things received into the record as exhibits. Certain things are not evidence and must not be considered. Because the lawyers are not witnesses, their statements, arguments, and questions are not evidence. You must decide which witnesses to not believe. To do this you must use your own common sense and good judgment.

All right Mr. Appleton, if you'd please call your first witness.

DIRECT EXAMINATION BY MR. APPLETON OF WALTER JOSSEN

Q. Good morning Mr. Jossen, are you currently employed?
A. No. I'm retired.
Q. Do you have any children?
A. Yes two, Richard and David. Richard lives in Westport.
Q. Now your son Richard, does he have a position at COMEX?
A. He was a gold trader I understand.

Q. Now I'm going to direct your attention to August of 1993. I'm going
    to ask you if you recognize that letter?
A. Yes I do. This is a letter I received in the mail back in August
    1993.
Q. Did you know the individual that sent you that letter?
A. No I did not.
Q. Mr. Jossen, I'd ask you to read government's exhibit 1 to the
    members of the jury.
A. It's dated August 26th, of 1993 and addressed Mr. Walter Jossen,
    40 East 9th Street, New York City. Dear Mr. Jossen: Please carefully
    review the contents of the documents enclosed with this letter.
    Your son, Richard Jossen, has been an integral participant of the
    copper pricing fraud clarified in those documents. It would be
    wise for you to suggest to your son that we solve this problem in a
    sensible manner.
    I was a victim of the copper pricing fraud. There are a very
interesting set of circumstances which have developed during the six
years since this story began. Page 7 of a Bureau of Prisons report will
give you a clue to parts of the story. As you should be able to deduce,
I have associates who are expert professionals in the art of making
people pay their debts. It would be much more sensible to resolve this
matter without their involvement. To be blunt, calling my bluff would
be the most stupid thing that the COMEX crooks could possibly do.
    This is a THREAT, (and he capitalizes the word threat). But
because the government has obviously covered up the COMEX crime,
the government would create their own scandal by prosecuting me
for making the threat. Consequently, the best bet is for us to become
coconspirators. I intend to use some of the ill gotten gains to help
homeless people who have been forced onto our streets. Therefore,
much needed social benefits will accrue from this crime. Please expect
my call. Sincerely, Steve Miller.
Q. Now Mr. Jossen, you indicated that you received a call the day
    before you received that letter, is that accurate?
A. Yes, he identified himself as Steve Miller.
Q. What if anything did the individual who identified himself as Steve
    Miller, say to you at that time?
A. He asked if Richard Jossen was home. I said no, you can reach him
    downtown. That was it at that point.
Q. Did you receive another call at some later point in time?
A. The next day I got the letter and second phone call. He identified
    himself as Steve Miller and I recognized the voice.
Q. To the best of your recollection Mr. Jossen what did Mr. Miller say
    in that phone conversation?

A. He said he wasn't fooling around, he meant business. I told him I had nothing to do with it. I was just as upset as my wife was. We knew that our son had nothing to do with this thing.

Q. And what did you do with the letter?

A. I called my son. We gave him the letter and he turned it over to the people at COMEX.

Q. Did you ever receive any more phone calls?

A. No.

Thank you Mr. Jossen, I have no further questions.

CROSS EXAMINATION BY MR. REEVE

Q. Good morning Mr. Jossen. My name is Mr. Reeve. I represent Mr. Miller in this case. I believe we met briefly for the first time this morning.

A. Good morning, we did.

Q. It seems pretty clear when you get this letter and these phone calls that you were upset.

A. Yes.

Q. And you didn't know at that time and had no way of evaluating the seriousness of the threats, correct?

A. Only from the tone of his conversation.

Q. And from the tone I take it you believed that there was a serious quality to these threats?

A. Yes.

Q. So you were upset and concerned about your son?

A. And my wife too.

Q. As a concerned father did you suggest to your son that he go to the police?

A. We discussed going to the authorities and he turned it over to the legal end of COMEX and they said they would take care of it. They would follow through.

Q. And just so we are all clear, can you tell us if you know what COMEX is?

A. The Commodity Exchange.

Q. Do you know if the legal department of COMEX made a decision, an intentional decision not to report this to law enforcement authorities or whether it just sat there?

A. I don't know.

Q. Okay. To the best of your knowledge did this letter ever get reported in 1993 to any law enforcement authorities, if you know?

A. I don't know.

Q. You don't know. No one, no law enforcement authority ever contacted you with respect...

A. No.

Q. ...to these calls and the letter until after December 6th of 1994, is that right?

A. Correct.

Q. In other words, the only time you were contacted by law enforcement authorities was in conjunction with your testimony in this case?

A. Yes.

Q. Okay. And so to the best of your knowledge someone at COMEX apparently made the decision not to refer this to any law enforcement authority?

A. I don't know.

MR. APPLETON: I'm going to object to that.

THE COURT: He's already said he doesn't know.

MR. REEVE: I'll go on.

Q. Now, did you try to convince your son to go to law enforcement authorities with respect to these threats?

A. I mentioned it to him. I said I think we should do it and he said he would talk to the authorities at COMEX.

Q. Okay. And you have identified government's exhibit 1, which was the letter you received?

A. Yes.

Q. And did in fact did you receive attachments as part of what is now being referred to as government's exhibit 1?

A. Yes.

Q. And did you turn those attachments over to your son?

A. Yes.

Q. And do you recall what those attachments were about?

A. It's so vague because I read them in a hurry. I was only concerned with the threats in the letter itself. I had no background in the copper trading field. I know there was something with a Congressman in Connecticut.

Q. Would that have been Christopher Shays?

A. Yes.

Q. Okay. And so if I understand you correctly, the attachments have to do with activities in the copper market?

A. I didn't try to analyze it. I have to be honest with you.

Q. You indicated in response to a question by Mr. Appleton that you knew that your son, Richard Jossen had nothing to do with any kind of fraud on the COMEX, is that correct?

A. I knew that he was clean.

Q. Now when you say, you know, are you expressing the hope of every father or are you expressing personal knowledge that your son is clean?

A. Let's say I know my son.

Q. And your gut tells you he's not involved in any fraud?

A. Right.

Q. Mr. Jossen, after turning this letter over to your son Richard, did you ever have any more discussions about the letter and the threats with Richard?

A. Once it was turned over to the people in his office at COMEX, it just faded away.

Q. So you really didn't discuss it anymore?

A. No.

MR. REEVE: Thank you Mr. Jossen.

MR. APPLETON: Government calls Richard Jossen your honor.

DIRECT EXAMINATION BY MR. APPLETON

Q. Good morning Mr. Jossen. Could you tell the ladies and gentlemen of the jury how you are currently employed?

A. Good morning. I'm an independent trader on the Commodity Exchange in New York which is a subsidiary of the New York Mercantile Exchange.

Q. What is an independent trader?

A. I trade for myself. I basically speculate on commodities contract prices of gold, silver, copper, bonds, and oil.

Q. How long have you been trading and speculating on COMEX?

A. Since 1979.

Q. Have you ever been elected to the COMEX Board of Governors?

A. I was Vice Chairman for about five years.

Q. And what did that involve.

A. The Board is empowered with the day to day operation of running the exchange. There is a budget of about $35,000,000 and about twenty people were elected from the membership to serve on the Board and to serve the public interest.

Q. Did you ever trade copper Mr. Jossen?

A. Occasionally. Not often but occasionally.

Q. Now I'm going to direct your attention to December 5th, 1994. Where did you reside then?

A. Westport.

Q. Where in Westport do you reside?

A. Two Twin Oaks Lane. Its about a quarter mile from the Merritt exit 41.

Q. On December 5th, 1994, I direct your attention to the evening.

Could you tell the members of the jury what happened that night?

A. I was watching a Knicks game about 10:30, and my bedroom window sort of faces the driveway. I saw a car drive into the driveway, headlights first and then back out up the road, which made me assume it was just someone making a wrong turn.

Q. What kind of a car was it?

A. The only thing I was able to see was that it looked like it was a sports car because of the way the lights bent down and had those light covers. It looked like a two door sports car.

Q. Did you see a license plate?

A. No.

Q. Could you see the color of the car?

A. It looked like it was white, but I couldn't be sure.

Q. What happened next?

A. A minute or two later the door bell rings and I went to my window which overlooks the bell, and there were two guys standing outside the doorway and there was no car.

Q. Two men?

A. Two men.

Q. What did they look like?

A. From my window all I saw was the tops of their heads. One wore a golf shirt and the other wore a dress shirt. I didn't see the car and I was wondering. So I went down stairs and I went to the door. Then I was pretty much face to face and said, "Can I help you?" They said they had come to deliver a letter and did I know anybody named Steve Miller? And I said, no. They said, do you know anything about trading copper, and at that point I remembered who Steve Miller was because of phone calls and a letter that my father had gotten prior to this.

So I said, look, I said to these guys, "I don't know what you're talking about." One guy was moving, the other guy was doing all the talking about three steps down from the landing. I was getting real nervous at this point. I'm trying to talk to one guy and keep my eye on the other guy. They went on to say that they represent Steve Miller and they are here to deliver this letter.

He said to me, "Steve Miller contends that you owe him six million dollars. He claims you were involved in some copper trading fraud." And they went on to say that if his allegations were true that they'd be back, somebody would be back. They are basically connected and they would have the power to collect if his allegations were true. **But they did say if I don't know what these guys were talking about, they said to call the F.B.I. because this is clearly extortion.**

They tried to get me to open the door. I wouldn't open the door. They kept trying to hand me the envelope. Open the door, let me hand you an envelope. I wouldn't do that. This went on and it seemed to me like a long time but was probably five or seven minutes. Finally they said we want to give you the letter, and I said, "Drop it and leave, and I'll deal with it."

Q. And did they leave?

A. Yes.

Q. Did you get a better description when you were down speaking with them at your door?

A. Yeah, they were 25 to 30 years old, dark hair. One guy was in decent shape. The guy standing off to the side was wearing dungarees and a golf shirt, the other guy who was doing all the talking had a mustache and Brooklyn accent I could recognize.

Q. Were they in possession of any weapons?

A. I didn't see any.

Q. And what did you do after they left?

A. I was scared. I think I first called the Westport police and then **I took their advice and called the F.B.I.**

q. Did you speak with Special Agent Skelly?

A. I guess.

Q. Mr. Jossen, now I'd like you to read government's exhibit 2.

A. It says Dear Mr. Jossen: For your personal benefit and on behalf of the Board of Directors you need to make your first consulting fee payment of $6,000,000 by wire transfer no later than today into my account.

Wire transfer instructions are: The Dime Savings Bank of New York, 9 DeKalb Avenue, Brooklyn, N.Y. 11201, Stephen A. Miller, Account #0710488024. These payments will cement our business partnership in the copper price fixing fraud which you have had in progress since 1987. We will begin meeting to determine the most profitable method to use your willingness to commit fraud in the copper futures contract market traded at COMEX. Sincerely, Steve Miller.

Q. Now, had you ever spoken to any individual Mr. Jossen, by the name of Stephen Miller prior to that?

A. No.

Q. After you contacted the F.B.I. did you agree to cooperate with the government in an investigation?

A. Yes I did.

Q. And what did you do?

A. When the F.B.I. agents came over the next morning, I called Mr. Miller to engage him in conversation to further the investigation by taping the conversation.

MR. APPLETON: Your honor, I would ask the court's permission to play the taped conversation, exhibit 5 for the jury. (Whereupon the tape was played.)

SM: Hello.

JR: Stephen A. Miller please. My name is Richard Jossen.

SM: Yes Rich.

JR: I got correspondence from you last night strangely delivered and I wanted to talk to you about it. Can you talk?

SM: Yeah.

RJ: A couple of years ago I remember receiving from my father a letter along the same lines. I'm just a little confused Mr. Miller. I don't know what you're talking about. I was a Governor on the Board of COMEX and I don't know what you mean.

SM: You don't know what I mean?

RJ: I don't know anything about copper. When I received your letter a couple of years ago, I referred it to the exchange and they said there was some sort of investigation by the CFTC at your request. It didn't turn up anything. I'm not a copper trader. I don't know what I can do for you. But I'd be happy to set the ball rolling again to have another investigation if that's what's warranted.

SM: I had a long conversation with John Moore last night. Did you speak with John?

RJ: No, you spoke to John Moore last night? He's now the Chairman of the exchange.

SM: He never discussed our conversation with you this morning?

RJ: No, I'm not at work.

SM: Do you know how to reach him?

RJ: No I don't, I really don't. I would have to go through the exchange. They're not going to give me his number, he's the Chairman of the Exchange. They don't give out numbers like that.

SM: You were the spokesman in the newspaper about COMEX. Now you're trying to make believe you're nobody and tell me you don't know anything about copper. You're playing stupid with me and you're insulting my intelligence Mr. Jossen. You would have contacted law enforcement in August 1993 when I sent my letter to Walter, your father, if you weren't guilty of rigging copper prices.

RJ: The reason why my name was in the newspaper is because I was on the negotiating committee that merged COMEX with NYMEX, but that's all I did. I have nothing to do with copper, John is a copper trader.

SM: Mr. Jossen, if you weren't guilty of rigging copper prices with John Moore, you and he and your father Walter would have had me arrested for sending you extortion threats. **I have shown copies of these**

letters to F.B.I. Special Agent, Ed Cugell and to Howard Heiss, the Chief of the Commodities and Securities Fraud Unit at the Southern District of New York. I would have been arrested long ago if the Justice Department was not allowing this fraud to continue. And I have the evidence which no one in the Justice Department wants put in a federal court for a jury to see. The two guys who came to your house last night are members of a crime family who will lean on you to take some of the money you are ripping off. You need to understand that. Have you ever heard of John Gotti?

RJ: I've heard of John Gotti.

SM: This is not a joke Rich.

RJ: Do me a favor, tell those guys not to come around my house anymore.

SM: Do yourself a favor Rich, you better get this show on the road with your ass hole friend, John Moore. Call the F.B.I. and report me and show them the letter I sent your father. Think up some more stupid shit to explain why Walter didn't call NYPD Blue, pal. I send all my letters to Howard Heiss at the Southern District of New York, United States Attorney's office. I faxed my letter to John Moore at his house. The same letter the two guys delivered to you at two Twin Oaks Lane. I gave John Moore your number so he could call you about our partnership with this crime family. Those guys become very greedy. They have never thought about ripping off billions of dollars in a Wall Street scam. You keep pushing your luck Richie boy, you need to call John Hancock right now.

RJ: Okay well let me call John, do you have his phone number?

SM: 908-957-0349, good bye, we'll be seeing each other, partner.

CONTINUATION OF DIRECT BY MR. APPLETON

Q. Now Mr. Jossen, after that conversation with Mr. Miller, what did you do?
A. I called John Moore.
Q. Was that in connection with the F.B.I. investigation?
A. Yes.
Q. After the call on December 6th, did you place another call on December 7th?
A. Yes, with the F.B.I. agents.

MR. APPLETON: Your honor this tape is government's exhibit 7 which I would like to play for the jury now.

THE COURT: All right go ahead.

RJ: Steve Miller please.

SM: Yes.

RJ: Steve, Rich Jossen. I went down there with John. I'm actually sitting here with him right now. We spent the morning and talked to a lot of people. We found out a couple of things that we didn't know. There was a whole CFTC investigation going on about this.

SM: It wasn't an investigation, it was a cover up Rich.

RJ: A cover up and a conspiracy.

SM: Correct.

RJ: That's what I told them. I said that you were alleging that this whole CFTC thing was a cover up and that there were a lot of people involved in it. On that basis I said this guy's got evidence and he's willing to show you what the evidence is.

SPECIAL AGENT, LISA SKELLY:

LS: Mr. Miller.

SM: Yes.

LS: This is Special Agent Lisa Skelly from F.B.I.

SM: Yes.

LS: I want you to go to your door, answer your door. There are agents there.

SM: Okay.

RM: This is Rich Meade, F.B.I. New York, who's this?

LS: This is Lisa Skelly, F.B.I. Bridgeport.

RM: Okay Lisa I'm gonna put the phone down while we finish clearing the room.

LS: All clear.

CONTINUATION OF DIRECT BY MR. APPLETON

Q. Now Mr. Jossen, did you actually go down to the exchange and make the statement that you made on the tape?

A. No.

Q. Was the purpose you made those statements for furtherance of the investigation and to engage the defendant in conversation?

A. Yes

MR. APPLETON: I have no further questions.

CROSS EXAMINATION BY MR. REEVE

Q. Good morning Mr. Jossen. My name is Mr. Reeve, and I represent Mr. Miller.

A. Good morning sir.

Q. First, the F.B.I. asked you to lie on those tapes to further the investigations in these conversations, right?

A. No they didn't.

Q. They didn't? Did you make up those things on your own?

A. Some of them, yeah. They asked me to get him to talk, the story was mostly my doing.

Q Now you indicate that your father received a letter from Mr. Miller. Do you recall when that was?

A. I think about eight months ago or a year prior, maybe longer.

Q. I'm gonna show you government's exhibit 1, and ask you if you can identify that letter?

A. Yes, that's the letter that was sent to my father. And there's the date August 26, 1993. So that would be 15 months prior to the letter to my house.

Q. Okay. And you indicated that you took that to the counsel's office for COMEX?

A. I took it to the Exchange counsel, Martha Brescher and she sent it to the Vice President, Mr. Goodwin.

Q. Did you have some conversations with Mr. Goodwin and others regarding this letter?

A. I did. I had conversations with both Mr. Goodwin and Martha Brescher explaining that this man had called my father a couple of times and scared my parents. I told them that my parents were nervous and I'm worried about it too. I asked them what they planned to do about it.

Q. What were you told about Mr. Miller?

A. They said they had a file on Mr. Miller and that he had written many letters creating an ongoing investigation. They told me that there was no substance to the allegations Mr. Miller continued to make.

Q. Was it your decision not to pursue contacting law enforcement with respect to the letter turned over to you by your father, government exhibit 1?

A. Well, I was under the impression that the proper agents were being contacted by the Exchange.

Q. All right. Were you ever contacted by a law enforcement agent between the date on that letter in August '93, and December of '94, with respect to that letter?

A. No.

Q. So to the best of your knowledge no action was being taken with respect to that letter?

A. **No. Because I repeatedly would contact the Exchange because my father would repeatedly contact me saying, "What's happening?" I would then ask her, "What's going on?" And she would stick to her story that something was going on and there was an investigation pending, and that. I think, the Brooklyn D.A. she said, or something like that, was looking into it.**

Q. When you referred to it as a story, did you reach the conclusion at some point that in fact nothing was going on?

A. Now.

Q. You were being told something by Martha Brescher. She was legal counsel, a lawyer in COMEX. **And she was telling you something that wasn't true?**

A. **My conclusion is that she was probably telling me something that wasn't true.**

Q. And as to why people in COMEX, either her acting on her own or upon instructions from somebody else, do you know why she failed to contact law enforcement authorities?

A. I don't know why.

Q. Between August '93, and December '94, when these two individuals came to your door, did you have discussions with anyone at COMEX regarding Mr. Miller?

A. Yes, two or three.

Q. Now when these two individuals came to your door on December 5th, is it correct that one of the first things that you said to them was that this guy Miller is crazy?

A. Yes.

Q. Okay, and what they said to you is, look if this guy Miller is not crazy then you owe him some money and ought to pay, right?

A. **Well they said more than that. They said if Miller is crazy you should call the F.B.I. and have him arrested for extortion. And they also said if I made that call, that a good thing for them is they'd get rid of Miller because he was a thorn in their side. I recall them saying, "If he's arrested he won't be our problem anymore."**

MR. REEVE: I have nothing else, thank you your honor.

At the time I heard Richard Jossen testify that Bobby DiNicola and his cousin Mark had told him to call the F.B.I. to have me arrested, I suspected that Bob Appleton had coached Jossen to say that because it would make me believe that these mobsters were ratting on me, making me want to retaliate by reporting them to law enforcement. **It appeared inconceiveable that Jossen's claim could be true**. Why would Tony Rosetti and Tommy Gambino the Gambino capo for the Connecticut crew, want to prevent grabbing their own share of a huge crime which was protected by the Attorney General, Janet Reno and other senior government officials?

This situation is going to surface in a very bizarre manner two years later when I learned that it was true.

Tony Rosetti had been very friendly with me. When the COMEX crime began in 1987, I kept Tony fully informed of each development from that point forward. In fact prior to my first meeting with U.S. Congressman Chris Shays in 1987, Tony suggested that we meet with Attorney Frank Riccio in a mob frequented restaurant in Stratford to ask Frank to accompany me during my first meeting at Shays' office in Bridgeport. Frank did this. It was Tony's favor that made Frank get involved. Now for me to believe that Tony would direct his own mob associates to have me arrested was impossible for me to believe at that time.

There was a series of incidents during my time in prison that began to indicate Tony abandoned me and was part of the scheme to get me arrested. The first incident happened in 1996 when I met John Palazola. I became friendly with John playing pinochle. When I felt I had John's confidence I asked him to contact Tony to confirm that Tony was my Rabbi. John began to act differently to me because Tony must have disowned me.

Then I had another incident in 1998, when I went to Fort Dix and met a guy from New Haven who knew Tony very well. The guy's name was Rooster and he became friendly also. Then all of a sudden for no reason Rooster turned his back on me. I still had strong doubts that I had been double-crossed by Tony. I didn't want to believe it and it made no sense.

I would learn directly from Gene Gotti when I was transferred in 1999 to FCI McKean that I was completely wrong and that the highest levels of the Gambino crime family ordered my arrest.

The reason the Gambino people became angry was that based upon personal experiences I had had with Bruce Cutler, the attorney confidante of John Gotti, I recognized that Cutler was the government's inside man with John Gotti and was then trusted by a variety of other LCN leaders in Philadelphia, Chicago, and Kansas City. My proof was not only undeniable, it was also known by Tony Rosetti. The problem I failed to consider before I made my declarations was that all the people who had trusted Cutler would be murdered for vouching for Cutler.

A few of the points I raised were widely known. Gotti's court had ruled that Cutler was not acting as the lawyer for Gotti but was part of the crime family. That decision was then contradicted when Cutler represented Joe Gambino. Judge Leisure never questioned Cutler's ties as a crime family member in Joe's trial 2 years later than John's trial in 1991.

Another point that seemed to go unnoticed by the Gambino's was that Cutler was credited for the acquittal in the first Gotti trial even though a juror plead guilty to jury tampering. It had been Sammy Gravano who went to the Westies to pay off the juror $60,000 to guarantee his acquittal. Giving Cutler credit for legal work that had no bearing on the verdict is ignorant.

What had focused my attention upon Cutler's infiltration of the Gambino crime family for the benefit of the government is a series of events that I had personally in Cutler's office in May 1991. My first hypothesis about Cutler's strange behavior proved wrong. I then recognized that Cutler wanted to be thrown off the 1991 case because he would not be blamed for the inevitable conviction of John Gotti. That conviction proved to boost Cutler's value when the mob chose to believe that Cutler would have won the case and that the government was afraid of Cutler's theoretical legal defense ability.

I was going to learn the hard way about mob myths. I have been intrigued with the mob from a very young age. I am a mobologist. I have read most of the books written about the mob and I enjoyed going to places which put me into contact with mobsters. This includes watching trials. In 1993, I watched the entire trial of John and Joe Gambino, which included the testimony of Sammy "The Bull" Gravano, and the infamous mob rat on the Pizza Connection, Tomaso Buschetta.

I met Tony Rosetti in 1983. We were both members of Mill River Golf Club in Stratford, CT. Tony was the Secretary Treasurer of the Teamsters, Local 191 in Bridgeport. He was very well liked and he was an influential person in a variety of circles, including political operatives in Bridgeport.

Tony trusted me and I trusted him. Tony was busted for some union business of which I know nothing about. He did a very short sentence. When he was released he bought a business in Stratford that packaged very close tolerance military aircraft spare parts. I introduced Tony to owners of a shop that produced about $5,000,000 of these parts, and Tony received their business packaging parts they made for prime military contractors.

There was no imaginable reason to suspect that Tony would have told Bobby DiNicola and his cousin Mark to tell Richard Jossen to call the FBI on me.

DIRECT EXAMINATION BY APPLETON OF JOHN MOORE

Q. Good morning Mr. Moore, how are you currently employed sir?

A   Good morning, I am a self employed floor trader at the New York Mercantile Exchange, COMEX Division. I am also co-chairperson of the overseers of the COMEX fellowship.

Q. What are your duties as Chair?

A. To make sure that the merger of both exchanges gets fully knitted, and on top of that I am Chairman of the Board of COMEX, where we make the rules. I am Chairman of the Rules Committee For New Rules, Chairman of the By-Laws Committee, Chairman of the Corporate Advisory Committee, and basically I'm the COMEX staff.

Q.   What is COMEX?

A.   COMEX is a futures exchange. It's the largest metals exchange in the world.

Q.   Did you ever receive a call from someone who identified himself as Stephen Miller?

A.   To the best of my recollection in 1988, Congressman Christopher Shays contacted me about price movements in the copper market. After explaining things to him he asked if I would speak to one of his constituents because he was sure that I would be able to explain things. I was on the settlement committee at that time. This committee at the end of the day, settles prices for margin purposes. About five minutes later I got a call from a man who identified himself as Steve Miller who had just gotten my number from Congressman Shays.

Q.   What if anything did Steve Miller say to you at that time?

A.   Basically he felt that prices that we posted at the end of the day had no basis in fact. He said that I was manipulating the prices and making a lot of money out of it.

Q.   Okay, the call you received on December 5th, 1994, what happened then?

A.   I was downstairs in my office, my wife was upstairs. It was 10:30 at night and I heard the family phone ring. I guess not wanting to wake up the kid my wife said, "Steve Miller is on the phone." At that time Mr. Miller said, "I've sent somebody with a message over to Mr. Jossen's house. I'm going to send them over to your house too with the message."

I said, "There's no need to do that, I'll give you my fax number."

He said, "Okay, what is it?"

I gave him the fax number. Then he says, "Listen, I want $6,000,000, that starts our partnership, but I also have other partners now. If they don't like what you have to say, they'll show up at your door." When he hung up, the fax came through.

Q.   This will be government's exhibit 3. Mr. Moore, will you read this letter to the jury. The other letter you received on your fax, addressed to Mr. Jossen has been read to the jury before by Mr. Jossen.

A.   It says. Board of Governors, COMEX. Dear sirs: I have a New York Famiglia as our new partner in your copper scam. They met with Richard Jossen to deliver my message. This is not a bluff. Don't be completely idiotic. The only sensible thing for you to do is to share a little of your stolen property. The other two choices are real stupid. Nothing can protect you except a share of the loot. Richard has the directions.

Q.   Were you upset by this call?

A.   At this point, I didn't take anything that Mr. Miller said seriously. I didn't bother to contact Richie Jossen. Richie and I had served on the same board for four years. When I was at work the next day and I'm sitting in the office, this time I was Chairman, and Richie Jossen's clerk came by and said, "Call Richie at home, he needs to talk to you."

So I called him up, and I said, "What's going on Rich?"

He says, "You tell me. There were two goons at my house last night. I got the F.B.I. here now."

And I said, **"You're kidding." And I went cold, I went cold.**

Just as he's telling me that, he said, "I got the F.B.I. here. Here they want to talk to you." He put Ms. Skelly on the line. Just as I'm starting to talk to her, I was being beeped by my wife. I put Ms. Skelly on hold while I dialed my wife. She said, "I'm going to the store, you need anything?"

"What are you bothering me for? Do you know what's going on here?" And I said, "Lock the doors."

Now that I know that somebody's done something really stupid, I said, "Lock the doors, don't answer the door, don't go out."

I called the Holmdel Police Department after I got off the phone with Ms. Skelly. I guess it was the next morning. I called the F.B.I. in Tittenfalls, which is their headquarters in our area, and they told me what to do if Mr. Miller called again. But I never received anymore calls from Mr. Miller because the very next day, December 7th, I believe he was arrested

MR. APPLETON: No further questions.

CROSS EXAMINATION BY MR. REEVE

Q.   Mr. Moore my name is Richard Reeve. I represent Mr. Miller and I'm going to ask you some questions.

A.   Fine.

Q.   First of all you indicated that when you got the call from Richie, as you refer to him?

A.   I made the call to Richie.

Q.   You got a message from Richie and you called him on the morning...

A.   I got a message from his clerk, he was at home. He wasn't on the floor that day.

Q. And you called him at his home?

A. Yes.

Q. All right and you indicated that you had been on the same board or committee for four years with Richie; what committee was that and when?

A. That was the COMEX Board of Governors. I initially started serving in March of '90, through the end of, until the merger which was August of '94. Richie came on sometime later but still in 1990, and served until the end, which was August of '94.

Q. Okay. Now you indicated that you personally were not put in fear as a result of any of the calls that Mr. Miller made to you, correct?

A. Correct.

Q. All right, have you ever seen Mr. Miller?

A. Not until today. I'm assuming that's Mr. Miller.

Q. When I tell you that's Mr. Miller sitting over there in the white tee-shirt, that doesn't mean anything to you, you've never laid eyes upon him?

A. No.

Q. Your area if I understand it correctly that you specialize in and have expertise is the copper market specifically, is that right?

A. In my professional career I've traded more copper than anything else. I wouldn't say that I have expertise. If I had expertise I would be retired a long time ago.

Q. I wasn't asking you if you knew where the price was going to go, although we'll get to that. But you have expertise as a trader in the copper market, is that right?

A. Twenty four years of it.

Q. Did you have a position in the copper market in May of 1987?

A. I'm sure I did.

Q. Do you remember if you were short or long?

A. By the end of the day I was net flat, but that doesn't mean I still didn't have a position. I could be long one month and short another, that's having a balanced position. But flat so I'm not net long or net short. For the most part as a floor trader I was a day trader. A spread trader where I wasn't going to take unusual risks over night.

Q. Why don't you tell us how much you made trading copper since May 1987?

A. Half a million dollars, pre-tax over a nine year period. These last six years, from between the Board and being Chairman really hurt.

Q. As I understand your testimony, most of your half million earnings would have been made between 1987 and 1990, is that right?

A.   Two thirds.

Q.   Please correct me if I'm wrong, one of the reasons you didn't take Mr. Miller seriously is because you didn't think he knew anything about the copper market, right?

A.   From his statements, correct. I thought he was totally misinformed. I thought he was a total rookie. And I thought maybe he had some bad advice.

Q.   And you thought he was crazy, right?

A.   No.

Q.   Did you ever call Mr. Miller a nut job?

A.   Probably.

Q.   Okay, did you call Mr. Miller a nut job when you were interviewed by Lisa Skelly of the F.B.I. on December 6, 1994?

A.   Probably.

Q.   So you did say and tell people that you thought Miller was crazy, right?

A.   No.

Q.   Oh?

A.   It's a colloquialism.

Q.   Are you distinguishing between a nut job and crazy, or what?

A.   Yeah, I consider crazy a term for mental illness. I consider a nut job somebody who is off the wall. Somebody who makes statements who has nothing to back them up.

Q.   So you believe Mr. Miller was a nut job but you didn't believe he was crazy?

A.   Correct.

Q.   Now the copper, gold, and silver market are different from soybeans, cotton, and other perishable commodities, right?

A.   Yes.

Q.   And one of the things that makes it different is that they are storage able, right?

A.   Correct.

Q.   The other thing that makes copper, gold, and silver different from a lot of other commodities markets is that they are not seasonal, correct?

A.   Copper is.

Q.   Copper is seasonal, in what way?

A.   Well usually during the summer, demand slackens off. The refineries shut down, so there's not as much production. Coming into the Spring, they start making wire for new homes, because construction usually picks up in the Spring time, slacks off in Summer, picks up again in Fall, from say December through March or May, that's usually the peak demand period.

Q. What's the first year you began trading copper?

A. 1974.

Q. For thirteen years, from '74 to '87, there was no backwardation in the copper market, isn't that correct?

A. Not true.

Q. When was there backwardation in the copper market during those 13 years?

A. 1974, 1970, 1980, 1983 through '84.

Q. And what's the longest period of time that the backwardation lasted in any of those prior to 1987?

A. I missed a year. The other—- the '80 backwardation started in '79. So two years.

Q. The longest period was a full two years?

A. Yes, that would be a pretty good guess.

Q. All right, what's backwardation?

A. Backwardation is when the nearby price is higher than a price further down the road.

Q. And what that means is the nearby price of the active month, as you've testified about, is the closest month to the day you make the trade right?

A. Not necessarily. That's the spot month. The spot is today, this month September. For instance today 1996, September is considered the spot month. If you bought copper for September delivery today, you might have it in your warehouse tomorrow, whereas if you buy December which is now the active month because it trades more, you have two and a half months to decide what you're going to do with it. You can liquidate your position or you can hold it. You can stand for delivery or if you're short, you can liquidate or make the delivery.

Q. Is it true sir, that since approximately May of 1987, that the copper market has been in backwardarion virtually the entire time?

A. Except for a short period in 1993.

Q. And you would also agree would you not, that backwardation, while it might have existed for periods of time prior to 1987, never went on for the period of time it is right now in the copper market, correct?

A. Only from 1948 to 1970.

Q. Okay.

A. 22 years.

Q. You're saying that during that entire period of time the copper market had backwardation?

A. Yes. Copper traditionally is a backwardation market. It's very rare that there's a surplus of copper. From 1970 to '74, under the government in Chili they had to pump out every ounce of copper they could. The COMEX warehouse stocks consisted of copper that nobody could use. It was wire bars, it wasn't state of the art copper. At that time COMEX became a dumping ground for copper and it just piled up.

Q. What's Black Monday?

A. That was the day the stock market crashed over five hundred points.

Q. November 19, 1987?

A. October.

Q. October?

A. It was October. I can tell you the exact date.

Q. October 19? Is it correct that the closing price for copper on the day before was somewhere around $.87 per pound?

A. Right.

Q. All right, and is it true that by the end of Black Monday it was at $.74 per pound?

A. No.

Q. All right. That was true the next day, October 20th?

A. Yes.

And when the market drops in effect $.13 in a two day period of time, that's a significant loss to a lot of people who are in the wrong position, isn't it?

A. Oh yes.

Q. I mean panic set in, in the copper market, didn't it?

A. I wouldn't call it panic. I would call what happened last June a panic. If you want to call it—- whatever term you want to use for it. London opens five or six hours ahead of us, by the time we opened, we already knew that the market was due ten cents lower.

Q. It opened that way didn't it?

A. It opened that way, rallied four cents and then went out on its lows.

Q. And what happened after October 21st, when it got down to seventy four cents? Over a ten week period the price of copper went from seventy four cents to above a dollar forty, correct?

A. Yes.

Q. It almost doubled didn't it?

A. Yes.

Q. And people who were in the market made a killing didn't they, if they were well positioned?

A. I believe some funds did pretty well.

Q. Yeah, maybe some individual investors too?

A. Maybe some individuals, maybe George Soros...

Q. And when the market doubled in price, is it also true that the number of open contracts more than reduced by half?

A. Yes.

Q. In other words while the market is going up, doubling, the number of open contracts on the market is going from somewhere around 80,000 contracts down to thirty thousand contracts, isn't it?

A. Yes.

Q. So at a time when the price is skyrocketing, people are leaving the copper market in droves, aren't they?

A. They are not leaving. They are trading less because of the volatility. You could make or lose the same amount of money with a lot smaller position and so you look at your risk and you trade according to that.

Q. All right.

A. Now let me point out one more thing about charts.

Q. Yes sir.

A. When we crashed that day the next day if you're a chartist, what we call the triple bottom, which is the most bullish signal you can get in the world. It signaled at least a rise to a dollar.

Q. All right. It is also true that at the same time the market price is down, open contracts are getting cut way back? There's less activity? The backwardation is growing during that ten week period?

A. Yes.

Q. In other words, the active contract is becoming in relation to the deferred months, there's more of a spread?

A. That's caused not only by the price increase but it is also—-

Q. Before—-

A. --can be caused by the 66% draw down in stocks or thereabouts.

Q. Okay, I understand your explanation. But just so that we're clear, your answer is yes, is that right? Yes there was a widening gap between the active and the deferred months?

A. Yes.

Q. Okay, and it was a very significant gap, wasn't it?

A. Yes.

Q. Okay. Now at the time all of this was happening, you were on the Quotations Committee, were you not?

A. I've been on the Quotations Committee it seems like forever.

Q. So your answer is yes.

A. Yes.

Q. The Quotations Committee is the group that sets the prices for settlement prices for each month in the copper market, right?

A. Yes.

Q.	You already told us that the active month, that's the month where there's more volume than any other month, right?

A.	Typically.

Q.	Typically it's either the next one or the one behind it as you get closer to the front month, right?

A.	Right.

Q.	Now the active month's price is decided on the basis of you take the sales during the last minute, the top price and the bottom price, that is the highest and the lowest price, and you divide by 2, right?

A.	Right.

Q.	And that's locked?

A.	Yes it is.

Q.	Now with respect to the deferred contract months, if I understand your testimony correctly, has some discretion in terms of how they set that price, is that right?

A.	The Quotations Committee uses some discretion. Anything that isn't authorized, that isn't set out in the rules, the Quotations Committee has to write on the actual settlement sheet why it is that they used discretion. Discretion is very very rare. There is a formula that's used and when it's not used it has to be explained.

Q.	Was discretion used from October 20th, 1987, through December of 1987, on any day in the market?

A.	I can't answer that.

Q.	You don't know?

A.	I don't know.

Q.	You just don't recall?

A.	I don't recall.

Q.	Fair enough.

A.	But as I say, it's a very rare occasion and I'll tell you why it's rare. It's because people have to—- the margin is based on settlement. I've always told anybody on my settlement committee—- it's not my settlement committee—- that you can't go wrong by following the rules. Nobody can fault you somewhere down the line and say well, why did you do this this way? You can always say I did it by the rules. You got a problem with it, petition to have the rule changed, but do it by the rules.

Q.	Let's take 1987, there were many times, and I'm focusing now on October 20th through early December of 1987. There were many days for example on which there wasn't much action in deferred contract months, right?

A.	That's typical.

Q.	Nothing unusual?

A.   No.

Q.   Just so that we're clear in what we're talking about, for example, the active month would be what?

A.   December.

Q.   December '87 was the active month, right? And that's where most of the trades were going on?

A.   Right.

Q.   Now the next deferred month would be what?

A.   The next active deferred month?

Q.   Yes.

A.   The next active deferred month would be March.

Q.   This would not be abnormal in the market that there might be a trade in the March '88 at ten o'clock in the morning and then no other trades?

A.   Well no. Typically you've got pretty decent activity through May and July.

Q.   As you get further out for example there wouldn't be much less activity for the December '88, would there be?

A.   No.

Q.   And the Committee would have to set a price nevertheless for the December '88 contract while you sit on the Committee on October 30, 1987?

A.   Right.

Q.   And you look at the contract's prices for any trades that occurred for the December '88 month, right?

A.   No.

Q.   You don't, you don't look at those?

A.   The rules say it's based on switch values. If you've got an active month, say December '87, what's bid and what's offered for the difference between December '87 and December'88. If there is a switch trade in the last fifteen minutes, again the switch trade is two hundred and trades at three hundred, settles in the middle at—- you know, the difference between the two Decembers will be two hundred and fifty. If there are no trades, you ask where are the orders? When somebody—- because you know what the March settlement is going to be, somebody said I could buy March and sell December '88, at such and such a deal, somebody else says, well, I can sell March and buy December '88, at such and such a deal, and now you know, you take the mid-point of that if there is no trades. This stuff is etched in stone, this stuff is in the rules.

Q.   You mean if I'm a trader—- if I'm a trader, a way that I could manipulate the market is just by making **an outrageously high offer to buy December '88 in this situation, deferred contract and**

then somebody else could take a low and you would just divide that by two and take it in the middle?

A. No, no.

Q. I didn't think so.

A. It would be the relationship of the switches. Just not the bid and offer for December, it's the relationship to the other months, and there are professionals in the market. Professional arbitrators and professional dealers who have orders in every day for every switch, whether or not the market gets to where they can do the trading, the orders in there everyday, you don't need floor locals to make those markets, although they do generally tighter than a dealer would make it.

Q. All right

A. And one other——-

Q. Go ahead.

A. The deferred months on the London Metal Exchange are much more actively traded even than they are on COMEX. It's a bigger market, and because of the character, nothing is allowed to get very far out of line before it gets knocked back into place.

Q. Just so things are clear——- its true now there's some dispute about whether or not prices in the copper markets have been manipulated in London and elsewhere, isn't that right?

A. What do you mean by manipulation? If you're talking about the Sumitomo incident.

Q. Yes.

A. I don't know if I would call that manipulation. They put up their money, they bought the copper. Once they've got it it's their problem.

Q. If I can have this marked for identification. I'm going to show you a document which has been marked as defendant's Exhibit C for identification. Without reading from that document, have you ever seen it before?

A. No, I haven't seen it before.

Q. I want to give you a situation and ask you if in your capacity as a member of the Quotations Committee if you can explain it? I'm just going to give you one day and this is October 23rd. The December '87, at 9:53 A.M. was eighty dollars and sixty five cents. That would be for a hundred pounds, or 80.65 cents per pound. At the same time the price at 9:53 for the December '88 traded at 76 dollars and fifty cents, or 76.5 cents per pound.

A. So we've got a spread of 415 points or 4.15 cents.

Q. So between 9:53 A.M. and the close at 2:00 P.M.the December '87, went up 1.5 cents, right?

A.   Right.

Q.   Even though the last trade on the December '88 was at 76.5 cents at 9:53 A.M. the committee , the Quotations Committee set the settlement price for that month down a full cent at 75.5 cents per pound, a cent less than it was before the active month traded higher by 1.5 cents for the day. So while the owners of the December '87 made money, the owners for December '88 lost money, even though no trades including switches were made after 9:53 A.M.

A.   I think I know what you're getting at. Why did that go down and the other go up? You would also have to look at what happened to the March contract on that day. What happened to the July contract on that day. What happened to the September contract on that day. Because there's all those relationships.

Q.   But what data would you look at that would authorize you as the committee to go a penny lower on the December '88, when the market for the active month is going up? Because obviously what's happening there, is, the spread is widening. The committee is creating backwardation which is supposed to be the sign from god that there is a shortage of copper. If there is this sign which fools people on October 23rd that there is a shortage of copper when three days before the world is in economic panic of the collapsing stock market. But three days later there is an incredible shortage of copper because builders need copper wire for a housing boom, is that what was happening Mr. Moore?

A.   One of the reasons that people trade spreads especially at that time, the spread market was as volatile as the outright market and sometimes more so. Perhaps something in the back wouldn't move at all, other than the spot. December kept going higher, higher, higher. That's a result of, you see what happens going on with the warehouse stocks, they were being drawn down. People who were short December had to buy back their shorts. People who needed metal had to buy on the COMEX hoping they'd be able to get some copper out of the warehouse because they needed to fill their orders, they needed to draw wire, they needed a lot of different things.

Q.   All right. I wanted to show you what's been marked as Defendant's Exhibit D for identification and ask if you can explain that one page document?

A.   This seems to have come out of the **COMEX rule book, and it describes I guess the makeup and the duties of the settlement committee.**

Q.   Does that page contain the rule with regard to setting of prices by the Quotations Committee for deferred months at the end of the day?

A. Yes.

Q. And based on your familiarity with the rules, is that in fact the rule that was in existence in 1987, '88, and '89?

A. Yes.

Q. And that is the rule that still exists in the market today or has it been changed?

A. We changed one aspect of the rule. The active month is now settled on the weighted average of what trades on the close instead of the midpoint.

Q. So I ask you again—- if you're saying it's based on the quotes in the last fifteen minutes, **it would be incredibly easy for me to just set a price for that December '88 that's way out of line, right?**

A. Only if I want to own it or sell it, because if you're out of line you're going to either own it or sell it. It's going to trade.

Q. **I understand what you're saying, but what you are forgetting is, at this point the market is closed and no trades are being executed.** Isn't the Quotations Committee trying to formulate a price for margin purposes on contracts which were inactive. Remember the December '88 contract didn't trade after 9:53 A.M. on October 23rd. But the committee decided to drop it's price by claiming that there were switch quotes which never were executed during the trading before the COMEX closed on October 23rd, 1987. Getting back to the example that I used about October 23rd where the settlement prices for the deferred December '88 contracts was set by the committee at 75.5 cents per pound. If I understand you correctly, what you're saying is that somebody offered to buy and sell at either side of the 75.5?

A. Based on it's relationship with another contract. The outright bids and offers for deferred months are usually disregarded because you don't have outright bids and offers for deferred months. For the most part you have the switch relationship which is why every month other than the spot and the active are all settled as a switch relationship.

MR. REEVE: I would ask that Defendant's Exhibit D, the rule for the Quotations Committee that Mr. Moore has identified, be admitted as an exhibit.

MR. APPLETON: No objection.

THE COURT: Full exhibit. (Whereupon Defendant's Exhibit D was marked full.)

Q. I want to show you what's been marked as Defendant's Exhibit E for identification. There is no date on this. Can you identify in general what that depicts?

A. Looks like a listing of commodities price settlements.

MR. REEVE: If I can have this marked also for identification. I apologize.

Q. I'm going to show you what's been marked as Defendant's Exhibit F for identification. Does that have the same figures that are within Defendant's Exhibit E for identification, sir?

A. Let's see, I would say so.

Q. All right, and there is a date on the top of Defendant's Exhibit F for identification that is a blow up of the commodity exchange numbers, right?

A. Thursday May 30, 1996.

MR. REEVE: Your honor, I would offer Defendant's Exhibit F.

MR. APPLETON: No objection.

THE COURT: Full exhibit.

Q. Now Mr. Moore, the numbers, the way that they are reported, and this is out of The Wall Street Journal. As you go across the numbers, and with the court's permission, I would ask you to label what the columns mean so that they are understandable to us.

A. First column is the contract months. The second column lists the previous day's settlement. The third column lists the high trade for the day. The fourth column lists the low trade for the day. The fifth column is the new settlement. The sixth column is the difference from the night before. The seventh column is the contract high. The eighth column is the contract low for the life of the contract. And the ninth column is the open interest as of the close the day before. The open interest is the number of longs and shorts that haven't been liquidated. For every long there's a short and that counts as one in the open interest, not two.

Q. All right. And in this chart for this particular day it shows in the column that you indicated, the sixth column, the difference from the day before?

A. Right.

Q. It indicates that the May, which is the closest contract, May of '96, had a net of minus 1.25 cents, correct?

A. Yes.

Q. Whereas all of the other months behind that had a significant rise in price, correct?

A. Yes.

Q. **Can you explain why that is?**

A. It was the last day of trading for May, the May '96 contract. If you still had an open position at the end of the day, you either had to take delivery or make delivery. This looks to me that some of the longs just stayed in the market a little too, you know, a—- they waited until the end of the month to get out and now they've got to pass it on to somebody else at whatever price they'll pay,

Q. Now you indicated I believe, correct me if I'm wrong, that the backwardation process has been in existence in the copper market since sometime around the middle of 1987, correct, with one exception in 1993?

A. Right.

Q. As I understand it, one of the things that you have indicated to others explaining that backwardation is that there's a shortage in supply, is that right?

A. There has been, yes.

Q. And in fact that's one of the reasons you've given in the past as to why there is backwardation in the market?

A. Yes.

Q. And in fact, two days ago when you were interviewed by Agent Skelly, you told her that, didn't you?

A. Yes.

Q. You said the reason for this is because there's a shortage of copper, is that right?

A. Right.

Q. Okay, and that there still continues to be a shortage of copper, is that right?

A. Not as severe. Somewhat because of the higher price levels over the last nine years, a lot more production has come on line and its just starting to make its way down the pipe line. It takes a long time to open up a copper mine.

Q. In 1987 there was nothing in the rules that prohibited you, as a member of the Quotations Committee, from trading in that copper market that you were setting the prices for, is that right?

A. As long as I wasn't trading against any of my customers or ahead of my customers orders.

Q. But that would be a different rule, wouldn't it? I mean can anyone do that?

A. Can anyone trade ahead of a customer order?

Q. That applies to all traders doesn't it? I am specifically asking about the rules which only apply to the members of the Quotations Committee concerning the correct choice of settlement prices for the purposes of margin calls for all the positions, both long and short in each contract on a daily basis?

A. No, there was nothing prohibiting me from trading in the rules.

Q. You've already told us as a member of the Quotations Committee you were trading. To your knowledge, how many people are on the Quotations Committee?

A. No less than five.

Q. How many were on it in 1987?

A. Who was on in '87, that stuff is archived so I couldn't get it for today. The names I can guess, it doesn't change that often.

Q. Do you know how many there are, four or five other members, were they actively trading in the market?

A. Back in October of '87?

Q. Yes.

A. Nobody would miss a day.

Q. No one would miss a day? And when you say no one would miss a day, that's because there was a tremendous amount of money to be made then, wasn't there?

A. It's because if you had any sort of a position, you'd have to be there to protect it.

Q. I don't understand. If no one would miss a day, why did the open contracts drop from 80,000 to 30,000 during that period of time?

A. Again due to the volatility of the market and you had a lot of fund business that would not trade in copper after what happened on October 20th. They'd been along for the ride from $.70 up to almost $.90. And then overnight they're forced to liquidate because they are all trading by computer and the computer tells them when they have to get out.

Q. So if I understand you correctly nobody would miss a day, but a lot of people did?

A. I'm talking about floor traders, the people on the settlement committee.

Q. I want to show you what's been marked for Defendant's Exhibit F for identification. Can you identify that document?

A. Oh, yes.

Q. What's that from?

A. It says here, source is U.S. Bureau of Mines.

Q. Are you familiar with the Commodity Year Book?

A. I've heard about it, but I've never looked at it.

Q. Can you tell us if that chart appears to be an accurate summary of the production of copper on a worldwide basis?

A. This is the production of mine ore, this is not refined copper. As the production of mine ore expands, smelter capacity does not increase. It is very difficult to build a new smelter. I would say over the last ten years or so the average production of refined copper is about ten million tons a year.

Q. So if I understand you correctly, the supply of copper over the last ten years has been roughly at the same level?

A. Yeah.

Q. So your explanation of backwardation by a shortage of copper must have to do with the demand side since it doesn't have to do with the supply side?

A. Yes.

Q. Or maybe I'm missing something here?

A. No there's the demand side also. As the demand goes up the supply stays static.

Q. So it's your position that the demand has increased significantly and that's what caused this rise in prices since 1987?

A. Definitely.

MR. REEVE: Your honor, I have some more questions of Mr. Moore. I wonder if this would be an acceptable time to break so I can consult briefly with Mr. Miller and try to do this quickly after the lunch break?

THE COURT: All right, we'll suspend now for our lunch break and resume at 2:00 o'clock

[134] Stephen A. Miller

CHAPTER SIX
HELLO is anybody home?

I didn't want to make any part of this story dull for anyone. I decided to include almost the entire verbatim testimony of John Moore for a few reasons. Mr. Moore rambles a lot so I cut out as much as I could to keep from torturing my readers. I kept in as much as possible so you would be able to appreciate the brilliant work of Dick Reeve, one of the finest litigators ever to be in the legal profession. During the hours Dick and I spent together in the Bridgeport jail, he really learned most of the fine points concerning the technicalities of futures trading and copper in particular. **This was a surprise to me** because Dick kept being confused by the terms long and short during our conversations preceding the trial.

It's impossible to know how much the jurors understood. I can only wonder what readers now think. I suspect that they might have been able to tell that John Moore was being trapped by Dick's style of letting John ramble on and on, while he offered obvious contradictions to points he had made. To me Moore's evasive answers and answers that contradict common sense make it clear that John Moore was committing a simple fraud.

There is going to be much more to come, and when I testify I will clarify many of the ridiculous claims that John Moore made. For instance the copper production reported in the Commodity Year Book which Mr. Moore has never seen before in his entire 24 years of specializing in copper trading, reveals the production of more than 18,000,000,000 pounds, or 9,000,000 tons of copper. The recovery of copper from copper ore is only about .2 to .6% of the ore. If the U.S. Bureau of Mines reported ore tonnage the numbers would go off the page. Ore tonnage is 99.8% dirt and rocks being dug by huge shovels.

What John Moore and his team of five manipulators on the Quotations Committee did on a daily basis was to drop the price on the deferred contracts by huge amounts which illegally created the backwardation. These changes were made daily after the close of the market. My best analogy to this would be to imagine that after every N.Y. Yankee baseball game, the score keepers changed the score of every game for ten seasons in a row. Would no one who watched the game notice this? What is beyond my understanding is how could the floor traders on COMEX and all the commodities traders and analysts, and reporters fail to see this? I forced some people to see this, including U.S. Congressman Chris Shays, two reporters for The Wall Street Journal, Peter Angrist and John Valentine, and a host of others. I put it literally under their noses in their offices.

People tend to accept the official version of things. They don't question what they suspect might be too complex. The official tried and true version of things in general may not make sense and often doesn't. But few people are willing to challenge the accepted when it fails to be what has been accepted. This is why fads come and go with regularity. If the final scores of baseball games were changed for one day there would be an eruption. **For ten years the prices were changed on copper after the market closed while a huge number of participants lost a ton of money, but it went unnoticed. We call this the information age, but this is a case of very simple information that failed to be understood. Did the jury understand it?**

The facts are that I am writing this again in 2005, and there have been many corporate exposes. Enron, WorldCom, Arthur Anderson, and dozens more, but the S.E.C. and the Justice Department are running away from putting the big crooks in prison. With the government's feet to the fire, they are slapping fines on a few, and making speeches about restoring faith on Wall Street. The government wants as few corporate crooks in prison as possible and we are being told that the government is tough on corporate crime. We the voters are going to reelect the incumbents in spite of their lies. This is our culture.

They like to tell us that these cases are very complex. The reason I pursued the copper fraud was because it was so simple. I still was told that it was too complex. If changing a price is too complex, you need to go back to first grade again.

When John Moore testified that when Richie Jossen told him that the F.B.I. was at his home, he stated on the witness stand, **"I went cold. I went cold."** I turned around to the U.S. Marshals sitting behind me and said, **"When are you going to hand cuff this guy?"**

HELLO is anybody home?

You can never know what a witness will say on the stand. If anyone had bet me and gave me 1,000,000 to 1 odds that John Moore would say that, I would have saved my $1.00. How could the jurors not understand that John Moore wanted to get nowhere near any law enforcement because John is a criminal. John Moore couldn't believe that his friend Richie called the F.B.I. That is why Mr. Moore never called the F.B.I. until after he knew the F.B.I. had already been called by Richie. Remember he said he called the F.B.I. in Titenfalls, New Jersey. He already knew that the F.B.I. was in the case.

My mission was to get John Moore in a federal court on a witness stand. Remember the last thing that Bob Appleton and Judge Nevas wanted was to allow me any trial. I had a couple of options besides going to prison for what would finally be more than 9 years on a 9 year sentence. One possible option was that because the most senior government officials in America wanted this fraud to continue, they might decide to make me a partner with them. That option entered into no one's mind but mine. When I had put this suggestion on the record to Judge Daly during the competency hearing Judge Daly pretended to not hear it. In the great United States of Hypocrisy you can't expect a Federal Judge is going to respond to his chance to get rich by being part of the crime. Let's not do this on the record but Judge Daly could summon me into his chambers if he needed to discuss getting paid for the crime he wanted to continue. But the hypocrisy allows the judge to make believe he is conducting a real competency hearing. The bottomless pit has no limit. Infinity is a hard concept to imagine but I have gotten a dose of infinity here on earth.

The conspiracy to conduct the competency hearing with the exalted Judge Daly and the good Dr. Kucharski is commenced without even a wink and a nod. When our government doesn't claim to know the obvious, they study the obvious forever. How long did our government study nicotine to learn if it is addicting? They can do these things with a straight face too. We let them by voting for these liars because the voters are brainwashed. I used to think that the voters are just stupid. I learned that we are not stupid, because no one can be that stupid. We are brainwashed and we vehemently deny being brainwashed because being brainwashed is considered a stigma.

I mistakenly believed that I could convince them that they were being short changed by John Moore and his many friends involved in splitting up a huge amount of money. In fact I would not be surprised that none of the judges and the prosecutors received any money for their efforts to protect a large number of elected officials who were taking bribes in the form of political campaign contributions. You will soon see what Congressman Chris Shays says to John Moore when he went to COMEX for his bribe. This comes out during Mr. Moore's testimony after the lunch recess.

The other possible chance I had to gain would be from my potential book I intend to write. A juicy, controversial story written about the most prominent, elite American judicial officers who decided to play stupid might sell. That's how Michael Moore made a fortune. Beside money I would earn from my book, I hope to use my exposure to prove my expert ability as a commodity price risk manager which in turn would bring me substantial clients. There are huge amounts of money to be made in this field if potential clients will hire a strategist who knows how to protect them from enormous risks of interest rate costs, fuel costs, and other commodities that will unexpectedly have adverse price changes. It is very hard to make corporate executives understand that there are very sensible strategies to use as opposed to the improper use of derivatives that have caused massive losses in the past.

Presently there are more than $100 trillion of derivatives accounted for, off the balance sheets of the largest banks in the world. Many of these positions are crazy speculations which are kept off balance sheet because they would bankrupt the entire world's financial system if they were put on the balance sheets of these financial institutions. Each time there has been a date proposed to end this off balance sheet accounting by oversight authorities those dates have been extended.

There are no victims of this crime except copper traders like myself. In a vehicle there is less than 30 pounds of copper. If copper costs doubled who cares? If General Motors passes their cost on to the consumer the cost only jumped $15.00 on a vehicle which cost $20,000 and more. This situation made this crime almost victimless even though the copper producers would profit by more than $9,000,000,000 per year. Copper producers always bribe elected officials anyway in order to get favorable treatment from the Environmental Protection Agency. So the bribes for rigging copper prices went completely unnoticed.

How do I know that more than $9,000,000,000 were generated by the illegal profits? That's easy, when $.50 per pound is added to the price of copper, and production is greater than 18,000,000,000 pounds annually, that generates more than $9,000,000,000 per year. The price jumped from $.65 per pound in June 1987 when this fraud began to a range of between $1.15 to as high as $1.60 for the entire period until it stopped after my trial in 1997.

John Moore remembers the drop in 1993, which only lasted a short time. He was right. That drop was right after I first spoke with Howard Heiss. Mr. Heiss was the Chief of Securities & Commodities Fraud Unit for the Southern District of New York. I caught him on the phone and convinced him to have investigators contact me. After I received a call from them, they were supposed to contact F.B.I. Special Agent Ed Cugell. I explained our meeting which Congressman Shays had arranged in 1989, followed up by Shays' letters to Thornburgh and Bowsher.. I feel confident to speculate that Howard Heiss learned that I was right about the COMEX fraud and he decided to let people at COMEX know that he wasn't going to tolerate this fraud to continue. This is why Mr. Moore remembers vividly that the market dropped in 1993, according to his testimony on the stand. Then I suppose that Mr. Heiss was told to look the other way again. The fraud started right back again for four more years.

This story is not about copper or about futures contract trading, it is about money. I stress this issue emphatically. I did not write this story for people interested in copper or futures contracts in general. I wrote this story for citizens in America and elsewhere. Huge sums of money being ripped off in a very unsophisticated manner by people like John Moore who are very fortunate that America has a very corrupt government, and a public who will believe preposterous nonsense. This week Senator Hillary Clinton had her book published. She claims to be **"dumbfounded"** to learn that Bill was having sex with Monica Lewinsky now that he finally admitted this to her. Every retard on planet Earth knew that Bill and Monica were having sex. For her to make up this obvious lie in a book, is an insult to our intelligence. Remember that she has an editor and a publisher who went along with this stupid lie, which should be an insult to our intelligence. The problem is that our American culture rebukes the truth and embraces the oceans of hypocrisy spewed out around the clock by the government's media.

As I transcribe the court reporter's transcription of the testimony, I have a desire to stop and explain the finer points. I continue to get feedback from people who fail to grasp the points I am trying to convey to a mass audience. If I am unable to give the reader enjoyment because of the beyond weird behavior of the most senior officials elected and appointed to govern America my mission failed. Of course when the reader is unfamiliar with technicalities it can present dry boring parts to wade through. If I fail to explain what went on throughout the legal process I'm trying to expose, then my credibility will be doubted.

There exists a C-span and trial junkie audience who enjoys the real thing. My hope is to get beyond that audience so that the average voter can see how the Judicial Branch of our government really works. My case opened up my eyes much wider than they had been previously even though I had watched every single government hearing since Watergate on the major scandals.

As my story continues you will come upon explanations of many other things you have read before. For instance, it will be hard for you to believe that Dick Reeve is in on the plan to get me convicted. You may want to believe that I am paranoid for making that statement. I am sure that if Dick really represented me the way he is capable of doing, that there was no chance for the jury to convict me. But Dick knew that Kent Moller guaranteed a minimum of a hung jury regardless of his best legal skills. I am also positive that Dick knew that my plan was to make it impossible to lose a fair trial and that it would be very unlikely that there would ever be a trial.

I choose to believe that objective readers who wait until they have read my entire story before they come to a conclusion will be convinced that I am not paranoid. I believe for me to be deemed paranoid, I would need to be incoherent too.

So now let's get back into the court room for the resumption of the trial phase of the story.

AFTERNOON SESSION

(2:10 O'CLOCK, P.M.)

MR. REEVE: Your honor, I have a number of charts which have been marked, I think there's seven of them. I've reviewed them with Government counsel and the parties I believe are in agreement that they can be full exhibits. Not all of them will be able to be authenticated by this witness but they will be by subsequent witnesses.

MR. APPLETON: I have no objection your honor.

THE COURT: All right, they may be marked as full exhibits.

Q.   Mr. Moore I want to show you two documents, which I believe I have not shown you, correct me if I'm wrong. One is defendant's A for identification, and the second is Defendant's B for identification. Are either of these documents familiar to you sir?

A.   No

Q.   You can identify them as letters on the stationary of Congressman Shays but beyond that you can not comment in terms of any knowledge you have other than just seeing them right now?

A.   Right.

Q.   Congressman Shays had a conversation with you, you testified. Can you place a time frame on that? Was it somewhere around July or August of '89?

A.   I believe it was '88. Shortly before I had my first contact from the defendant.

Q.   And Congressman Shays indicated to you that he had gotten complaints from constituents, plural, right?

A.   No sir.

Q.   Did you ever become aware on any conversations with Congressman Shays that there were in fact many constituents,

plural, who were complaining about copper price irregularities in their view?

A. No sir.

Q. I take it as someone in a position, an upper position in COMEX, that the fact that a Congressman was contacting you about concerns about prices is something that would be of concern to you?

A. Earlier that year, there had been a CFTC investigation, CFTC regulatory boards that oversees futures trading in the United States, and since I was basically the head of the copper settlement committee, Vincent White, one of the enforcement officers, and his partner Bill—- I can't remember his last name, asked me to sit down with them and we went over the way settlement prices were derived for a period in 1987, on a significant number of days, consecutive days. And I explained looking at the time and sales recently, and looking at the settlement sheets. I was able to explain how we arrived at each and every price for each and every day. To the best of my knowledge they were perfectly satisfied with my answers.

The above mentioned answer is not responsive to the question. Moore dodged the question for a reason and Dick Reeve failed to pursue his point. The point I had emphasized to Dick was that a meeting had been convened in Shays' office with the two CFTC officials. It was that meeting that exposed the CFTC to Congressman Shays and was the catalyst to the letters Shays wrote to Thornburgh and Bowsher that are the exhibits A and B that Dick had shown to Moore. At no time in the trial were those exhibits read to the jury because Judge Nevas prevented reading them.

Finally they are the only two exhibits not read to the jury. A United States Congressman writing a complaint to the Attorney General, a Presidential Cabinet member about rigging global copper prices being condoned by the Justice Department is a serious allegation that refutes a mythical investigation that found nothing wrong.

The question was did Congressman Shays interest provoking his contacting Moore concern Moore. If Moore isn't committing any crime then Shays contacting him shouldn't concern him. More people than just myself had complained to Shays and Shays stated that in his letter to Bowsher.

Q. Did you ever see a report that was prepared by the CFTC as a result of that investigation?

A.   I saw one on Monday. I didn't read it thoroughly but I saw one on Monday.

Q.   Was that in the form of a letter to Congressman Shays?

A.   I really don't remember who it went to but I do remember seeing that report.

Q.   Now I want to show you a document, which has been marked as Defendant's Exhibit N for identification. Can you identify that document sir?

A.   I don't think I've ever seen this before.

Q.   Were you made aware at any time in 1989 that Mr. Miller had sent a threatening letter, which he himself referred to as an extortionate demand to James Goodwin?

A.   I found out in 1994. Only when—- Jim Goodwin was no longer with the Exchange—- only when this whole incident in 1994 came up did I know that Jossen had ever been contacted by Mr. Miller, did I know that Jim Goodwin, a Tom Cohen and Nancy Minnet. None of us knew that anybody else—- I guess the three employees, Cohen, Goodwin, and Minnet knew about it but they didn't know about my involvement and never mentioned to me about theirs.

Q.   I want to show you Government's Exhibit 1. Have you ever seen that letter which is a letter addressed to Walter Jossen?

A.   No I haven't.

Q.   So during that period of time, you were aware of your interactions with Mr. Miller, but if I understand your testimony, you were not aware of other communications he was having with other officials in COMEX.

A.   Correct.

Q.   So when you got threatened with phone calls from Mr. Miller, you didn't contact anybody and tell them that?

MR. APPLETON: I'm going to object to that. I don't think that's the testimony. There is no foundation.

Q.   Well didn't you testify that you got some threatening phone calls from Mr. Miller before?

A.   What he said was if I didn't cooperate with this, I could end up in jail, he would help to keep me there. I didn't consider this a threat.

Q.   You didn't?

A.   I did not.

Q.   In any event you didn't contact anyone, any law enforcement agency with respect to your dealings with Mr. Miller at any time prior to December 6th of 1994.

A.   That is correct.

Q.   And why is that?

A. I never really took him seriously.

Q. I'd just like to show you one more document that's going to be marked for identification and ask if you can identify it. It's defendant's Exhibit O for identification. Can you identify that document, sir?

A. I've never seen this before. I know who Allen Hansen is but I've never seen this before.

Q. The backwardation issue has been the critical part of the fraud alleged by Mr. Miller. Mr. Miller claims that the Quotations Committee under your command, illegally concocted backwardation which in turn successfully gave a false signal to traders that there was a shortage of copper, which has never occurred during this entire time. There is no question in Mr. Miller's mind that the report by the U.S. Bureau of Mines accurately shows a substantial increase in the production of copper because the multi-national companies that mine copper on a world wide basis knew that COMEX intended to guarantee a stable high price due to your control of settlement prices and your ability to rig this constant backwardation. On the demand side of the equation, there is no discernable indication that there has been an expansion by industries which needed a greater supply of copper than was increasingly produced during the past nine years. As a matter of fact, one huge past user of copper wire has completely eliminated copper wire by their use of fiber optics for the expanding telecommunications industry.

So what I understand you to be saying is backwardation occurs when there's a low supply, right?

A. And it feeds upon itself. Backwardation is not unique and it is not unique to copper. The energy market is constantly in backwardation because people want to buy oil. Backwardation does not effect gold, and not silver, because there's such a tremendous supply in the world.

Q. Now, from sometime toward the end of December of '87, until within a month, the price crashed all the way back down from $1.40 per pound to $.88, $.87 per pound in a month. This price change is shown on Defendant's Exhibit J. Would you agree that this price drop is accurate?

A. Possibly.

Q. Well, do you remember that? Do you remember that?

A. I do remember that the January contract usually isn't all that accurate but we did come off after December. I think supplies might have come into the warehouse at that time. I'm not positive. Every once in a while if the backwardation gets steep enough it behooves someone to deliver the stuff to the COMEX warehouse. That's how you finally brave the backwardation is you put resources into the warehouse. When I say backwardation feeds upon itself, it doesn't behoove anyone to put COMEX speculators, the people who buy the copper, to lend it elsewhere. They are the buyers of last resort. You only get metal in the warehouse when there's too much to go around. So in times of shortage, even though you might not need that pile of copper you have sitting in your yard right now, there is no sense putting a warrant for an exchange because it gives people a false sense that there's surplus and that doesn't happen. If a commercial participant gets caught short and he just decides he doesn't want to pay the price to get out, he takes that pile of copper that he's got in his yard and he delivers it to the Exchange.

Q. If I understand what you're saying, you would expect that when there's a downturn in the market like that—- that's when backwardation is eliminated.

A. Not necessarily. Because when I say backwardation, backwardation feeds on itself. And so it continues to widen the backwardation even in a downward market.

Q. And that's what happened in the copper market, right?

A. I believe so.

Q. And in fact that's whats been happening in the last ten years, right?

A. Yes.

Q. Can you think of any other market or time when this process has occurred in a commodity similar to copper?

A. Commoditiy similar to copper? Copper is unique but I can tell you about the oil market.

Q. Has the copper market ever performed in this way?

A. You saw, you just saw

Q. No before this.

A. 1974.

Q. You're saying the backwardation levels as high as these, a premium of as much as $.30 per pound?

A. I think the '74 backwardation was much higher.

Q. It was higher?

A. I don't remember what it was. I know there was a lot of money in backwardation.

MR. REEVE I have no other questions, thank you.

THE COURT: Mr. Appleton?

REDIRECT EXAMINATION BY MR. APPLETON

Q.   A few questions Mr. Moore. Did you cause a backwardation?

A.   No, I did not.

Q.   Could you cause it?

A.   Not by myself, that's for sure.

Q.   Why couldn't you cause it?

A.   A number of reasons. First of all, I don't have the capital. Second of all, in the U.S. Commodities markets, no individual, be it the largest metals company in the world would be allowed to control such a portion of the open interest to affect a price that much. We have position trading limits and especially when you come into the spot month, you have a position limit of 2,500 contracts. The Exchange officials, not members of the Exchange but our market surveillance and compliance staff, they are constantly on the phones with the market participants that have some of the biggest positions in the spot, and the CFTC for these last nine years has done the same thing every month. People are getting tired of getting the phone calls, what are your intentions? We need to know your intentions so that we know that there's a stability in the market.

Q.   So the issue that Mr. Reeve raised earlier or alluded to in that other case which was an alleged issue of manipulation. Could not occur on COMEX?

A.   Again, nobody would be allowed to control that amount of stocks under the U.S. regulatory rules.

Q.   Mr. Moore going back to 1987, through the present, have you ever not followed the rules as promulgated by the Exchange in setting the prices?

A.   No. I do not set the price. The price is—- the prices are arrived at in open outcry auction market. We just follow the rules and write them down at the end of the day.

Q.   And on October 23rd, 1987, were the rules followed with respect to the price settlement?

A.   I believe so. That was one of the days that was included in Mr. White's investigation.

Q.   Okay, you understand the defendant's allegations here?

A.   I understand them, I don't accept them.

Q.   Let me show you what's been marked Government's Exhibit 9 for identification. I ask if you've seen that before?

A.   I saw this on Monday.

MR. APPLETON: I'm going to offer 9 your honor.

MR. REEVE: No objection.

THE COURT: Full exhibit.

Q.   What is 9, Mr. Moore?

A.   It's a daily account statement. It's something again under U.S. Regulatory rules.

Q.   Whose account is that?

A.   This is Michael A. Miller.

Q.   Now can you describe as best you can in layman's terms what kind of activity, buying and selling activity is reflected on that account statement?

A.   On this particular statement, November 5th, 1987, 3 nearby Decembers, December '87 contracts were sold. Three December '88 contracts were purchased, doing the math real quickly 985 points.

Q.   The trading practices reflected on that document, are they consistent with or opposite the trends in the market?

A.   It's opposite the trends in the market.

Q.   Fair to say that that trading was exactly the opposite of what the market was doing?

A.   Obviously.

Q.   Now you had more than one conversation with Congressman Shays, correct?

A.   Yeah, but they were all centered over no more than a two day period.

Q.   Did you ever have a conversation after that with him?

A.   I had a conversation, he was down visiting the Exchange a couple of years ago afterward.

Q.   Okay, what was said at that time?

A.   I was introduced to him, I had never met him. I don't know that I'd ever seen him on TV. I was introduced to him because I was a representative of our **political action committee, being on the Board at the time**. So I was introduced to him and I just said, **"Whatever possessed you to give out my home phone number?"** And he said, **"What are you talking about?"** I said, **"To Stephen Miller, what was it that made you move mountains for him?"** He said to me, **"It doesn't matter, he moved out of my district."**

MR. APPLETON: No further questions.

RECROSS BY MR. REEVE

Q.   Mr. Moore, I want you to focus on one situation and tell me what documents exist, okay? And here's the situation: Let's go to the situation we were talking about before the break. It's October 23rd, the last sale for the December '88 contract happens at 9: 53. You, the committee set a price for the December '88 contracts which gets published in the newspaper and everybody relies on, right, is that right?

A. Yes.

Q. And in fact that price determines who—- as you testified I think at the start of your testimony, that determines who has to pay money and who gets money, right?

A. Yes.

Q. So that price is really critical to everybody in the market, right?

A. Yes it is.

Q. And you're saying the committee set that price on the basis of spread offers—-

A. Spread offers that are in the ring, orders that people have.

Q. All right, and my question to you is your committee sits down, right, market closes at 2:00 o'clock?

A. We're standing.

Q. You stand?

A. All right we get together.

Q. You're together in a room right?

A. In the trading pit with all the other traders around.

Q. And you then set a price for the December '88 contract?

A. Yes.

Q. What physical pieces of documentation do you have, that you rely on to set that price, given that the last sale was at 9:53 and you're now setting it at a different price from what it traded at, at 9:53 A.M. on that day?

A. I can't tell you what—- if you have the times and sales. Obviously you can say that that was the only print or that was the last print for that day. I don't know if there were any spread transactions involving the December '88, unless I have the time and sales in front of me. If there were spread transactions that would affect the close, they would have to occur in the last fifteen minutes. Lacking any of those spread transactions, you yell out to the participants in the market. We might have a lot of transactions for September '88, relative to December '87. So then you go announce to the ring, does anybody have any market in September, December? Because now we have the September settled. We know where September is supposed to settle relative to everything else. Did anybody have any spreads working in the September, December? Now that is the narrowest we can get. If somebody were to say yes, I have one sixty bid, somebody says I am offering one eighty, boom, it settles for one seventy. We never do anything negative.

Q. So what I hear you saying is, if an investigative body investigates your committee, **there's no documents. What you do is you sit**

down and say, well, Jones over in the corner said one sixty and Tommy Smith said one eighty, so we did it at one-seventy, is that what you're telling us?

A. Market surveillance investigates every complaint about settlement prices.

Q. Sir—-

A. And what happens if someone pretends that he has an order to buy a switch at one-sixty, to sell a switch at one-eighty, just for these investigations he's required to keep these unfilled orders for five years.

Q. I'm not asking you what he's required to do. My question was a very simple one, which is when somebody comes and investigates, do you have any documentation when there are no spread transactions within the last fifteen minutes that says this is why we set the prices at X or Y or Z? Yes, or no?

A. The only time we have to do that is when we are not following the rules.

Q. No, no, that's not a question of the rules. I am asking you, do you have anything to show an investigator from the CFTC, from the F.B.I., from any other body, where you can say with documentation, this is why we set the price for the December '88 contract?

A. I have my rules. Want me to read the rule?

Q. **No, I'm asking you—- is it that you're having a difficult time answering?**

A. I'm not having a difficult time.

Q. I'm not asking you for the rules. **I'm asking a very simple question and try to listen to the question.**

THE COURT: Try to listen to the question Mr. Moore.

Q. Is there any documentation which would corroborate or support a specific price that you set in circumstances where there's no active trade or spread transaction in the last fifteen minutes? **Yes or no.**

A. **I would have to say no to that question.**

MR. REEVE: Right, thank you. I have no other questions, thank you.

THE COURT: Thank you Mr. Moore, you're excused.

MR. APPLETON: Call Special Agent Schulte, your honor.

Special Agent Francis J. Schulte, Jr. told the jury that he worked for the FBI for 24 years and that he remembered arresting me on December 7th, 1994, at my apartment in Brooklyn, N.Y. There was no importance to his testimony because by this time it was very apparent to the jury that I had been arrested.

THE COURT: Thank you you're excused. Next witness please.

MR. APPLETON: Agent Skelly your Honor.

THE CLERK: State your name and address for the record.

THE WITNESS: Lisa A. Skelly, 35 Courtland Street, Bridgeport, Ct.

DIRECT EXAMINATION BY MR. APPLETON

Q. Agent Skelly, could you tell the members of the jury your current employment?

A. I'm a special agent with the FBI.

Q. How long have you been a special agent?

A. For six years

Q. In your six years with the FBI have you been assigned to a unit?

A. I am assigned to the reactive unit here in Bridgeport

Q. And what is your role in that capacity?

A. The reactive squad handles what is considered violent crime major offender program, crimes to include bank robbery, fugitives, extortion, kidnapping, interstate property theft and the like.

Then agent Skelly went on to explain all the details as to what she did which led up to taping the phone calls and having agent Schulte arrest me in Brooklyn.

CROSS EXAMINATION BY MR. REEVE

Q. Good afternoon Agent Skelly.

A. Good afternoon.

Q. Now you indicated that you're the case agent. What does that really mean?

A. I'm assigned to investigate this case.

Q. It was part of your duties to familiarize yourself with the whole situation?

A. Yes.

Q. You have examined the letters which are exhibits in this case and in each of the letters they contain Mr. Miller's phone number, his bank account number, his signature and his name, right?

A. Its all in here.

Q. Makes it a pretty unusual extortion case in your experience, doesn't it?

MR. APPLETON: I'm going to object to that.

MR. REEVE: She can answer that. She's the case agent.

THE COURT: Overruled, she can answer.

THE WITNESS: **It was certainly unique**.

Q. Yes, in fact Mr. Miller gave himself to the FBI and you on a silver platter, didn't he?

A. He even suggested it, as previously testified to.

Q. He suggested—- what?

A. Suggestions made by the two individuals that appeared at Mr. Jossen's doorstep.

Q. They identified him as Steve Miller, nothing secret about this was there?

A. No sir, it didn't take a great deal on the part of the FBI to find Mr. Miller.

Q. I want to show you what's previously been marked Defendant's Exhibit C and ask you based on your knowledge of this case as case agent, can you identify that document?

A. This document appears to be a letter which was sent from the defendant to David Furtak. He's a Special Agent with the Bridgeport office of the FBI. It's dated January 3rd, 1989, and it is containing information concerning the copper market. On the second page it's entitled copper prices rigged by the Commodity Exchange and a list of numbers and dates and amounts and differences, and so forth.

Q. And that's a copy of the letter but that letter is contained within a file, an FBI file, correct?

A. Yes it is.

Q. And in fact, in response to that Agent Furtak prepared a memorandum, didn't he?

A. Yes, I believe he did.

Q. I want to show you what's been marked Defendant's Exhibit P. Can you identify that?

A. This appears to be a memorandum dated January 5th, 1989, from Special Agent David Furtak of our office concerning Stephen Miller. It sets forth his contact with Agent Furtak and it goes on to list other individuals that the defendant had contacted concerning his allegations of manipulation of the copper market.

Q. There had been meetings between Agent Furtak or other agents in the Bridgeport office and Mr. Miller, until the end of 1988, right?

A. Yes, according to this document it appears that Agent Furtak met with Mr. Miller and had a discussion regarding the alleged manipulation of copper closing prices and Mr. Miller also informed Agent Furtak of the other individuals that he had voiced his complaint to. Others including Congressman Shays, the General Accounting Office, the CFTC, the United States Attorney's office in New York, the FBI in New York, and various news media and agencies.

Based on that documentation it was indicated that the CFTC had already conducted an investigation into copper price fixing and determined that Mr. Miller's allegations were unfounded.

Q. Hasn't Mr. Miller offered himself to the government as an investigator who can pursue the fraud in the copper market?

A. I don't recall that. I recall Mr. Miller wishing to speak to me **but I'm prohibited from speaking to him. I suggested that he ask you and go through you to speak to me.**

Q. I understand, and there have been a number of occasions on which I have made requests of you to sit down with Mr. Miller and talk about his allegations of fraud since his arrest on December 7th, is that fair?

A. I don't remember unless you went through the Assistant.

Q. Has any law enforcement agency ever done an investigation of any of Mr. Miller's allegations? The FBI took absolutely no steps as far as you know to talk to witnesses or do anything with Mr. Miller's claims, right?

A. Correct.

Q. Did the FBI ever tell Mr. Miller that they were going to do nothing with his claims, they were going to defer to the letter written by the CFTC to Congressman Shays and that's it? It's gone, it's history. To the best of your knowledge as case agent, was that ever communicated to Mr. Miller?

A. I don't believe so. Oh wait, I correct myself. Agent Furtak prepared a memo concerning Mr. Miller and forwarded it to New York.

Q. I want to show you what's been marked as Defendant's Exhibit Q. for identification and ask you, Agent Skelly, if you can identify this document because I think this is the document you're referring to at this point.

A. This appears to be a memo dated July 11, 1989, to Bob Paquette who's the senior supervisor resident agent at Bridgeport FBI office and its from Raymond A. Hassett, a Special Assistant United States Attorney.

Q. All right with the Court's permission if I can stay up here and ask some questions about these documents?

THE COURT: Go ahead.

Q. Mr. Miller provided documentation in a letter which is Defendant's Exhibit C dated January 3rd, 1989, correct?

A. Yes it appears so.

Q. This document has voluminous data regarding trading dates on COMEX for copper from September 1, 1987 all the way through to November 30, 1987, correct?

A. Yes sir.

Q. Your knowledge would allow you to state that that letter,

Defendant's Exibit C, represents a great deal of work on the part of Mr. Miller in supplying that information to the FBI?

A. Yes he appears to have spent a considerable amount of time on this.

Q. This memo dated July 11th, 1989, approximately 7 months after the voluminous documentation that Mr. Miller has provided the FBI which is contained in Defendant's Exhibit C appears that Agent Paquette suggested to Mr. Miller on July 10th that he provide further documentation of the fraud, is that the way you read that?

A. Yes it appears that Senior Supervisor Resident Agent Robert Paquette requested more information be provided by Miller.

Q. To your knowledge is there anything in writing in the file that indicates that Mr. Miller was ever advised that the FBI was not going to conduct an investigation of his allegations?

A. I believe that there was a letter from the then United States Attorney, Stanley Twardy informing Mr. Miller that there would be no investigation concerning this matter and to seek a civil remedy.

Stanley Twardy has been appointed a Federal District Court Judge in Connecticut. Twardy had no problem obstructing justice while he was the United States Attorney. He played ball with his boss, Attorney General Richard Thornburgh. Thornburgh ran for the United States Senate in Pennsylvania where he had been Governor. President Bush replaced him with William Barr who worked for the C.I.A. and commanded the Iran / Contra scam that sold missiles to Iran. Most of that money was diverted into secret Swiss bank accounts for the benefit of Ollie North and other individuals. They falsely claimed that the money was being used to illegally fund so-called freedom fighters in Nicaragua.

Mr. Reeve questioned Agent Skelly in detail to be able to show the jurors that all of the government's agencies included:

1) The Commodities Futures Trading Commission
2) The F.B.I.
3) The General Accounting Office, and
4) Specific United States Attorneys.

Concluded that they all decided to stonewall the evidence provided to them, by raising the bar, effectively obstructing justice. Reeve's strategy for his excellent cross examination of Agent Skelly proved that my intent was not to extort money from Jossen and Moore, but was to prove that the officials of these agencies allowed and condoned the rigging of copper prices by COMEX officials.

The United States Attorney who controls the FBI wanted to rely upon conclusions which refuted my allegations except the letter from U.S. Congressman Shays to the Attorney General himself which contends that the CFTC and the GAO was wrong, but Dick did not confront Agent Skelly with Shays powerful letter.

The jurors who sat on my case were all accomplished people. They were well educated and had good jobs. They were very capable of understanding the picture Dick Reeve was painting for them. They refused to deliberate the evidence and the testimony they heard and saw. They reached their verdict in 25 minutes from the time they began. It would be impossible to deliberate this case in 25 minutes.

As you will learn by the end of this story, Judge Nevas placed a juror on my jury who guaranteed at least his own guilty verdict. I would love to be able to question all the other 11 jurors as to why they went along with juror #74. They elected him to be the jury foreman and reached their verdict in 25 minutes. I would like to ask the other 11 jurors to explain what happened in that room during the 25 minutes they spent to reach their verdict. I doubt they would speak with me about anything and if they did I doubt they would tell me the truth.

When the lengthy cross examination of Agent Skelly ended, the government rested it's case at the end of the first day of trial. Dick Reeve was very effective in convincing the jury that the government was part of the conspiracy to allow the crime to continue. Because the jurors decided to not deliberate before their verdict, none of that mattered to them.

Because I believe that this subject is now apparent and will be more apparent during the rest of the trial and during the appellate phase of the case, I've decided not to burden the readers with the ponderous testimony by Agent Skelly contained in 43 pages of the transcript.

The defense would call six witnesses all of whom would be quite interesting, contained in 157 pages of transcript. Again I will delete the boring parts because the story after the trial ends becomes even more fascinating.

As you will soon learn, the jury will be deprived by Judge Nevas to learn about the government's ploy to deprive me of any trial by falsely claiming that I was incompetent, and used the insanity defense to attempt to incarcerate me without benefit of any trial. This also deprived me of using the statement by Dr. Kucharski whose opinion validated my defense.

DIRECT BY MR. REEVE OF JIM GOODWIN

THE CLERK: State your name and address for the record.

THE WITNESS: My name is James Goodwin, I live in Verona. New Jersey, 3 Newman Avenue.

Q. Can you summarize your employment history?

A. Out of college **I worked for about ten years for the Commodity Futures Trading Commission** which is the government agency that oversees futures trading. In 1980 I went to work for The Commodity Exchange Incorporated as a manager of market surveillance. Then from about 1983 through 1989, I was Vice President of the Compliance Department at the Exchange.

Q. And those positions were at COMEX?

A. That is correct.

Q. Do you know Stephen Miller?

A. Yes.

Q. How is it that you have come to know Stephen Miller?

A. I met Stephen Miller sometime in the late 1980's when I was manager of the Compliance Department at COMEX, when he came to complain about the copper market.

Q. Do you recall if he was requesting rules on how the Committee sets settlement prices?

A. I don't recall that.

Q. I take it one of your primary goals is to insure the integrity of COMEX and the markets?

A. Correct.

Q. I want to show you Defendant's Exhibit N and ask you if you can identify that document?

A. It's a letter on the letterhead of MILLER ENTERPRISES dated July 21st, 1989. It's to people at COMEX myself being the first listed and the signature on the second page is Stephen A. Miller. There is one reference in here to the Miller Foundation for homeless people, which I do recall having seen. Other than that I don't have a specific recollection of the letter.

Q. Can you read that letter please?

A. July 21, 1989, fax copy to Jim Goodwin, V.P. Compliance, COMEX. Mr. Tom Cohen, Commodity Exchange Board of Governors and Officers.

People think commodities trading is a risky business. Cheating commodities traders is like walking a high wire with no net from the top of the World Trade Center. In full payment for cheating, COMEX is given the opportunity to donate $15,000,000 to the Miller Foundation for homeless people. To take advantage of this generous offer, wire funds by Monday, July 24, 1989 to—- (and there is a bank address and account number there.) Remember there were 85,000 copper contracts in May 1987 before the COMEX copper fraud began. Now there are only 24,356 COMEX copper contracts.

Make no mistake, this is an extortion threat. If you fail to pay or you fail **to report this extortion threat, this letter will break this case into the open. I will take my chances on the court.**

Enjoy your weekend, signed Stephen A. Miller.

Q. Do you recall discussing this letter for example with John Moore or other individuals who are identified?

A. No I do not.

Q. Did you report the receipt of this letter to anyone within COMEX?

A. I don't recall.

Q. Did you report the receipt of this letter to any law enforcement agencies?

A. I don't recall that I did but I'm fairly certain that I did not.

Q. Were you ever questioned by a law enforcement agent about that letter to the best of your recollection?

A. No.

Q. I want to show you what's been marked as Defendant's Exhibit S for identification and ask you if you can identify that document please?

A. It's a letter, it reads Steve Miller, phone number, commodity price risk management. Do you want me to read it?

Q. Yes please.

A. Dated August 28, 1993, addressed to Mr. Jim Goodwin, Vice President of Compliance, COMEX.

Dear Mr. Goodwin:

It is a fact that you actually believe that you can ignore the problem you created and it will disappear. Ignorance won't work in your best interest because I intend to be reimbursed by COMEX. Bring this into criminal court, negotiate, or watch out.

My deadline is September 1, 1993. Talk to Richard Jossen, Walter Jossen, and John Moore.

Sincerely,

Steve Miller

Q. Did you talk to any of those three individuals about your receipt of this letter?

A. I believe that I did. I don't have a specific recollection of the letter other than I do remember the letterhead and the stationary. So on that basis, I would think this is a letter that I did receive. I do remember at some point in time discussing Steve Miller with Richard Jossen. I knew John Moore quite well at the time so I'm sure I spoke about it in general terms with him. Although I don't have a specific recollection of discussing this letter with either of them.

Q. To the best of your knowledge did you ever report your receipt of this letter to any law enforcement agency?

A. I did not.

MR. REEVE: I have nothing further.

Mr. Goodwin would need to know the rules in order to perform his job and to be able to determine that he was able to understand if Moore was violating the rules. I am trying to stay away from the technicalities as best I can. I truly believe that it is very easy to understand that if Goodwin, Moore, and Jossen were not violating rules and not rigging prices, that they would have had me arrested. That's just common sense.

Mr. Goodwin's primary job is to insure the integrity of The Commodity Exchange. There are many frauds perpetrated by outsiders on Wall Street exchanges but I have never heard of any Wall Street exchange controlling a fraud. The exchanges are self regulatory bodies themselves and they register and regulate members of their respective exchanges. When Goodwin was threatened by me and simultaneously accused of being part of the ongoing settlement price fraud, common sense would dictate that he would protect the integrity of the exchange by having me arrested.

Arresting me would have been a denial by him, and a contradiction by him of the allegation I had been making. To my way of thinking, Goodwin's refusal to report me to law enforcement proved that Goodwin and his colleagues had made a decision to not report me because it would draw themselves into a federal courtroom where their obvious and unsophisticated crime would be exposed.

Suppose I was only a foolish nuisance. Suppose there was no fraud and that I am some fool. When I set up meetings with major media officials and show them Congressman Shays' letters to the Attorney General, and I show them copies of my extortion threat to Goodwin, the story by the media would have been bizarre and potentially entertaining.

When I mention the media I'm referring to meetings with THE WALL STREET JOURNAL reporters John Valentine and Peter Angrist. I'm referring to 60 Minutes Producer Philip Scheffler who authorized my meeting with Errica Stewart. I'm referring to WASHINGTON POST business editor Jerry Knight. There were many other reporters too.

The media is not now going to expose itself for their cover-up of

Shays letters. It is up to the readers of this book to spread this story to their friends and business associates for the sake of democracy. The government controlled media is the essential reason for bloggers who are trying to combat the propaganda machine controlling our minds and political system.

It is not common sense for legitimate officials of a Wall Street exchange to ignore someone who threatens to black mail them or to extort money in conjunction with violent threats. When I sent my first letter to Goodwin in 1989, I gambled that I likely would not be arrested. When a few days elapsed and no arrest was made, my gamble was correct. That gamble set into motion all the succeeding steps. Those steps focused upon law enforcement officials in addition to COMEX officials.

In my possession were the two letters Congressman Shays had written, the first to G.A.O. Controller General Bowsher, the second to D.O.J. Attorney General Thornburgh. Shays unequivocally put the fraud into those two senior officials' laps. My intentions from that point consistently emphasized the behavior of Goodwin, Moore, Bowsher, and Thornburgh. These people have obligations to perform legitimate functions required by their jobs.

It is more interesting and much more important to focus on their behavior than to focus on the rules and the technicalities. This story would be dull if it was about the rules and the technicalities. I became convinced that I had two pieces of evidence, which made it impossible for any jury to convict me for an extortion charge. The first piece were the letters written by Congressman Shays. The second piece of evidence were the extortion letters I had written to Goodwin and to Walter Jossen because they had decided not to contact law enforcement. Their actions deduce that they wanted nothing to do with law enforcement because they were afraid to contact law enforcement.

I was dead wrong. I still can not imagine how 11 jurors can all be stampeded into a guilty verdict in 25 minutes after they were exposed to each witness. The government's witnesses were extremely convincing. I only needed one juror to start considering their testimony to force a deliberation.

We live in a culture that accepts farfetched behavior. Try to remember that for decades there were studies to determine if cigarettes were addictive. That charade finally ended when the CEO's from the tobacco companies were subpoenaed to testify to a Congressional Committee. One of the Congressmen asked each CEO if he knew if nicotine was addictive. They were testifying under oath and they all denied that nicotine was addictive. That Congressman should have had the United States Marshalls handcuff all the CEO's and arrest them for perjury.

Who doesn't know that nicotine is addictive? What is the purpose for swearing people under an oath to tell the truth but when there is no doubt that they are lying their lies are ignored? How can professional commodities traders watch outrageously manipulated settlement prices, close their positions (that is why the open interest dived from 85,000 contracts to under 20,000 contracts) but fail to report this fraud to law enforcement? Do they have no clue for why they closed their positions?

Picking a settlement price is similar to a football referee spotting where to put the football after each play. The rule is simple. The ball is spotted at the point where the forward progress of the ball stopped. There is one exact spot on that field to spot the ball to start the next play. There is a 10 yard chain to measure if the offense made a first down, or not. If the nose of the ball is beyond the chain, there is a first down. This simple rule is just as simple as the rule to establish the settlement price for each futures contract of copper. When the rules are followed by the Quotations Committee the price they choose is either exactly right or its wrong.

When a price is established on anything that price is precise. Any amount either higher or lower than that price is wrong. To make the price of a copper contract appear too complicated for people to understand is beyond weird. When copper is bought and sold there are impurities to evaluate. The same holds true for corn or cotton. But there is a minimum standard grade required for delivery of copper, corn, or cotton. The standard to meet the futures contract delivery is precise.

There is no logical reason that September and December contracts of copper would have huge variations every day, which is what began on October 23rd, 1987, all of a sudden. These huge variations continued for ten years until after my trial in 1997. I was sentenced December 6th, 1996.

In 1995, while I was being housed in the federal prison in Otisville N.Y. a writer for The Wall Street Journal began to quote experts who were making ridiculous statements about copper futures trading. Did this writer and her editor know that the information they were publishing was being written to condone the daily manipulation of copper spreads? I suppose they did because I find it hard to believe that they were just ignorant.

Why would readers of THE WALL STREET JOURNAL knowingly want to be deceived? Will there ever be a time that the American culture will change? When a man like Governor Mario Cuomo makes this statement, "By any measure, America's social well-being is at a dangerously low point, and it's not improving. From our economy to our culture, we are facing problems that are big, awkward, expensive, even repugnant. They will never get better on their own. They will never get better if we pretend they don't exist or insist that they are not our responsibility. And they will never quiet down if we just shout at them to shut up," and people ignore Cuomo what chance can I have to change the culture?

A sensible question would then have to be, why didn't all the traders complain. For the first months from May '87 into March '89, the open interest dove. The traders got out of the market. They got out because it was being rigged by the Quotations Committee. These traders reacted by closing their positions. Did they contact regulators and law enforcement to complain? I don't have the entire answer excepting the written statement by Congressman Shays to Bowsher that other traders had come to him. Why would traders come to only Congressman Shays and not go to regulators and law enforcement first? I went to Shays only because the regulators and law enforcement had stonewalled my complaint.

From that point in time I can't understand why traders came back into the market, but they did. The CFTC should have questioned the traders. The problem was that the CFTC was part of the fraud. The G.A.O. was part of the fraud. The Justice Department was part of the fraud. Judge Nevas and the other judges much later became part of the fraud. The B.O.P. psychologists were part of the fraud. And a huge number of media people at THE WALL STREET JOURNAL, and a host of other media companies were part of the fraud.

This conspiracy became so huge that it contradicts the theory of checks and balances of our political and economic system. **This is the big picture.** It is the big picture that is so confounding to me. It's very hard for me to imagine that people can be so irrational, but now I can see how irrational our society has become. America has had spectacular cultural changes. These changes have evolved gradually and that is why they go unnoticed and become accepted.

When a trader orders a spread, which means the same thing as a switch, he puts in an order which demands that he wants either more of a spread or less of a spread. These are examples. Sell December '87 at a 200 point premium to December '88. Let's say that December '87 is at $1.00. If December '87 is sold at $1.00 then December '88 must be bought for $.98 or less. If December '88 is bought lower than $.98 the premium is wider than the 200 point premium limit. Has your mind glazed over yet after that explanation? Who could read a book written like that?

Now let's assume that during the day December'87 traded as low as $.98 but when the trade was being executed December '87 had moved up to $1.02. There must be actual prices on each leg of the spread, so to make it appear that December '88 had traded lower than it really did, they would fill the order at December '87 at the low$.98 and December '88 was bought at $.96. This would fill the spread at the 200 points difference, but it made the December appear to have traded lower than it had. This would break a rule during the trading day.

Their game was to make the spread, or what Moore call backwardation look larger. It is an accepted theory that when there is a tight supply of a commodity, people who need that commodity will pay more (a premium) to get it right away. If you are sitting in a line to get gas for your car and there is no line across the street for $.05 more a gallon, some people will pay more to reduce their waiting time.

Was there a waiting line to buy copper for ten years? Was there a waiting line for copper on October 21st, 1987, after the stock market crashed? Who was in that waiting line? Were they all invisible people only seen by John Moore? Has mass irrationality swamped all our minds in America?

It was simple to see that the Quotations Committee never followed the rules. Congressman Shays obtained the Time & Sales Registers for the outright trades of copper and for the spread trades. Using the recorded prices from this evidence, which was subpoenaed from the COMEX computers, I proved to Congressman Shays that the prices were rigged. Shays wrote his letters complaining to Attorney General Richard Thornburgh based upon his observance of the official data and the rules. His letters were unambiguous.

Shays had had meetings with me that will be discussed in the testimony, along with his letters that were official Exhibits for the jury. Even if the jury couldn't understand John Moore, or myself, they surely understood Congressman Shays' letters to Thornburgh. Shays also wrote a letter to the Controller General of the GAO (General Accounting Office). Again, this letter was based upon the proof that Shays had seen himself. Shays had appointed staff people to work with me, and then his letter was written after he saw the evidence personally.

Agent Skelly was the Case Agent. She sat next to Appleton at his table. She observed John Moore testify. So she had first hand knowledge by observing his testimony during cross-examination by Dick Reeve. Reeve proved clearly that Moore didn't follow the rules during his cross-examination. After she observed Moore's testimony, Skelly had to know that the claims by the CFTC were false. This was the basis for the defense. The jurors couldn't help but know that COMEX rigged copper prices and they couldn't help but know that Agent Skelly and Assistant

United States Attorney Bob Appleton knew this from Moore's testimony and the exhibits presented during the trial.

CROSS-EXAMINATION BY MR. APPLETON

Q. Good morning Mr. Goodwin I just have a few questions for you. Were you concerned by the defendant's allegations that he raised about the copper prices being rigged?
A. I was not.
Q. Did you have any evidence whatsoever that there had been manipulation on the market?
A. No.
Q. Did a class action lawsuit ever sue COMEX?
A. Not to my knowledge.
MR. APPLETON: No further questions.

REDIRECT EXAMINATION BY MR. REEVE
Q. Did you investigate the complaint by Mr. Miller in any manner?
A. I don't believe I did.
MR. REEVE: No further questions.

RECROSS EXAMINATION BY MR. APPLETON
Q. Did the defendant have any paperwork to back up his claims that you remember?
A. I don't recall.
MR. APPLETON: No further questions.
MR. REEVE: I have nothing further thank you. Your honor, the next witness on behalf of the defense is Special Agent Edward Cugell with the FBI

DIRECT EXAMINATION BY MR. REEVE

Q. Agent Cugell did there come a time in 1989, when you had an occasion to interview Stephen Miller?
A. Yes there was.
Q. Can you tell us where the interview took place and what prompted the interview?
A. The interview took place in Mr. Miller's office in Fairfield. I was asked by my supervisor upon information that had been conveyed to him from the Connecticut FBI office.
Q. Can you tell us what the substance of that interview was please?
A. His complaint centered around his belief that settlement prices, closing prices had been manipulated by the Quotation Committee

of the Commodity Exchange. Also that the effect of that manipulation would be to create an impression in the market for copper that there was a shortage of copper, when in fact copper supply was high or at least adequate according to Mr. Miller.

Q. Do you recall at that meeting if Mr. Miller provided you with some documents?

A. Yes he did and I listed them in the report I prepared.

Q. What were the documents?

A. In essence they were a series of communications between himself and Congressman Shays, correspondence from the CFTC, I believe it was Gary Madsen to Shays on Miller's behalf. Another letter from Christopher Shays from Miller and a letter from Christopher Shays to Richard Thornburgh. At the time he was the Attorney General. And a letter from Miller to a Mr. Jim Goodwin.

Q. Now I want to show you what's been marked as Defendant's Exhibit N and ask you if you can identify that letter, sir?

A. Yes.

Q. That is the letter that you testified earlier dated July 21, 1989 to James Goodwin. What was the date of your interview?

A. August 8.

Q.. Your interview with Mr. Miller was then 18 days after the date on the letter to Mr. Goodwin and that letter contains some demands for money, does it not?

A. That's what it states there.

Q. And there are threats in that that letter, are there not?

A. He states that he would bring a class action suit.

Q. Well he states a lot more than that too, doesn't he? He says, "Make no mistake, this is an extortion threat," correct?

A. Yes.

Q. Did you consider this to be an extortion letter?

A. No, not a physical threat to harm someone, he didn't intend to harm someone.

Q. Do you recall what Mr. Miller said to you at the time that you discussed that letter to Mr. Goodwin? Do you remember what he said after he showed the letter to you?

A. He in substance said that he's very frustrated with this whole thing.

Q. Do you remember that Mr. Miller said to you that you have three choices. The first choice is that you can investigate this fraud honestly on the basis that the reason that COMEX officials decided not to report him for his extortion threat is most likely because COMEX is guilty and prefers not to get involved with law enforcement because they will expose themselves. The second choice that Mr. Miller clarified to you was that you decide to arrest him for extortion, which would force the government to expose itself because Mr. Miller is confident that in order to prosecute him, the government would need to use the COMEX officials as witnesses. **In fact the process we are in today in this court room is the product of this second choice he explained to you during your meeting at his Fairfield office on August 8, 1989.** The third choice he explained is the choice you chose. That was to continue the government's decision to stonewall Mr. Miller and allow the fraud to continue. Do you recall the points Mr. Miller made to you?

A.   No I don't.

MR. REEVE: I have nothing further.

CROSS EXAMINATION BY MR. APPLETON

Q.   Why didn't you pursue an investigation in this matter?

A.   I spoke with my immediate supervisor and with an Assistant U.S. Attorney in Manhattan. Once the U.S. Attorneys decide not to go further, we can't go further. At the time Mr. Miller contacted the F.B.I. he had already caused his complaint to be brought to the attention of an Assistant Attorney General in Washington, to the Department of Justice, which is a level far above mine. Again through the Congressman's office this information had been conveyed to the CFTC for review. In addition in discussing this with the AUSA, I had learned it had also been previously brought to the attention of the U.S. Attorney's office in the Southern District of New York.

MR. APPLETON: Thank you, no further questions.

REDIRECT BY MR. REEVE

Q.   **Agent Cugell in your experience, does it appear that the letter, Defendant's Exhibit N, might refer to a blackmail extortion letter?**

MR. APPLETON: Your honor, I'm going to object. I didn't ask that on cross examination. It's beyond the scope of cross.

THE COURT: Sustained.

MR. REEVE: I have no further questions. At this time we would call Richard Wisot.

DIRECT EXAMINATION BY MR. REEVE

Q.   Good morning Mr. Wisot can you tell us under what circumstances you know Stephen Miller?

A. I was at Echlin as their Director of taxes and Assistant Treasurer when Steve joined Echlin.

Q. Do you know where Mr. Miller was employed prior to joining Echlin?

A. I believe he had a brokerage background.

Q. What was your relationship to him within the company?

A. We had a coworker type of relationship.

Q. Was he to your knowledge an individual that the corporation relied on in financial matters?

A. **Given the financial responsibility of running the price risk management of interest rates and copper costs, he had to be relied upon by the senior management of Echlin.**

Q. Do you have any recollection of a meeting that occurred right after the stock market crashed on October 19, 1987?

A. No I don't.

Wisot had created that meeting for me to address his boss Dick Patterson, the Chief Financial Officer of Echlin. In addition Bill Bowman was invited because Echlin paid him for being a financial consultant for the pension fund. No executive would have a follow-up meeting for his boss to evaluate a proposition unless the proposition was deemed to be highly worthwhile for the stockholders and the executive's career.

I would have no purpose and Mr. Reeve would not have agreed to call Mr. Wisot or any other witness who had no way to substantiate my defense. I could never have expected for Mr. Wisot to lie about an incredibly memorable meeting. I had called Rich two weeks before the infamous collapse of the stock market on October 19th. Rich invited me to his office to discuss the copper market. My purpose was to establish consulting business with Echlin at that time because of the creation of backwardation of copper prices. Copper prices were still low trading under $.80 per pound. Never has legitimate backwardation ever occurred in any commodity until the price had risen to very high levels.

After I made my presentation to Rich he decided to have a follow-up meeting with the C.F.O., Dick Patterson and also to invite Bill Bowman to attend. Bowman had left Echlin years before '87, but he still had a consulting contract to oversee the pension fund. It would be impossible for Rich Wisot to have forgotten that we had, not one meeting, but two meetings, which he had convened with his boss, the C.F.O., Dick Patterson and an outside consultant.

The coincident fact that Wisot had suggested 2 weeks prior to having this meeting which happened to be on the day after the massive world wide stock market panic and collapse, October 20, '87, but then completely forgot that it took place is preposterous. During this meeting I made it clear to them that copper prices along with all other commodities had collapsed that day. The stock market collapse had a domino effect upon all commodity prices except gold, which rose because people panic into gold.

Dick Reeve was not prepared for a complete denial by Wisot about the meeting he had convened with his boss. No executive in their right mind would convene a follow up meeting with the CFO unless that executive was confident that the follow up meeting had considerable merit to make himself look good.

If this trial were being heard by a legitimate jury the testimony of Rich Wisot would have been extremely important to my defense either way. I say either way because if Wisot had testified truthfully he would have proved my intent was based upon the legitimate business deal that we were meeting about. I have no idea why Wisot decided to lie on the witness stand. But as a hostile witness he could have been just as effective and maybe more effective for my defense if Reeve decided to tear Wisot apart. After Dick had established Wisot was a liar on the stand, he could have forced Wisot to explain his purpose for committing perjury.

Wisot had to know that Bill Bowman was also called as a witness and Bowman could easily corroborate that Wisot was lying about not knowing that we had had this meeting because Bowman was called by Wisot to be in the meeting.

There must have been a reason that Rich Wisot decided to lie about both meetings we had had in October 1987. He wasn't in any position that telling the truth to this jury would adversely effect him in any imaginable way. He knew that I was alleging that the federal government had decided to allow the fraud to continue. Maybe he believed that it was in his interest to extricate himself as a witness by claiming he had no part in the meeting, which was the purpose for being called as a defense witness.

Wisot was a tax accountant for Echlin, maybe he believed that the I.R.S. would ruin his life. But he must have considered some reason to lie about forgetting there had been a meeting he himself had convened.

The next witness would be a much bigger disappointment to me. I had worked side by side with Bill Bowman at Echlin for two years. While I was a broker for Smith Barney in their New Haven office I had opened an account for Bill Bowman. After I left Smith Barney in 1979 and was hired by Echlin, I worked with Bill and I was friendly with Bill. We played golf in the Echlin golf league. We had occasionally skied in

Vermont. We socialized after work and I had been a guest at Bill's home in Madison, CT. a few times.

Bill was very well liked by the office staff at Echlin because he was a friendly person with everyone in the corporate headquarters. During the years I worked with Bill, I shared information on three investment opportunities that were very successful for Bill. The first one was in 1981 when sugar, legitimately went into backwardation after it hit it's highest prices over $.40 per pound. A few months later the price crashed and the backwardation disappeared, exactly the way I had predicted it would. Legitimate backwardations only last about four to six months. I was an expert on backwardations and made substantial profits on two prior occasions.

During the ten years of our friendship Bill had good reason to respect my ability as an expert trader and as a professional risk manager. But there was more to our friendship I believed than the money he earned by exploitng the backwqrdation opportunities I had advised him on.

Bill and I both reported to the CFO, Chet Russ. In 1982, Chet fired Bill. This story is both interesting and it shows my true character. Chet went on vacation to Nova Scotia and while he was gone another fellow in the financial group decided to quit working for Echlin to accept a better job working for Wendy's. His name was Tony Rodalakis and he worked with the insurance underwriters for Echlin. When the C.E.O. Fred Mancheski learned that Tony was going to leave, Fred asked Bill to learn if Tony would accept a counter offer to remain at Echlin. A deal was worked out to keep Tony.

When Chet returned from his vacation and learned what had happened, he fired Bill because he decided that Bill should have contacted him during his vacation. To help my friend Bill keep his job; I visited with John Echlin, Jr. to ask him to intervene. John, Jr. was a Director and a large stockholder. Bill was asked to return to work and I know that Bill learned that I had played a part in helping him keep his job.

If someone had bet me that Bill Bowman would lie on the witness stand in an effort to hurt my case, I would have given him or her five to one odds. I would have lost another bet.

I never advised Bill to trade copper, but after our meeting at Echlin, Bill put on a copper position to profit from the backwardation. I did not advise or suggest to Bill to position the copper spread. Bill didn't know about the fraud at the meeting because I never spoke about the fraud then. When Bill told me later that he executed a copper spread to profit from the backwardation, I explained that the backwardation had been created artificially. The spread began to go wild 2 days later on October 23rd and Bill lost $80,000. Bill could not have possibly forgotten about his loss from the copper spread that he claims he never had. Why would Bill lie under oath about his copper spread? Surely there must be a reason, but it seems irrational to me unless the government pressured Bill to lie or more likely that Bill believed that the government wanted him to lie.

I wanted Bill to join my effort to have the government investigate and intervene but Bill refused. He claimed that if his clients learned he had lost money that his reputation would be hurt. He also told me that Echlin didn't want him to be involved in my effort to seek justice. I tried to make him understand that he lost money due to a fraud, not to poor judgment. But Bill refused to make that distinction. Bill told me that he believed that he would jeopardize his consulting income being paid by Echlin. By the time of my trial Dana Corporation had acquired Echlin and none of the Echlin management were part of the new company. Bill no longer had his consulting business from the Echlin Pension fund, so that was not at stake as a reason for him to lie.

On one area which we worked together was to coax the Echlin General Counsel to meet with an attorney friend of mine, Gary Mastronardi in Bridgeport. I wanted Echlin to hire Gary to recover the $100,000,000 Echlin eventually lost due to the higher prices it was forced to pay for the copper wire it purchased for the parts Echlin manufactured. Gary had told me that he would file the case for a retainer of only $250,000 and he would seek penalties under the civil RICO Act.

I don't know why Echlin refused to recover its shareholders' money. I went to other corporate giants, which also bought copper, including General Electric, Burndy, and Harvey Hubbell. They all refused.

There have been a huge number of massive corporate frauds, which have made the national news because they resulted in bankruptcies which the media, couldn't cover-up. WorldCom, Enron, Adelphia, Global Crossing. The huge Wall Street firms including Solomon Smith Barney, J.P. Morgan, Morgan Stanley Dean Witter and others which were assessed $1,400,000,000, for touting stocks which they knew were having major financial problems. The accounting firm of Arthur Anderson collapsed after the Enron debacle but each of the other big four accounting firms has been caught cooking the books. The American culture treats these crooks as royalty.

The lame excuses I keep hearing by government officials and media reporters should insult our intelligence by their consistency of falsely claiming to get tough with the crooks that ride to their offices in limousines. The workers lose their jobs and the stockholders pay the fines. The news media spews out baloney about get tough laws and

the regulators claim to be restoring the faith in the American capital markets.

There is clearly a bottomless pit when it comes to having voters recognize this morass. Until a new political party puts corporate crime at the top of it's platform by attacking malfeasance, nothing will change. It is doubtful that the American voters want to kick the bums out even if there was a political party that campaigned on the corporate crime issue. American voters seem too narrow-minded to become angry about corporate crime. If the Enron, WorldCom, series of scandals failed to wake up American voters, they just fail to get it.

They all decided to stonewall the evidence provided to them, effectively obstructing justice. Reeve's strategy for his excellent cross examination of Agent Skelly proved that my intent was not to extort money from Jossen and Moore, but was to prove that the officials of these agencies allowed and condoned the rigging of copper prices by COMEX officials.

The jurors who sat on my case were all accomplished people. They were well educated and had good jobs. They were very capable of understanding the picture Dick Reeve was painting for them. They refused to deliberate the evidence and the testimony they heard and saw. They reached their verdict in 25 minutes from the time they began. It would be impossible to deliberate this case in 25 minutes.

As you will learn at the end of this story Judge Nevas placed a juror on my jury who guaranteed at least his own guilty verdict. I would love to be able to question all the other 11 jurors as to why they went along with Kent Moller by refusing to deliberate any part of the case presented to them, but I doubt they would be truthful with me. I have tried to interest a collaborator who would question these jurors. So far I have failed to find a collaborator.

When the lengthy cross examination of Agent Skelly ended, the government rested its case at the end of the first day of trial. Dick Reeve was very effective in convincing the jury that the government was part of the conspiracy to allow the crime to continue. Because the jurors decided to not deliberate before its verdict none of that mattered.

Mr. Goodwin would need to know the rules in order to perform his job and to be able to determine that he was able to understand if Moore was violating the rules. I am trying to stay away from the technicalities as best I can. I truly believe that it is very easy to understand that if Goodwin, Moore, and Jossen had not been violating rules and not rigging prices, that they would have had me arrested. That's just common sense.

It is not common sense for legitimate officials of a Wall Street exchange to ignore someone who threatens to black mail them or to extort money in conjunction with violent threats. When I sent my first letter to Goodwin in 1989, I gambled that I likely would be arrested. When a few days elapsed and no arrest was made, my gamble was won. That gamble set into motion all the succeeding steps. Those steps focused upon law enforcement officials in addition to COMEX officials.

In my possession were the two letters Congressman Shays had written, the first to GAO Controller General Bowsher, the second to D.O.J. Attorney General Thornburgh. Shays unequivocally put the fraud into those two senior officials' laps. My intentions from that point consistently emphasized the behavior of Goodwin, Moore, Bowsher, and Thornburgh. These people have obligations to perform legitimate functions required by their jobs by pursuing criminals. The Justice Department allocates resources for much smaller Wall Street crime regularly.

It is more interesting and much more important to focus on their behavior than to focus on the rules and the technicalities. This story would be dull if it was about the rules and the technicalities.

Picking a settlement price is similar to a football referee who spots the football after each play. The rule is simple. The ball is spotted at the point where the forward progress of the ball stopped. In other words if the ball was carried to the 25 yard line and then the runner was knocked back to the 24 yard line, the ball is spotted at the 25 yard line. There can be good spots and bad spots by the referee if he makes a mistake. If the ref spots the ball for one team's favor the coach of the other team is going to holler at the ref and may report the ref if the bad spot loses the game.

A sensible question would then have to be, why didn't all the traders complain? For the first months from May '87 into March '88, the open interest dove. The traders got out of the market in droves. They got out because it was being rigged by the Quotations Committee. From that point in time I can't understand why traders came back into the market, but they did. The CFTC should have questioned the traders. The problem was that the CFTC was part of the fraud. The G.A.O. was part of the fraud. The Justice Department was part of the fraud. Judge Nevas and the other judges later became part of the fraud 7, years later in 1994. The B.O.P. psychologists became part of the fraud when Judge Nevas and Judge Daly handed me to them to prevent my trial. And a huge number of media people at THE WALL STREET JOURNAL, THE WASHINGTON POST, 60 MINUTES, and more big time media companies (presumed by me to be reliable) covered up this story after I brought my story to their attention in face to face meetings

This conspiracy became so huge that it contradicts the theory of checks and balances of our political and economic system. I looked under every stone imaginable to find a maverick writer to break ranks for notoriety. **This is the big picture.** It is the big picture that is so confounding to me. It's very hard for me to imagine that people can be so irrational, and/or frightened, but now I can see and accept that we live in an irrational society. People want to be accepted. Acceptance by the irrational is the way our minds have been trained.

It was simple to see that the Quotations Committee never followed the rules. Congressman Shays obtained the Time & Sales Registers for the outright trades of copper and for the spread trades. Using the recorded prices from this evidence which was subpoenaed from the COMEX computers, I proved to Congressman Shays that the prices were rigged. Shays wrote his letters complaining to Attorney General Richard Thornburgh based upon his observance of the official data and the rules. His letters were unambiguous.

Shays had had meetings with me which will be discussed in the testimony, along with his letters which were official Exhibits for the jury. Even if the jury couldn't understand John Moore, or myself, they surely would have understood Congressman Shays' letters to Thornburgh. Shays also wrote a letter to the Controller General of the GAO (General Accounting Office). Again this letter was based upon the proof that Shays had seen himself. Shays had appointed Betsy Hawkings his Chief of Staff, to work with me, but his letter was written after he saw the evidence personally.

Agent Skelly was the Case Agent. She sat next to Appleton at his table. She observed John Moore testify. So she had first hand knowledge by observing his testimony during cross-examination by Dick Reeve. Reeve proved clearly that Moore didn't follow the rules during his cross-examination. After she observed Moore's testimony, Skelly had to know that the claims by the CFTC were false. This was the basis for the defense. The jurors couldn't help but know that COMEX rigged copper prices and they couldn't help but know that Agent Skelly and Assistant United States Attorney Bob Appleton knew this from Moore's testimony and the exhibits presented during the trial.

There have been a huge number of massive corporate frauds, which have made the national news because they resulted in bankruptcies which the media, couldn't cover-up. WorldCom, Enron, Adelphia, Global Crossing, and the huge Wall Street firms including Solomon Smith Barney, J.P. Morgan, Morgan Stanley Dean Witter and others which were assessed $1,400,000,000. The accounting firm of Arthur Anderson collapsed after the Enron debacle but each of the other big five accounting firms have been caught cooking the books. The American culture treats these crooks as royalty.

The lame excuses I keep hearing by government officials and media reporters should insult our intelligence by their consistency of falsely claiming to get tough with the crooks that ride to their offices in limousines. The workers lose their jobs and the stockholders pay the fines. The news media spews out baloney about get tough laws and the regulators claim to be restoring the faith in the American capital markets.

CHAPTER 7
THERE IS NO WAY TO KNOW THE TESTIMONY OF ANY WITNESS

The morning after we returned from the 4th of July weekend, 1982, at Echlin, Bill Bowman, my immediate supervisor walked into my office and said, "Steve don't ask any questions, you need to liquidate the T-bond position."

My main job at Echlin was managing the risk of interest costs and copper costs. I offset Echlin's risk by using futures contracts. This program was developed by me when I joined Echlin in November 1979. The interest rate market had become its wildest in history during the next 4 years. Treasury bill rates skyrocketed from 7% to 18% and then began to drop. They dropped below 1% by 2003. The prime rate topped out at 20% in 1981. The long-term 30-year Treasury rate topped out at 15.5% in August of 1981. This rate hit bottom in 2003, 22 years later at 4.3%.

Interest costs to Echlin were much greater than copper costs. Copper costs could easily be passed onto the customers, interest costs could not. More importantly Echlin's debt structure was entirely short term, therefore rising rates had an enormous negative impact on Echlin's earnings. During the spring of 1980 Paul Volker, the Chairman of the Federal Reserve created a sharp drop in short-term rates. That opened a window to either hedge rates or sell long-term debt to hedge the risk of the impending steep increase of interest rates. When I tried to discuss this reprieve from the higher rates we had just experienced, my boss CFO Chet Russ had no interest.

By the end of 1980, rates had skyrocketed again to even higher levels. By this point in time Chet Russ and Bill Bowman finally met with me to discuss a strategy. This meeting came about after I had heard that Chet was about to have Echlin's investment bankers, Dean Witter underwrite a long term debt offering. I bluntly told them that locking in stratospheric rates for the long term was idiotic. I explained that the super high rates had to buckle the economy which in turn would reduce rates to much lower rates.

When they finally agreed that I was right, I offered them a strategy to profit from the impending drop we had just concluded would be inevitable. The strategy was to buy long term Treasury (T-bond) futures contracts because they would rise as interest rates fell.

Without going into the complete details, on the very Monday following the 4th of July weekend, I was ordered to liquidate the entire interest rate risk management program. Interest rates began their precipitous dive that very day. Echlin failed to capture a $30,000,000 overnight gain from the position I had created during the prior year and a half, by my very skillful, disciplined management. My potential 6% bonus would have been $1,800,000 if Echlin management hadn't pulled the rug out from under me and our shareholders.

By early 1984, I had made more than $1,000,000 from trading my own account. One of my greatest regrets now is for not having sued Echlin for wrecking my job performance. I believed then that I had good relations with Echlin management and I believed those relations would be valuable to me in the future. I was completely wrong then.

The Chief Financial Officer, Chet Russ, was fired shortly after the interest rate risk management program had been dissolved. Besides Chet's ridiculous idea to fire Bill Bowman because of the Tony Rodalakis negotiation, Chet had approved a number of financial disasters for Echlin's stockholders. Chet was an accountant and he might have been a terrific corporate controller bean counter, but he didn't have a clue about corporate finance or any other facet of his position as a chief financial officer.

I never found out who made the decision to abort the interest rate risk management strategy that I had created and successfully performed during the two and a half years I managed it. My speculation is that Chet got angry at me when he learned that I had gone to John Echlin, Jr. to save Bill Bowman from being fired. Then Chet convinced the Chairman, Fred Mancheski, to approve his order to abort the program on the spot. After that, no one in the know wanted to discuss the reasons or the merits of reestablishing the program.

I still had the copper risk management program to manage, but I had nothing else to do, which made my days boring. In September 1982, I left Echlin with a severance payment, traded copper for the rest of 1982, for my own account and earned $260,000, net. My big regret will always be that I didn't file a lawsuit to recover the bonus I would have earned and to establish the record of success I could have used to market the consulting business I tried to initiate when I left Echlin.

With this background about my years of experience working for Echlin, let's get back to the trial.

CROSS-EXAMINATION BY MR. APPLETON

Q. Good morning Mr. Wisot, I represent the government in this case. Do you know the reason why the defendant, Mr. Miller, left Echlin?

A. The specific reason, no. I know the program he ran didn't turn out positively for the company, the interest rate futures contract program. The market had swung the wrong way and the company decided to cut its losses and got out. I recall the losses for the copper futures contract program weren't significant. They may have decided to cut the program at that point and then Steve, you know, just wouldn't have a position.

Q. Was he fired?

A. I suspect he was released. He didn't report to me so I don't have firsthand knowledge of that.

Q. By the way, do you know what the allegations are in this case, the government's allegations?

A. I am vaguely familiar with them.

Q. Are you familiar with the government's evidence?

A. No.

MR. APPLETON: No further questions.

REDIRECT BY MR. REEVE

Q. Mr. Wisot, if you know, tell us if Mr. Miller received severance pay when he left Echlin?

A. I don't really know, I was not responsible for payroll at that time.

Q. Do you get severance pay if you're fired from Echlin?

A. Usually you do.

Q. You do?

A. Usually.

Q. With respect to the loss of money in the interest rate futures, is it correct that Mr. Miller was strenuously advising the company to keep with the interest rate futures program?

A. Yes.

Q. If the company had continued and followed that advice, what would have happened to those investments?

A.   The company would have recovered all that it had lost. I'm not sure of the time span but it was a short period of time.

If Dick Reeve had had a better knowledge of the market he would have known that Echlin would have had a spectacular gain of $30,000,000 in the next two months. For the truth, when we liquidated on the Monday after the 4th of July 1982, Echlin was even including all costs (brokerage commissions, interest on capital, and my salary).

Dick could have destroyed Wisot's credibility. The position was placed for the long term decline of interest rates. By the time of my trial in 1996, rates had declined from its high of 15.5% to 8%. The profit on that position would have been $64,000,000.

One of the most unsavvy, unsophisticated corporate decisions I witnessed first hand was a decision by Echlin's CEO, Fred Mancheski that I had argued against. Echlin's fiscal year ended in August. On August 30, 1981, Echlin had an unrealized loss of $4,000,000 in the T-bond futures account. Price Waterhouse, Echlin's auditors demanded booking the fiscal year-end loss. For that reason I liquidated the complete position, realizing the loss, and immediately rebought the position at a brand new cost that was at the dead bottom price. I then recommended to change our accounting to lower of cost or market, replacing a mark to market accounting. By the end of the November quarter the position had an unrealized gain of $4,000,000. Fred Mancheski demanded that I take a $1,800,000 realized gain. That forced me to rebuy the position at a higher price, which increased our cost basis. All of this was psychological nonsense for the long pull.

MR. REEVE: I have nothing further. At this time your honor we will call **William Bowman.**

DIRECT EXAMINATION BY MR. REEVE

THE CLERK: State your name and address for the record.

THE WITNESS: My name is John William Bowman, I live at 30 Georgetown Circle, Madison, Connecticut.

Q.   Sir, can you summarize your educational background?

A.   I went to undergraduate school at Penn State, graduated in psychology, went to graduate school in business administration.

Q.   Can you summarize your employment experience?

A.   I've been involved in corporate finance since I got out of graduate school through the end of 1985 and since that time I've been an investment advisor.

Q.   When did you get out of graduate school?

A.   1971.

Q.   So for 14 years you were in corporate finance.

A.   Yes.

Q.   After 1985 did you maintain any kind of working relationship with Echlin?

A.   Yes, I've been an independent consultant since that time for Echlin until the present.

Q.   Can you tell us what the circumstances were of your first meeting with Mr. Miller?

A.   I think when we first met, Steve was working for a brokerage firm and he called me in my capacity as Assistant Treasurer of Echlin. I think he had some strategies and suggestions with regard to how Echlin could better manage its exposure to potential adverse moves by interest rates.

Q.   Do you know where he was employed at that time?

A.   I think it was Smith Barney.

Q.   Did in fact Mr. Miller gain an employment position at Echlin?

A.   Yes.

Q.   And what was that if you know?

A.   I don't recall the exact title but was involved in purchasing and other corporate supply functions.

Q.   Did his position change at a future time or his duties?

A.   Yes. He suggested and was involved in coordinating some various hedging activities for Echlin.

Q.   Did those involve interest rate futures?

A.   Yes.

Q.   Did he do that with your approval?

A.   I'm not sure what you mean exactly by approval.

Q.   Were you supervising him on that or was it someone else?

A.   I believe that I had,—- originally Steve reported to another individual and at some time the reporting relationship did change to me and I think that for most of the time when he had responsibility for the futures related hedging activities he did report to me.

Q.   So in your capacity as an employee of Echlin you relied upon Mr. Miller's advice?

A.   Yes.

Q.   Did you get approval of people in the company above you in order to go into these interest rate futures?

A.   Yes.

Q.   Can you tell us briefly what happened to the interest rate futures and what might have happened had Echlin made a decision to stay in it a little bit longer?

A.   Yes. The strategy was basically a strategy to hedge long-term debt expense. Its success relied on interest rates declining. The strategy was to gradually establish a larger position as interest rates increased, which Echlin did for sometime. I don't recall how many months it was, but it was months prior to the 30-year bond reached an all time high. I believe that was 1981. If in fact management stuck with the program there would have been profits on it.

Q. Did you and Mr. Miller ever discuss, and did you ever rely on his advice in terms of personal financial transactions?

A. Yes.

Q. Can you briefly tell us what those were in?

MR. APPLETON: Your honor, I'm going to object to the relevance of this.

THE COURT: All right.

MR. REEVE: Did you rely on Mr. Miller and make investments in commodities markets?

A. Yes.

Q. Why did you rely on him in making those investments?

A. **My opinion is he was very knowledgeable about those markets.**

Q. Was some of your investment in the copper market?

A. Personally?

Q. Yes.

A. **I don't recall.** (He lost $80,000 and he doesn't recall.)

Q. But you recall there was some commodities, sugar, and soybeans?

A. Sugar and soy beans.

Q. Did there come a time when Steve Miller shared with you his beliefs about the copper market?

A. Yes.

Q. Can you pinpoint or give us a ball park figure about when that would have been that he first brought that to your attention?

A. Early eighties.

Q. Did you have discussions with Mr. Miller regarding his beliefs about fraud in the copper market?

A. Yes.

Q. How would you characterize the strength of his beliefs?

A. On a scale of zero to one hundred, one hundred.

Q. Did he request that you assist him in his efforts to uncover what he believed was a fraud in the copper market?

A. Yes.

Q. Can you tell us a little bit about that, sir?

A. He asked me to attend meetings with him. He asked me to engage the support of others. In one instance he asked me to help him write a letter because he thought that I could express his thoughts on paper better than he could.

Q. Did you in fact write a letter on his behalf?

A. Yes, I helped him prepare a letter.

Q. Do you recall who that letter was to?

A. No, I don't.

Q. Did you attempt to arrange for Mr. Miller to meet with other companies or individuals regarding his efforts to expose what he believed was a fraud in the copper market?

A. I think in one instance.

Q. Can you tell us about that?

A. Yes, I happen to know an individual in a financial capacity at Harvey Hubbell and suggested that he have a conversation with Steve.

Q. Did you ever attend any meetings with Mr. Miller and perhaps others from Echlin regarding the possibility of Echlin participating in or funding a civil action regarding and related to the fraud?

A. Yes.

Q. Can you tell us about that?

A. There was a meeting where the Assistant General Counsel of Echlin and I met with an attorney that Steve was having discussions with about this.

Q. Do you recall the name of the attorney?

A. No, I don't.

Q. If I indicated the name, Gary Mastronardi, would that refresh your memory?

A. Yes.

Q. Was it in Bridgeport?

A. Yes it was in Bridgeport.

Q. And the purpose of that meeting sir?

A. It was to explore and try to understand what Steve's thoughts were and how Echlin might potentially participate.

Q. If Mr. Miller was correct in his theories about the copper market, did Echlin as a company sustain losses in that market?

MR. APPLETON: I'm going to object to the foundation of that question.

THE COURT: Sustain the objection.

Q. Did Echlin make a decision regarding their possible involvement in a civil action related to the alleged copper fraud?

A. Yes their decision was to not participate.

Q. Based on your knowledge did that end Mr. Miller's efforts to pursue this issue?

A. No.

Q. How long would you say Mr. Miller has pursued this issue based on your knowledge?

A. Constantly since the early eighties.

Q, Do you recall a meeting on October 20, 1987, at Echlin the day after the 500 point crash in the stock market that was attended by you, perhaps Mr. Wisot, Mr. Miller and others?

A. I don't recall the exact timing of the meeting. I do recall a meeting with those people.

Q. Do you recall the substance of that meeting?

A. Well there was one meeting that I recall that had to do with, I believe soy beans, backwardation in that market, and there were meetings from time to time about copper.

MR. REEVE: I have no further questions.

CROSS-EXAMINATION BY MR. APPLETON

Q. My name is Robert Appleton, I represent the government and I just ask one question. Is it your testimony that the defendant's complaints about the copper market were prior to 1987? I think your testimony is it was way back to the early eighties. You mentioned that twice. Is that accurate?

A. Well I don't recall exactly when the complaints started. There was involvement with Steve in copper futures that I was aware of starting in the early eighties.

Q. Complaints about what?

A. No, I said involvement. I don't know about when the complaints started.

Q. You're not here to share your opinion on the merit of Mr. Miller's complaints or his theories about the market, are you?

A. Well, I haven't been asked that.

Q. Well, I'm asking you.

A. I shared his view at the time he pointed it out to me.

Q. And that was based on what?

A. It was based on the logic of his arguments.

Q. Anything else?

A. He had some closing prices on certain days and how the settlement prices had been determined and that was part of the logic that I'm referring to.

Q. It was his logic, correct?

A. Yes.

Q. Do you have extensive experience in the copper market?

A. No.

MR. APPLETON: No further question.

MR. REEVE: At this time we call Gary Mastronardi.

THE CLERK: State your name and address for the record.

THE WITNESS: Gary Mastronardi, my address is 2112 North Avenue, Bridgeport.

DIRECT EXAMINATION BY MR. REEVE

Q. How long have you been an attorney?

A. I've been practicing law in Connecticut since March 1983, about 13 years. Before that for seven years I was a Special Agent in the Federal Bureau of Investigation, New York City office.

Q. Do you know Steve Miller?

A. Yes I do.

Q. As a result of meeting Mr. Miller, did you have discussions with him regarding the copper market?

A. Yes I had a number of discussions on that subject. Over a period of six to nine months there were dozens of discussions.

Q. And what was the purpose of those discussions?

A. Mr. Miller was convinced that there had been a major fraud committed by the Commodity Exchange and the purpose of the discussions was to convince me that this was so. Because I lacked understanding of the complexities of commodity transactions, I insisted that Mr. Miller explain it to me in very simple terms and we had a lot of meetings on that subject.

Q. As a result of those meetings did there come a time when you met with Mr. Miller and other individuals?

A. Yes, I recall one specific meeting that I recall took place sometime in the year 1988, and it involved two individuals, one of whom for sure was an official of a company called Echlin.

Q. And the purpose of that meeting?

A. Mr. Miller was convinced that Echlin had sustained a major loss as a result of the fraudulent dealings of the Commodity Exchange. The purpose of our meeting was to convince them to fund a civil action against the Commodities Exchange.

Q. Were you prepared at that time to pursue a civil action if there was funding?

A. Yes, absolutely.

Q. Did that funding come to fruition?

A. No it did not. After that meeting I never heard from the Echlin people again.

Q. Do you have any recollection of meeting with Mr. Miller and an FBI agent named Cugell, at Mr. Miller's office in Fairfield.

A. I'm not saying that didn't happen. If I saw Mr. Cugell face to face,

I'm pretty good with faces, I would be able to tell you for sure. We're talking nine years ago.

MR. REEVE: I have no other questions.

MR. APPLETON: Good morning Mr. Mastronardi, it's correct that no lawsuit was ever filed?

A. That is correct.

Q. Your role as a lawyer is to advocate a position to advocate your client's position.

A. Not blindly, but when I'm convinced that there is an arguable position, then I will.

Q. But it is in fact a responsibility under the canons of ethics to zealously advocate the position of your client?

A. Yes.

MR. APPLETON: No further questions.

MR. REEVE: Our next witness is Steve Miller

THE COURT: We'll take our recess here and then we'll start with Mr. Miller.

DIRECT EXAMINATION BY MR. REEVE

THE COURT: All right Mr. Reeve, swear the witness.

THE CLERK: State your name and address.

THE WITNESS: Stephen A. Miller, I'm now incarcerated at the Bridgeport Correction Center on North Avenue, that's my address.

Q. Mr. Miller could you provide us with a summary of your educational background, employment, and tell us what it is that's brought you here today?

A. Yes Mr. Reeve, briefly before I begin on that I wanted to say to the members of the jury——-

THE COURT: Just answer the question Mr. Miller.

THE WITNESS: Fine your honor.

THE COURT: No speeches.

THE WITNESS: Your honor, my educational background is extremely important to the defense of this case. You know——-

THE COURT: Mr. Miller, we're going to get along just fine if you listen to the questions and you answer the questions. Don't embellish, don't add, don't subtract. Just answer the questions. Mr. Reeve asked you a specific question, and that's the answer that you're to give. And every time you stray I'm going to jump right on top of you, you understand?

THE WITNESS: Sure your honor, I'm going to answer the questions, as I believe the answers——-

THE COURT: Mr. Reeve asked you to give your educational background. That's a very specific question. Now answer the question.

A.   Okay, my educational background is that I graduated high school in Stratford, Connecticut in 1960 at Stratford High. I then attended Columbian Prep in Washington D.C., which is a military prep school. Then came back to Connecticut and went to the University of Bridgeport for about a year. Then after returning from the Navy I began my education at Wagner College in Staten Island. While I was at Wagner I also worked part time at E.F. Hutton & Company in New York City and I have continued my education right up to the present. I left Wagner to continue courses at the Bernard Baruch School of Finance, part of City College in New York City. I attended courses at Memphis State after my wife and I moved to Memphis in 1970. When I returned to Connecticut in 1977 to work at Smith Barney and later at Echlin in 1979, I took courses at Fairfield University.

But my primary education has been self-education concerning finance, economics, statistics, trading securities, securities analysis, the subjects that concern business, economics, finance, and criminal investigation. I feel that I've had a very extensive education and I'm still trying to learn.

Q.   Can you tell us about your employment background?

A.   After returning from the Navy in 1966, I began my career in the brokerage industry at E.F. Hutton. I worked as the administrative manager for Hutton's training department where potential brokers were trained in addition to management seminars for the most senior executives. Two years later in 1968, I became a trainee, passed my licensing examinations, and became a registered broker at Hutton. The two years I had worked for the training department was an invaluable educational experience because it put me into close proximity with the finest minds on Wall Street. I made friendships with all the top management people with Hutton, which gave me access to them and their wise counsel for business deals I developed.

In 1969, the stock and bond markets began an 18-month collapse. It was this collapse that influenced me to develop a commodities trading business. My commodities trading business preceded John Moore by 5 years, my knowledge of futures contracts is far broader than Mr. Moore's, and it's been entirely legal. If the government allowed me to settle prices of copper illegally, I would be able to earn $500,000 per day. Mr. Moore claims he only made $500,000 for the past 9 years. **(Can this jury sit there and believe that the Chairman of a major commodities exchange on Wall Street only earned $500,000 during the past nine years because he was so busy running the exchange?)**

At the end of 1972, I correctly predicted another major stock market collapse. At this time I decided to leave the brokerage business to avoid the financial disaster which happened during 1973 and 1974. I went to work for a well-financed company, which leased Xerox machines. This was a novel idea at the time and it was ahead of its time making business almost impossible. Therefore, I decided to go to sea in the merchant marine. I entered a school run by the union called the Marine Engineers Beneficial Association, MEBA and remained in that program until I believed the stock market was extremely oversold in September 1974. I was right again when I went to work for Reynolds Securities in September '74 at the bottom of the stock market collapse. This resumed my brokerage career.

By 1979, I began to hate selling securities for commissions. It was a conflict of interest that couldn't be circumvented. My mission then was to convince Echlin that it needed me to manage a price risk management effort using futures contracts to shift their risk from potentially adverse price swings of interest rates and of copper. I had opened an account for Bill Bowman at Smith Barney where I began to work in 1978, in the New Haven office. I had brought a pension expert into conference with the Echlin CFO, Chet Russ, and I had also tried to compete for investment banking business. By prospecting business with Echlin executives they had come to know me and my abilities to be a valuable member of their financial team.

I became familiar with a number of Echlin executives including Bill Bowman and Chet Russ. Echlin profits had dropped in 1979 and a hiring freeze was mandated. I was the only exception hired during that freeze. When I came on board in November '79, I was assigned to report to the Director of Purchasing, Harry Tice.

(The primary reason Echlin hired me was to manage their messenger. This sounds extravagant and bizarre because it is weird. The messenger was a kid named Doug Bonyai. Doug's mother Shirley was the secretary for the CFO, Chet Russ. Doug was a bit wild but was tolerated because Shirley was a nice lady. The office manager complained about Doug's work habits so I was hired to supervise Doug. In the end I had to fire Doug because I caught him in an embezzling scheme to split fake gasoline charges with the gas station that he used to gas-up the messenger's vehicle.)

My first assignment was to write the business plan which needed approval by top management and the Board of Directors before Echlin could open a brokerage account to implement the price risk management operation. Finally it was decided to open an account with Prudential Bache in order for John Echlin Jr. who was a broker in the New Haven office, could share half the commissions generated by the account. John Echlin, Jr. was also a Board Member and large stockholder of Echlin shares.

Inflation in America was running about 13% in 1979, and the gold and silver prices were on the launch pad to explode. Silver would zoom from $6 an ounce to $50, and gold would zoom from about $200 an ounce to $870. For no other reason copper would tag along from about $.80 per pound to $1.40 per pound. The copper price rise would eat into Echlin profits if the risk wasn't offset by using futures contracts. At that time interest rates were about to move from 7% to a top at 18% basis U.S. Treasury Bills, which is the rate which sets off all other interest rates in tandem with fed funds controlled by the Federal Reserve.

MR. APPLETON: Your honor, I'm going to object. It's not responsive. You're asking for employment history, we're getting a dissertation.

THE COURT: What were your job responsibilities at Echlin?

THE WITNESS: My job responsibility was to manage this hedging operation, to control the cost, to manage the risk of copper purchases. At the time Echlin bought millions of pounds of copper.

THE COURT: How long were you there?

THE WITNESS: I was there exactly until September 1982.

THE COURT: Mr. Miller

THE WITNESS: There is more that I did at Echlin. I'd like to tell the jury that the reflections of Mr. Wisot and Mr. Bowman—-

THE COURT: Mr. Miller

THE WITNESS: was not accurate

THE COURT: Mr. Miller—-

THE WITNESS: Yes sir?

THE COURT: What did you do after you left Echlin?

THE WITNESS: I did a lot before I left Echlin.

THE COURT: What did you do after you left Echlin?

THE WITNESS: I ran my own business.

THE COURT: What was the business?

THE WITNESS: I ran a consulting business.

THE COURT: Tell the jury about the consulting business.

THE WITNESS: Well I guess you're closing me out on the Echlin experience, which is extraordinarily important to this whole case.

THE COURT: Keep going.

THE WITNESS: So can I go back to the Echlin please?

THE COURT: Tell us about the consulting business

MR. REEVE: Your honor may we approach?

(Side bar discussion follows)

MR. REEVE: I object to the court's interruptions and cutting Mr. Miller off. I think that there are lot's of ways that witnesses proceed in giving testimony and its especially critical when it's a defendant and one who's been in jail for over twenty months to give him the opportunity to tell his story. Indeed there are ethical rules that would require me if I didn't believe my client, to put him on the stand and to simply say, tell us your story. And there is nothing wrong with that. I am not in that position; I am not suggesting that to the court. What I am suggesting is he has a right, and I believe it's a Constitutional right to be heard subject to—-

THE COURT: He doesn't have a right, Constitutional or otherwise, to make a speech.

MR. REEVE: Your honor, I think that what is the only issue in this case is what Mr. Miller's intent in sending these materials to Mr. Jossen, Richard Jossen, and to Mr. Moore.

THE COURT: Then ask him.

MR. REEVE: And he has a right to give the jury a sufficient understanding of his background and what led him to this position so that they can gage his intent.

MR. APPLETON: Well respectfully your honor, this is a witness like any other witness, who's bound by the rules of direct testimony and cross examination. There are no special rules because he is a criminal defendant. He's not allowed to give a speech. He has to confine his answers to the scope of the question, and a direct question at that.

MR. REEVE: Well I am requesting, just so that the record is clear, that he be given leeway to tell his story. And I don't think there is a requirement that I have to ask him specific questions or that I have to cut off my client who has been in jail for twenty months and who wants the jury to know enough background so that they can gauge his intent.

THE COURT: This courtroom is not going to be a forum for him to expound on his theories about the copper trading and the Commodities Exchange.

MR. REEVE: Judge I agree with that, but I also think he has to be given room. The government opened this door wide open yesterday in their questions of Mr. Moore, who was fully able through both direct and then cross in response to the government's examination. He expressed his opinions, he expressed what he thought was in the copper market. The court allowed that the government open the door. You can't deprive Mr. Miller to say his position.

THE COURT: You haven't asked that question yet.

MR. REEVE: No we're going to get there.

THE COURT: Then I'll let him answer.

MR. REEVE: Right.

(Side-bar discussion)

Q. Mr. Miller, do you recall what it is that you were testifying about before we had a conference?

A. Yes I do. It was about my employment at Echlin.

Q. I believe that the court advised you to move on. Can you talk for now about the consulting situation that you began to discuss and tell us what your duties were there, what you did?

A. I've been held for 21 months without a trial and I'd like to have a fair trial to be able to testify to this jury. I have a chronology and I'd like to not step over a very critical part of my testimony. That happens to be Echlin. There were two witnesses that claimed certain things that didn't happen and forgot a lot of things that did happen. The jury heard that—-

THE COURT: Mr. Miller.

THE WITNESS:—- and I need to be able to clarify that.

THE COURT: Mr. Miller, Mr. Miller—-

THE WITNESS: I don't want a mistrial.

THE COURT: You have a lawyer. He is a very able lawyer. He will ask you questions and you will answer his questions. You are not going to make a speech.

THE WITNESS: This is a government cover-up and that's the whole point of this.

THE COURT: Do you understand what I'm saying?

THE WITNESS: Yes sir your honor, and my defense—-

THE COURT: Just keep quiet.

THE WITNESS: The government is covering up this whole thing and that's clear as day.

THE COURT: Keep quiet Mr. Miller, go ahead Mr. Reeve.

Q. Mr. Miller, was there something that happened at Echlin that impacts on the actions that you took in this case and that brings you into this courtroom?

A. Of course.

Q. And could you tell us what that is?

A. Because Richard Wisot had me come to his office in 1987 to talk about the copper market, and back again two weeks later on October 20th, the day after the stock market crashed five hundred and eight points, which most people can remember. The reason for his invitation was because of my expertise in the copper market which he claims under oath that he totally forgot about. Consequently, I have been called a nut case and so on. So the question here before this jury is, am I really a nut case or am I not a nut case? Does Steve Miller, who made decisions involving tens of millions of dollars based upon a business plan which I had written for Echlin, know what's going on in the copper futures market? Is there a fraud continuing now which began in 1987, because John Moore is rigging settlement prices with the blessing of the government? Is the government covering-up this fraud to aid and abet John Moore? Of course this is germane for the jury to deliberate so they can make a correct verdict as to my purpose and intent. Was Steve Miller trying to extort money by using his own letterhead when he wrote his threats? Or was Steve Miller setting up a trial which forced John Moore and Richard Jossen to testify, which included a series of attempts to have the FBI and the Justice Department investigate not only COMEX but also the CFTC.

Q. Mr. Miller were you relied upon by individuals at Echlin as an expert in the copper market?

A. Every quarter I met with Fred Mancheski, the Chairman of the Board, with Chet Russ, the Chief Financial Officer, along with Bill Bowman, to brief Fred for his speech to the Board of Directors concerning the futures contract operation that I managed. Some Board members were concerned due to their ignorance of the strategy I created and followed to manage the risk due of volatile price swings. In my judgment I was much better prepared to address the Board on this subject, than Fred was. I believe I might have made them understand that I eliminated the risk instead of their misguided assumption that I created risk. Richard Wisot and Bill Bowman got up on this witness stand and lied to this jury about my job and their direct involvement with me.

Q. Now moving into the next employment position that you had, is there anything else that you want to tell the jury about that?

A. I don't want to take a whole lot of time because I want these people to get out of here as fast as possible along with myself. There was testimony concerning what I did and it wasn't correct and I'd like to correct it for the jury's knowledge.

Q. Please do that.

A. About what I did at Echlin in the interest rate futures and the copper futures. It will only take a few minutes.

Q. Why don't you go ahead.

A. We began in copper at the end of 1979, and that built up to about an eight hundred contract position, which is a very large amount of copper. We never managed the interest rate problem until a year later. The interest rate problem was huge compared to the copper. Interest rates had massive swings in 1979, '80, '81, and '82 the entire time I worked for Echlin. Interest rate futures contracts were new in the late '70's. Chet Russ brushed me off when I tried to discuss the risk Echlin had because all their debt was short term. They were completely exposed. When interest rates had skyrocketed in the late part of 1980 Chet told me that he was going to float a long-term bond. Chet, Bill, and I then had a meeting about the potential bond financing. I argued that locking into a very high interest rate for the long term would prove to be very poor judgment. The main reason was that the sky-high rates would put us into a recession, which in turn would drive interest rates back down.

My argument prevailed. Then I argued that because they agreed with me, we could make the decline in interest rates very profitable for Echlin if we got long interest rate futures contracts. As rates dropped the price of our contracts would go higher. I won that argument too. After I wrote the business plan, which had to be approved by the Board, we entered the market at about the 14% level. I don't have a crystal ball, and we now know that the highest yield on T-bonds was at 15.5% about eight months later in August 1981.

Echlin's fiscal year ended in August. By my strategy of trading I raised our yield to 14.5%, which produced an unrealized loss of about $5,000,000 on our position. We had a meeting with Pricewaterhouse, our auditors, who demanded that Echlin book this loss even though we were in a long-term position. So I then decided to sell our contracts, realize the loss for tax purposes, and reposition immediately at the higher yield. In our first quarter the position had a $4,000,000 gain and Fred wanted me to sell enough to show a profit of $1,800,000. I tried to explain that was a bad decision because it would raise our cost base. In addition I changed our accounting from a mark to market, to a lower of cost or market. I did this to eliminate the anxiety that our Echlin Board of Directors had with posting losses. It is now a fact that our cost basis was at the very bottom of the market.

We were so far out of the woods that we wouldn't ever need to discuss taking a loss again. I wanted to put the Board at ease. But Fred demanded we book the gain for the quarter and which then raised our cost base. When the interest rate futures contract position was closed on the day back from the July 4th holiday, Echlin was even for the entire time including all costs. There was no loss. Wisot's statement was wrong. The market took off that day and never looked back. Whoever decided to close that position cost the stockholders of Echlin $30,000,000 by the end of the year, and a whole lot more after that.

I reported to Bill Bowman and he knows that story like he knows his own name. I doubt that Bowman had any part of that decision, he was just the messenger. I have been close friends with Bill Bowman, so for him to come into this courtroom and lie is a big surprise to me. I can't imagine Bowman's purpose for lying but I wouldn't have called him to testify if I had any idea that he would commit perjury.

Bill Bowman also put on a copper spread right after our meeting on

October 20th, 1987, with Dick Patterson the CFO who replaced Chet Russ. Bowman told me that his loss on that position was $80,000. I know he didn't forget that. Bill Bowman got on this witness stand and committed perjury for no reason that I can understand.

For this jury to understand my true intent for writing not only the letters in December 1994, which have brought me before them in this court room I need to explain another very important incident. The court never interrupted John Moore as he rambled on and on about his job at COMEX. Mr. Moore claimed that I am unqualified to judge the copper market. My ability to analyze and investigate Mr. Moore's actions have been disputed by the government, which I contend is fully aware of the COMEX very simple, unsophisticated fraud.

In June 1982, I also managed a huge copper position for Echlin. The price of copper had sunk like a rock due to the recession caused by the super high interest rates. On June 21st, 1982, I created a spectacular series of events in the copper market. I made a call to the Chairman of Western Pacific Industries, a man I have known for two decades named Mickey Newman.

Mickey Newman's father Jerome was a partner of Benjamin Graham. Ben Graham was a professor at the Columbia Business School and Ben became Warren Buffet's mentor. Warren Buffet, the most successful investor on planet earth also had an association with Mickey and Jerry Newman.

Mickey Newman wouldn't have invited me to his office on a few occasions if he considered me to be a fool. It is important now for this jury to understand that John Moore refused to respond to my threats and call law enforcement because he knew I had the knowledge to get him convicted if law enforcement decided to do its job. I may not have a college degree but this jury can bet that John Moore and Bill Bowman know I have in-depth knowledge of the copper futures contract market.

THE COURT: Mr. Reeve?

THE WITNESS: This is part of my employment, it's my expertise in the copper market, and it's the whole subject of my defense.

Q. Mr. Miller, could you explain it and try to be as—-

A. I'm going as fast as I can and the deliberations will be much quicker if the jury is allowed to hear what I have to say

Q. Okay.

A. Mickey Newman, his father Jerry, and Ben Graham had created a conglomerate in the 1950's. They were the pioneers of acquisitions. Their company was called Philadelphia & Reading. One of the acquisitions Mickey Newman made was Fruit of the Loom. Fruit of the Loom was owned by my Uncle Mike's in-laws. My closest cousin Richard Farr got a job working at Philadelphia & Reading during his summer vacation from Wharton. This connection served to introduce me to Mickey Newman. When I got Mickey on the phone I told him I had a very profitable acquisition. He asked what it was and I told him it was copper. He immediately stated he wasn't interested but I asked him to allow me to explain why it would make sense if he gave me an opportunity. My argument was that many mines had been closed because the price of copper had dropped far below even the most efficient producers' cost.

Then I made an analogy I knew Mickey would understand. I said suppose it cost $6,500 to produce a Chevrolet and no company could build them for less than $6,500. Then suppose all the Chevrolets in the world were on sale for $5,200. If we acquired all of them we would have an advantage over the manufacturer because their cost was $6,500.

The same thing holds true today with copper at $.52 per pound. We could easily buy 10,000 contracts and take delivery. We would own the world's supply and therefore all buyers would have to buy from us at our price because the mines wouldn't reopen unless they knew they could sell copper for more than $.65 per pound.

Mickey said he would think about it. A couple hours later Mickey called me back because he understood the value of my strategy. It turned out that that would be the all time low price. I then suggested to Mickey that he consider what other experts had to say on a conference call. I went to Fred Mancheski's office and told him I'd like him to listen to the conference call too. When the call ended I called a broker from Hutton who was the biggest copper trader in the world and he was a Director of Hutton. His name was David Johnston, and I knew him from my work at Hutton. I began to feel Dave out and mentioned that I had a client interested in a large copper purchase. I learned quickly that Dave was short and I knew that when Dave believed a large buyer would take delivery of all the copper in the world, I knew Dave would cover his short position in a hurry. The minute I hung up the phone I called my broker to buy another 300 contracts. In minutes after I bought that position which is 7,500,000 pounds of copper, worth about $4,000,000, I went to explain what I had done to Bill Bowman.

Now I told Bowman that we needed approval from Chet to hold this position. Chet was involved in a very important meeting, but Bill called him to explain we had something very urgent to explain. After I explained my situation to Chet he gave us the special permission needed to expand our limits. By the end of 1982 copper was trading for more than $.80 per pound and Bill Bowman will never forget that day for the rest of his life. By the end of 1982, my personal investment of $6,000 was worth more than $260,000.

John Moore wants my jury to believe that I am a rube and a nut job who is imagining a fraud because I was putting on a copper position without understanding what I was doing. The exhibit which he looked at is part of the position. Mr. Moore mislead the jury. The position began with 4 short copper contracts. I was short at $.86 right near the highest price at that point in time, which was at $.87 or $.89, I can't remember the exact number. The next day the market collapsed with December '87 crashing to $.74 and the December '88 crashing to $.72. Instead of just taking my profit on the December '87 by buying it at $.74, I did what Mr. Moore claimed he had always done because it was safe, I bought the December '88 contract. That means I closed the day neutral. I was long 4 contracts and short 4 contracts. My reasons were two. First I knew that the manipulators who had created this illegal backwardation were broke and would be closed out by the clearing house because they had no money to meet their margin call. Second, there was an additional profit of about $.07 to be made without any risk.

Of course the risk I could not expect was that Mr. Moore and his Committee of five other traders would rig backwardation by changing prices by 3 and 4 cents per pound every day. This was done in full view of all the traders in the copper world and the CFTC regulators. This completely defies simple basic common sense. The spectacular liquidation of contracts is an action by both sides. That is the buy side and the sell side. Both sides were afraid to be either long or short because everybody saw the daily manipulation.

Imagine if everybody in your neighborhood got burglarized, but no one called the police. What happened here is the reverse. They all called the police, but the police refused to respond. Can it get much more weird?

For me to suspect that the most senior people at the Justice Department would protect John Moore doing his flagrant crime for the next 9 years, would make me a nut job. I just sat in this court room watching Mr. Moore convict himself in front of Mr. Appleton, Judge Nevas, and the United States Marshals, but we are all watching this together.

Q. Now Steve, I want to go to the end and then I want to go back and fill in, okay? There are a lot of letters, specifically a couple letters to Mr. Moore and the letter that was delivered to Richard Jossen. Did you send those letters?

A. Did I send them?

Q. Yeah.

A. I faxed the letters to Mr. Moore and I had two guys deliver my letter to Richard Jossen, just like he said.

Q. Have you ever denied that?

A.   No.

Q.   Can you explain to this jury now and then fill in, why you did what you did. Why you had the letter delivered to Richard Jossen and why you faxed the other two letters to Mr. Moore?

A.   Sure. As the jury knows, prior to the situation on December the 5th, 1994, I had done other things. Because my complaint was stonewalled by the Attorney General who received Congressman Shays' letter in 1989, I decided to try to trap COMEX, the CFTC, and the Justice Department. My letter to Mr. Goodwin and my follow-up call to Agent Cugel was my first attempt. Each time I tried a strategy, I believed I would end the problem I was trying to solve. I never imagined that they would keep going like this.

The Justice Department in the Southern District of New York has a special unit. That unit is directd by the Chief of Commodities & Securities Fraud Unit. In 1987 and '88, Bruce Baird was its chief and Rudy Giuliani was the United States Attorney. I have a letter which I hope the court puts into evidence signed by Mr. Baird directly for Mr. Giuliani.

Q.   Would you like that letter to be introduced into evidence?

A.   I certainly would.

MR. REEVE: Your honor could I have that document marked for identification?

MR. APPLETON: No objection to admission.

THE COURT: The government doesn't object to it being marked a full exhibit?

(Whereupon Defendant's Exhibit U is marked.)

THE WITNESS: This is to Mr. Baird.

Dear Mr. Baird, Securities & Commodities Fraud Unit:

I am writing to you at the suggestion of Ms. Gloria Calabrese. I request to meet you in person to discuss evidence which clearly indicates a manipulation of the copper prices on the Commodities Exchange, COMEX. I have already met with officials of COMEX and the CFTC. Unfortunately, these men have decided not to do the job they have been entrusted to do. Furthermore, due to a lack of experience, they are incapable of understanding even the incredibly unsubtle methods which have been employed by the operatives involved in this crime.

I have been told directly by David Johnston, a Senior Vice President at E.F. Hutton, and a Governor of COMEX, in a meeting at his home in Southport, Connecticut, on November 7th, 1987, that he knew people who were, quote, "Playing a game in another metal and were possibly playing a game in the copper market." end quote. When I later asked him what the other metal was, he claimed that it was aluminum.

There have been fictitious prices printed used to create

backwardation in the copper market. A backwardation has only been associated with a scarcity of a commodity in the past. This manipulation is still in progress now. Consequently, immediate attention to this crime should be exerted..

Sincerely, Steve Miller.

Bill Bowman mentioned a letter in his testimony that he helped me write. I would like to read it to the jury too, please.

Q. That is part of the same 4 page Exhibit U entered into the record?

A. Yes it is.

Q. All right its already in evidence.

A. This letter was written shortly after our meeting at Echlin with Wisot, Bowman, and Echlin's CFO Dick Patterson.

Dear Directors:

Written notification is hereby given of the blatant violations of COMEX rules which has occurred since, on or about October 13, 1987, and continues through this date. This follows my verbal notification to Mr. Thomas Cohen, Manager of Floor Surveillance and James Goodwin, Vice President of Compliance which occurred in their office on Thursday, November 5th, 1987.

Having been given formal notice of these blatant violations, it is hereby demanded that you immediately exercise the responsibilities of your office by taking direct action to remedy this illegal manipulation of prices by a group of insiders. It is my sincere hope there will be no blind endorsement of the actions of the violators by those in a postion of authority and responsibility.

Sincerely, Stephen A. Miller

Q. What's the date on that letter?

A. November 9th, 1987. I hand delivered it to Cohen in his office. Then he told me to leave and don't return.

The next letter in this Exhibit was written to Herbert Sue, dated December 11th, 1987. It is written by Bruce Baird, Chief of Commodities & Securities Fraud Unit from the office of United States Attorney, Rudolf Giuliani.

Herbert Sue, Regional Counsel, CFTC

Dear Mr. Sue:

Enclosed for whatever action you deem appropriate is a complaint this office received from Stephen A. Miller, Fairfield, Connecticut concerning allegations of fraud on the COMEX.

Sincerely,

Bruce Baird

Rudolph Giuliani

United States Attorney

Mr. Baird was fully aware that I had been to the CFTC and was dissatisfied by the actions of Mr. Sue who met me personally. This letter tells Mr. Sue that the Justice Department is not interested whether or not the CFTC decides to allow the fraud to proceed. That had been the reason I notified the office of the Southern District of New York. It is clear that Mr. Baird and Mr. Giuliani have direct oversight into Wall Street crimes. Mr. Baird mistakenly mailed his letter for Mr. Sue, to me. He doesn't tell Mr. Sue that he expects him to investigate my complaint legitimately, or he too will be in trouble. He authorizes malfeasance by the CFTC.

Q. Let me ask you Mr. Miller, when did you first come to believe that prices in the copper market were being manipulated by insiders?

A. Around June and July of 1987.

Q. Do you still have the same belief now.

A. Yes, can I clarify why?

Q. Absolutely.

A. This fraud is so simple. There have been many frauds in the past. I have been interested in a few of them. One of the most prominent was the manipulation of silver prices by the Hunt family. They drove silver prices from $6.00 an ounce to $50.00 an ounce. The Hunts had accumulated a lot of silver for years in a quiet way. When the time was right in December 1978, they began to manipulate the price. They enlisted super rich Arabs to conspire with them by driving the price higher. At the time of this crime it would have been impossible to see evidence of this fraud. Evidence unfolded when the scheme failed and the price collapsed.

It should be noted that the CFTC nor the Justice Department ever pursued criminal indictments of the Hunts. In 1988, a civil law suit brought by the Peruvian government won a judgment for $130,000,000 against the Hunts, because that jury became convinced that the Hunts were guilty of fraud. I don't have the capital that the Peruvian government has to hire a law firm.

The evidence in this case is so simple and clear, that each time I have approached law enforcement and they have turned their back to me, it makes me more determined to open up this case.

Try to consider this scenario. Suppose all of our homes were burglarized. I'm speaking of the jurors' homes, the U.S. Marshals' homes, and your homes. Also suppose we all had surveillance cameras in our homes which captured these burglaries on film. Then suppose we called 911 to report the burglary to law enforcement and supplied the video tape. Then suppose law enforcement did nothing, even though these burglaries continued every day and every day the victims called 911 to report their loss and supplied video tape. Also suppose that none of us knew who the others were but we all knew that law enforcement ignored our complaint and ignored the identity of the burglars on video tape.

Then suppose I was able to locate a few of the victims and I tried to convince these victims to band together to expose this to the media, but the media refused to publish this constant series of burglaries. That would piss me off. Also I would wonder why none of the victims would proceed further. They all decided to forget it.

I'm different, I'm more curious, I'm also tenacious or determined. This type of thing drives me to wonder why all these other people are ambivalent and disinterested. So as time went by, and from time to time I would get a brainstorm about a strategy, and when I was convinced that my new strategy would work, I went into action.

Well my strategy finally got us all together in this courtroom. And I've heard some amazing testimony, which seems very clear to me. I just hope that these jurors aren't employed by the CFTC, disguised as local citizens.

Q. When you met with Special Agent Cugel back in August of '89, can you tell the jurors why you gave him your letter that you had sent to Mr. Goodwin in July, the prior month?

A. Sure. Five months had passed since Congressman Shays had written to Attorney General Thornburgh. I was convinced that the Attorney General was ignoring a Congressman's request to order a legitimate investigation of a huge fraud. It was silly to imagine that the government would ever say that their resources were stretched to thin for them to allocate manpower to this major crime. I initiated this meeting with Agent Cugel by calling Congressman Shays to ask him to direct an FBI agent to contact me.

I got the call from Cugel a few days later and he agreed to come to my office. I told Gary Mastronardi that I wanted him there too, and Gary came for the meeting. I believed that Gary's work at the FBI would influence Cugel favorably.

At the meeting I laid out my documents to show Cugel the trades and the settlement prices, which were way out of line and violated the rules. Cugel listened but never agreed or disagreed. I pressed Cugel for a response and he refused to offer any response. At this point I presented the extortion threat letter to Goodwin and Cohen. I made a copy of the letter and gave it to Cugel. Then I told him that he had three choices. The first was that I hoped he would decide to investigate the COMEX fraud. The second was for him to arrest me for extortion because then I would have both COMEX officials and government officials in a courtroom where I could trap them in their criminal conspiracy. And the third choice was to continue the cover-up, eventually proving my point.

This episode shows my intent to the jury now. No criminal is going to call the FBI and give them evidence of extortion and then ask to be arrested. The reason that Goodwin and Cohen didn't want me arrested was because they were part of the COMEX fraud and wanted no contact with law enforcement. Now we know from Cugel's testimony to this jury that the United States Attorney in New York stopped him from doing any investigation of COMEX and the CFTC. I kept making it clear to Cugel that the CFTC was protecting the fraud from the beginning.

Q. Then you continued to make a series of efforts from that day all the way up until December 5th of 1994, to bring this situation to a head?

A. Wrong.

Q. Okay.

A. There were very large spans of time when I did absolutely nothing about this case. On October 1st, 1989 I moved to Memphis from Fairfield,. I had other business involvements. I dropped the copper case for two years until 1991.

Q. Now when you sent the two faxes to Mr. Moore and had the letter delivered to Richard Jossen. What were the options that you believed were possible and what were you hoping to accomplish when you did that?

A. Before I did that I contacted Bruce Baird's replacement, the new Chief of the Commodities & Securities Fraud Unit. His name is Howard Heiss. I had been in touch with Mr. Heiss about this case since early 1993, and before I had contacted Walter Jossen at his home.

Of course it was established that Richard Jossen had done nothing to contact law enforcement even though his father Walter and his Mother were very upset. I expected that the two people who went to Richard's home would give Richard a different perspective. I expected it was very likely that $6,000,000 would be wired into my account at the Dime Bank pursuant to the directions in the letter. I guessed wrong but I believed that that would be the most likely possibility.

In my letter to Mr. Heiss, I explained to him that we would split the proceeds and be partners, since he didn't mind allowing this crime to continue. My intention was to mail a personal check for the full amount of the wire to Mr. Heiss. It would then be up to him as to what he wanted to do with the money from COMEX.

Surely there could be no doubt that if COMEX wired the money it would be construed that they were paying money they had ripped off. My suspicion was that Howard Heiss wasn't being paid by COMEX to continue allowing COMEX to keep rigging copper prices, but either way Mr. Heiss was obstructing justice. This behavior is very perplexing to me. And if it doesn't ring a bell with the jury that will be even more perplexing to me. Why commit a crime to make others rich for nothing in return.

Maybe Richard Jossen and John Moore will ignore me again, but that seemed very doubtful to me. I definitely never thought they would contact law enforcement, so I was completely wrong. It has been stated on this witness stand before this jury that Walter Jossen was extremely concerned about the danger he feared and yet all the COMEX officials prevented any contact with law enforcement. The claims by Mr. Goodwin and Mr. Moore that a large group of people who worked at Comex and were contacted by me decided to remain mute and never discussed my allegations, I find that not likely and unbelievable.

It is now the obligation of this jury to decide if these witnesses are committing perjury under oath. On this subject we heard a contradiction between Walter Jossen and Richard Jossen. One of them lied. Walter wants the jury to believe that his son is innocent, but if Richard was innocent he would have contacted law enforcement at least to put his own father and mother at ease in August 1993. These were two opposing forces. The first to comfort his parents, and the second was to force law enforcement to bring this case into a courtroom which demanded both him and John Moore onto the witness stand.

Something changed dramatically in Richard's mind to contact law enforcement after he was visited on December 5th, after 10:00 at night.

Q.   You stated that you contacted Howard Heiss. What were you going to tell Howard Heiss was the source of the money after you mailed your check for the proceeds in case COMEX wired money into your account at Dime Bank.

A.   I set this up with a letter to Mr. Heiss dated November 22, 1994.

Q.   Would you like that letter to be introduced as evidence?

A.   I certainly would.

MR. REEVE: All right your honor, could I have that document marked for identification?

MR. APPLETON: No objection to its admission.

THE COURT: The government doesn't object to it being marked a full exhibit.

MR. REEVE: All right if it could be marked as a full exhibit and then Mr. Miller, I'll return it to you.

(Whereupon Defendant's Exhibit V was marked full.)

Q.   Its been marked as Defendant's Exhibit V and could you read this letter to the jury.

A.   Sure. The letter is dated November 22, 1994

Howard Heiss, Esq.

Chief of the Commodities & Securities Fraud Unit

United States Attorney for the Southern District of New York

1 St. Andrews Plaza

New York, N.Y.

Dear Mr. Heiss;

On February 12, 1993 I informed you by phone and in writing of the COMEX copper pricing fraud which began in May 1987.

On Monday, November 21, 1994 I met with the principles of Corplex concerning my ability and knowledge to help them with certain corporate fraud cases, especially derivative fraud.

The principles are: 1) Jeffrey Schlanger, President and 2) Joseph Pepe, Director of Investigation.

Among other factors of our meeting, I mentioned you and your participation in the ongoing cover-up of the COMEX copper pricing fraud. They decided to contact certain people for their response to my allegations and the evidence which clearly proves this fraud still continues.

In this regard I made it obvious to Mr. Schlanger and Mr. Pepe that if they contacted you, quite naturally you would deny any wrongdoing and therefore deny that COMEX was committing a crime. Furthermore, I made it clear to them that it is normal for government officials such as yourself to attack and defame citizens who allege malfeasance by officials.

My interest in this case is two fold.

1)   I want to recover my financial loss.

2)   I would like to force the government to honestly police financial markets.

Realistically my goals will never be achieved. The next best thing I can hope to achieve is to receive a payoff from the COMEX officials to share with you personally. To be perfectly clear I want to be partners with you and your friends at COMEX. As soon as my kickbacks begin I will forward a check for the entire proceeds I receive from COMEX. It will be for your discretion as to your disposition of my check to you.

Sincerely, Steve Miller

Q.   So what did you think would happen on December 5th, when you delivered the materials to Jossen and Moore?

A.   I believed that COMEX would authorize a payment wired to my account. Once my account was credited with funds from COMEX it would be easy to prove where that money had come from. Then I intended to mail a personal check in payment to Howard Heiss, and learn what he would do next. I believed my letter written to Mr. Heiss on November 22, 1994, would convince a jury that my intent was not to extort money from Jossen and Moore, but that it would force the government to deal with the crime by COMEX.

Q. That payment wasn't wired, did you factor that into your strategy?

A. Yes.

Q. Please explain that?

A. I have been put under certain constraints by the court to present special issues which fits my entire strategy.

Q. What were you going to tell Howard Heiss was the source of the money?

A. I was going to show him the letter I had delivered to Richard Jossen and John Moore.

Q. Did you believe that would be evidence?

A. No question.

Q. Evidence of what?

A. Evidence that Moore and Jossen had capitulated by wiring the money instead of complaining they were being extorted because they were guilty of the fraud. And evidence that I didn't extort them because I relayed the money to Mr. Heiss.

Q. Did you believe that if they sent you money, that would be a sign of guilty knowledge on their part?

A. I think you'd have to be a total simpleton not to know that. I also was confident that if I received credit for my role in ending this ongoing fraud, that my credentials as a consultant would be enhanced. If I could get work because of my expertise in risk management, my earning power would exceed $6,000,000 quite quickly.

Q. Did you feel that was your loss?

A. No.

Q. No?

A. Of course not. I picked $6,000,000 out of the air but for a few reasons. First of all I needed a fairly large number because Moore and his friends were dealing with huge amounts of money. I believed that if I chose, let's say $60,000 or even $600,000, they would suspect that I had no idea of the enormity of their fraud. There's more to it than just that. The mining industry knew that the grossly inflated prices were derived by the benefit of the COMEX fraud. As I had stated earlier, there was an average surplus price exceeding $.50 per pound on more than 18,000,000,000 pounds annually. The executives of these mining companies weren't going to blow the whistle on this bonanza.

In addition I explained the enormity of this fraud to the guys who visited Richard Jossen. They thought $6,000,000 was crazy too because they had no concept of the size of the COMEX fraud.

Q. You heard Mr. Moore yesterday when he was questioned by Mr. Appleton and then by me explain his beliefs that there is not fraud in the copper market. Right?

A. He's a criminal, who would expect him to admit that.

Q. Could you explain to the jurors, hopefully in the simplest way that you believe is appropriate, what the basis of your belief in the fraud is?

A. Do you want me to go into the rules and the prices which violate the rules?

Q. I'd like to give you an opportunity to explain to this jury what the basis of your belief is, just as Mr. Moore yesterday testified as to the basis of his belief that there is not fraud.

A. The basis is that the prices were changed after the market closed. You did a superb job on cross examination when at the end he finally admitted that traders would make up spread prices out of thin air which had never been executed. First of all there are very few spread trades ordered or executed. Listening to Mr. Moore you would think that most people trade spreads. To prove how few spread trades are executed we would need the separate Time & Sales spread register as evidence. I can't produce the register in evidence so its up to the jurors to decide who is telling the truth.

Without knowing anything about futures trading or copper futures trading, John Moore contradicted himself and made comments which the average person would know indicates that he is a criminal. The best one is when he called Richie when the FBI was at his house. He said, "I went cold, I went cold, you're kidding." I turned around to the Marshals and asked them when are you going to put the cuffs on this guy.

John Moore is telling us under oath that he went cold when he learned that Richie called the FBI. He wasn't supposed to call the FBI no matter what. To me this type of behavior is better than the number and the rules. Remember when O.J. left in the Bronco with cash and his friend Al Cowling. Didn't everybody on earth conclude he was going to run away instead of turning himself in because he was guilty.

Maybe I shouldn't use that example because O.J. got acquitted. But it seems that the rest of the people on earth besides the 12 jurors were convinced that O.J. was guilty because of circumstantial evidence.

I understand the prices and the rules. To me they are very simple because I have lived my life as a commodity trader for many years. To explain the prices and the rules it is necessary to look at 3 or 4 documents at the same time and you really need a table to spread all the documents out for observation.

We all buy items at stores. For example at the super market you see a price posted on the shelf for a bottle of ketchup at $1.00. When you go to the register and the cashier wants $1.10 you know there is a mistake. Any other price other than $1.00 is wrong or else the sign on the shelf is wrong. Its just that simple. John Moore tried to make you believe that prices on two different months are going to vary and that a committee of experts are necessary to decide complexities that average people are incapable of deciding. To all of a sudden after October 23, 1987, watch prices going in different directions for the same commodity is on its face ludicrous.

Let me go through some evidence for the jurors to view.

Q. Yes if at any time you need the charts that are part of the evidence in this case just let me know and I'll put it up for you.

(Because there were charts to aid my explanation to the jury the testimony recorded can't represent to readers of this book what the jury **heard and saw simultaneously.** For this reason I am forced to omit this part of the trial because it can't be reproduced and it is very dry as it stands alone.)

I believe it is common knowledge that prices rise because there becomes greater interest and increased bidding for any asset or commodity. For this reason I will publish the average open interest of copper contracts provided by COMEX for each month in 1987, 1988, and 1989.

MONTH	1987 / 1988 / 1989
January	77,851 / 43,177 / 33,397
February	77,433 / 41,220 / 33,756
March	76.967 / 35,505 / 34,464
April	70,108 / 34,787 / 35,694
May	74,628 / 31,410 / 30,459
June	84,725 / 35,949 / 27,606
July	**85,**391 / 31,750 / 24,462
August	75,725 / 29,520 / 25,128
September	65,678 / 34,946 / 23,742
October	59,073 / 35,724 / 19,439
November	47,279 / 36,606 / **14,955**
December	41,787 / 33,094 / 22,898

The highest open interest for the six years ending in 1992 was 48,700, reached in March 1992. The decline reached its nadir in November 1989 at 14,955 contracts. The massive decline in open interest which coincides with a daily noncompliance with the simple rules **indicates a**

huge number of traders eliminated their copper positions while this fraud continued. Whether or not they complained to the government can't be proven without enormous effort. Congressman Shays wrote in his letter to GAO Controller Bowsher that he had complaints from other traders. Traders not in Shays district wouldn't complain to him, they would go to the Congressman in their own district. Furthermore it is more likely for traders to complain to the CFTC or the Justice Department before going to a Congressman.

When you try to explain a concept, especially a concept which the jury suspects is too complex or remote, it is difficult when they can't ask questions. When you are able to listen to questions it is more likely that you can learn if the points that are being made are being understood.

During my testimony I tried to address points, which John Moore had made because he was misleading the jurors. When I concluded that portion of my testimony I went into my efforts about trying to interest corporations headquartered in Connecticut that bought huge amounts of copper wire. These companies were forced to pay the inflated price. It was in the interest of their stockholders to recover their excessive payments for copper. These companies were passing off the higher costs to their customers so it wasn't a severe problem for them.

My purpose for my defense was to inform the jury that I had gone to great lengths to resolve the problem. My purpose supported my defense in that my intent was not to extort money from COMEX. Also I was not only fighting COMEX, I was fighting the government too. Then to my surprise the media was actively covering up the story, which I was confident they would publish.

I had many encounters with media sources including 60 Minutes, The Wall Street Journal, The New York Times, The Washington Post, and many others. The encounters I had were fairly strange and I testified about a few of my meetings. My primary ammunition which I believed validated my story were the letters written by Congressman Shays to Thornburgh and Bowsher.

CHAPTER 8
THE COMPETENCE STIPULATION

The luncheon recess broke at 12:55 and we resumed at 2:05. During this recess I told Dick that it was critical for my defense that the jury learned that the reason it had taken 21 months for me to go to trial was because Judge Nevas stopped me with his incompetence ploy. It was now plain to the jurors that I had been an articulate witness and they would recognize this to be the cover-up I was trying to prove. Dick met with Judge Nevas about my plan and Judge Nevas forbade me to mention anything about mental health.

My reply to Dick was that I needed a stipulation for an appeal put on the record in case I lost my trial. When there is a problem resulting by a court's ruling, that problem must be addressed or the Circuit Court will refuse to decide that issue. I couldn't get Dr. Kucharski's admission on the record that his analysis was that I was not a criminal without being allowed to present the competence / mental health ruse by our fair judicial system. My acquittal was almost guaranteed with this evidence.

MR. REEVE: Could we address an issue?

THE COURT: All right.

MR. REEVE: The issue is that I've discussed with Mr. Miller and he would like to testify about what has happened in this case procedurally since December 7th of 1994 when he was arrested. Including the government moving for his competence, his being found competent by this court. That competency ruling then being vacated a few days after the original jury selection. His examination by another psychiatrist, Dr. Kucharski from M.C.C. New York along with a re-examination by Dr. Amble. The hearings before Judge Daly. His transfer down to Butner for another determination of his competence and the determination by Butner that he was competent.

He would like to go into that so that the jury has a full understanding of why there has been a delay and why he's been incarcerated for about 20 months from December 7th, until now.

MR. APPLETON: Respectfully your honor I think that testimony is completely inadmissable and irrelevant. The government would stipulate that the defendant is seeking a speedy trial. I think its dangerous and impermissable to get into the psychiatric information.

THE COURT: All right. As long as the government will stipulate that the defendant's been seeking a speedy trial, I think its adequate.

MR. REEVE: My understanding is that is what the court's ruling is and I'm preserving this issue. I mean I understand the court's ruling.

THE COURT: I thought we understood there is to be a stipulation that you were agreeable.

MR. REEVE: Given the court's ruling that there can't be testimony about that, I'm agreeable to the stipulation. I'm not trying to whipsaw-- the court indicated that that testimony was not going to be admitted. Mr. Miller still desires and would like to pursue that testimony but my understanding was the court was going to rule that it is inadmissible and agree with the government.

THE COURT: No I don't think that's what happened. What happened was I asked you why you wanted to do that and you said you wanted to do that because Mr. Miller wanted the jury to know why its taken so long to get to trial. He wants the jury to know that he's wanted a speedy trial all along.

MR. REEVE: Right.

THE COURT: And I said to Mr. Appleton, well you'll stipulate that he wanted a speedy trial and has wanted a speedy trial, won't you? And Mr. Appleton said yes.

MR. REEVE: That is correct judge.

THE COURT: So I don't know that I ruled one way or the other on whether or not there should be psychiatric testimony because I assumed when I asked Mr. Appleton that question he said yes. That the jury would be told that Mr. Miller has been all along seeking a speedy trial and that everyone was in agreement, including you Mr. Reeve.

MR. REEVE: Your honor just so that the record is clear, after that, I did discuss it with Mr. Miller and the other basis for the pursuit which I did not raise in chambers, is that as the court is aware through a number of correspondences from Mr. Miller, he believes that that is part of an ongoing government conspiracy or cover up and it is in that context that he would desire to introduce that evidence. I did not go into that in chambers.

THE COURT: All right.

MR. REEVE: And so that's the position and I'm kind of caught in the middle here.

THE COURT: I understand, I understand, that's the way we'll proceed.

MR. REEVE: Your honor, given those rulings, I believe we will be able to wrap things up.

THE COURT: Fine.

MR. REEVE: Your honor could I have just a moment with Mr. Miller? Thank you. (Pause)

MR. REEVE: Your honor Mr. Miller would like me to put on the record that if he's convicted, that this is an issue that he might wish to pursue on appeal.

THE COURT: He doesn't have to do that. He can appeal any issue he wants to appeal.

MR. REEVE: And as long as its in the record, I've advised him he has the right to appeal and I believe he's satisfied with that. I appreciate it.

(Whereupon the jury entered the courtroom at 2:15).

MR. REEVE: Mr. Miller, I want to direct your attention to your contact with Congressman Christopher Shays. There has already been testimony about this but I wonder if you could summarize how that contact started, what the purpose was, and what happened?

MR. APPLETON: I'm going to object, its irrelevant.

THE COURT: What's the claim?

MR. REEVE: Your honor there has been a great deal of testimony about this already and, number one, it establishes that Mr. Miller was making significant efforts to uncover the fraud. That those efforts are legitimate efforts that were pursued through the course of many, many years. And I think its very appropriate, relevant evidence.

MR. APPLETON: That is absolutely irrelevant to the charges. The charge is whether or not the defendant committed the acts in the indictment. That is extortion. It's irrelevant.

MR. REEVE: Well your honor I'm going to object to that. The government knows that there is a lot more and the only issue in this case is Mr. Miller's state of mind. That is his intent and for the government to stand up and say the only issue are his acts, is a misstatement of the law.

THE COURT: All right I'm going to overrule the objection.

MR. REEVE: Thank you your honor.

THE WITNESS: Thank you your honor.

A.   I went to Congressman Shays because I was looking for another avenue because of the road blocks by the CFTC and the Justice Department. First I met Congressman Shays at a town meeting he held in Fairfield. I mentioned the problem in front of the group at the meeting and Congressman Shays invited me to his office in Bridgeport. We had a half hour meeting in Bridgeport during which Congressman Shays was asking me to declare my motive. This led to his invitation for me to meet with him in his Washington office.

At that meeting he explained that he served on the Government Operations Committee. This Committee had oversight on the GAO. Mr. Shays introduced me to Russell Mathews who worked for the Republicans who served on the Committee and Mr. Mathews would help me by getting vital information presented to the GAO for its investigation. Mr. Shays requested that the GAO investigate the CFTC to learn if the CFTC performed its oversight on the COMEX. Congressman Shays also introduced me to Betsy Hawkings. Betsy worked for Shays on his staff and she helped me also.

The primary evidence which was turned over to me is called the **TIME & SALES REGISTER.** This was a record of every single copper trade at each minute of the trading day. These records were for a three month period which began on September 1st, 1987, through November 30th, 1987. My purpose for asking for these three months was that it would and did show the sharp change which occurred at the mid point in October 1987, which was triggered by the stock market crash.

I reduced the data contained in the huge number of pages I received to help the GAO investigators best understand how COMEX was illegally setting the settlement prices. Even though the fraud was being committed before the October 19th, "Black Monday" crash, the dimension of the fraud was magnified beginning on October 23rd. There was an unmistakable difference which was impossible not to see.

In addition there is a separate **TIME & SALES REGISTER** for spread trades. Switch and spread are synonymous words meaning that the trade executes a buy and sell of two different months simultaneously. I make this point for the jury because Mr., Moore testified about how switches are used to derive the settlement price on each contract except the active month.

Congressman Shays was very helpful when gave me access through Russ Mathews to the GAO. Maybe if I had been given direct access to the GAO investigators we would not be in this courtroom now. But that did not happen and unfortunately the CFTC was able to convince the GAO that COMEX was abiding by the rules and that the CFTC had done their job properly.

About a year expired. In early 1989, I got a call from Congressman Shays and I will never forget his precise words. He said, "Steve this is Chris. They said you're full of shit."

Congressman Shays has a very distinctive voice so I knew it was him on the phone. I was really shocked. So I said, "I want to ask you one more thing and then I'll drop the issue. Please set up a short meeting in your office with the GAO investigators, the CFTC officials, you, and me. We'll see first hand who's full of shit." He agreed.

I was on my way back to Washington and I had all my documents ready for our meeting. We all shook hands with introductions. The 3 GAO investigators sat on a couch and never said a word. The 2 CFTC officials sat at the conference table facing Congressman Shays. And I sat in a chair facing the 3 of them at the conference table.

For about 10 to 15 minutes the CFTC officials took turns spewing out jargon and statements which sounded very erudite but were not understandable by me. It appeared to me that they would filibuster the meeting and my chance would never happen. I decided to interrupt and I said that I don't know what they're talking about.

Chris Shays said, "We're not here to point our fingers at anybody."

I said, "I'm here to point my finger at both of them, and I'd like to put the evidence on the table."

When I finished showing Chris the rules and the different documents which needed to be seen so you could point to prices on different pages, Chris understood that I was right. It was right after that that Congressman Shays wrote his letters first to Charles Bowsher, the Controller General of the GAO, and second to Richard Thornburgh, the Attorney General.

When I received copies of our Congressman's letters to these senior officials, I was convinced the fraud would stop.

I would like to read these defense exhibits to the jury. Can I please read this to the jury and into the record your honor?

THE COURT: How long is that letter?

THE WITNESS: It's four pages.

THE COURT: No the jury can read it if they want to read it, its an exhibit.

THE WITNESS: Can I read just part of it?

THE COURT: It's a full exhibit?

MR. REEVE: It is your honor, yes. It will go to the jury.

THE COURT: It will go to the jury, they can read it.

THE WITNESS: Can I read one paragraph?

THE COURT: One paragraph, yes. You can read one paragraph.

THE WITNESS: The February 9, 1989 letter to Charles Bowsher said this:

"In addition, other futures traders have confidentially expressed to my office their concerns about the way copper prices have been set in recent months. One of them specifically stated on several occassions the day's settlement prices were set consistently higher than the day's closing price for no apparent reason."

I don't know if there were one or two others, or five thousand other traders, but these letters leave nothing to the imagination.. They completely agree with the allegations I have made. Specific rules were sited. These two letters contradict the notion that the FBI and the Justice Department should be satisfied by what they are told by the CFTC.

Q.   Are you referring to Defense Exhibits A and B?

A.   Yes and there is one other letter that came from Congressman Glenn English that was written to Shays. I'd like to make a comment concerning Congressman English's involvement with the CFTC. May I do that please your honor?

THE COURT: Just a minute.

MR. APPLETON: No objection.

THE COURT: Full exhibit.

(Whereupon Defendant exhibit W was marked full.)

MR. REEVE: Thank you your honor.

THE COURT: Mr. Reeve will read the letter.

MR. REEVE: This is Defendant's Exhibit W. It's dated July 17th, 1989, addressed to the honorable Christopher Shays, House of Representatives, Washington D.C.

Dear Mr. Shays: Recently you sent information regarding the settlement prices established at COMEX and the election of Board Members who have been disciplined for trading violations.

After studying the material you included about settlement prices, I have concluded that our staff does not have the expertise to conduct an investigation into the matter and therefore it would be necessary for us to turn to the CFTC. Your letter indicates that you have done this in the past and are not satisfied with their conclusions.

Last Wednesday Tom Coleman and I introduced the Commodities Futures Improvements Act of 1989, (H.R. 2869) which addresses the question of board member election. Our bill prohibits the election to self regulatory governing board or disciplinary committees, of any person who has been disciplined for major trading violations. This provision will prevent the situation you described in the future.

I am enclosing a copy of H.R. 2869 as introduced. I have scheduled hearings for this week and markup by the subcommittee next week. When it reaches the floor I hope you will be able to support it.

Thank you for your help.

Sincerely,

Glenn English

Chairman

MR. REEVE: Mr. Miller, do you have any additional knowledge with respect to that letter?

A.   Two separate items. First Congressman English is telling Congressman Shays that his staff doesn't have enough knowledge to perform their job. He claims I can't investigate the issue but must rely upon the CFTC. Secondly, Congressman English refused to reauthorize the CFTC after it had completed its 15 year authorization period because he knew that the CFTC had been complained about repeatedly for allowing the industry criminal abuses.

Q.   Steve I want to direct your attention to another point in time. There was a time in 1989 when you discontinued your efforts to pursue COMEX. Explain what you did then?

A.   Sure, by September 1989 I gave up. I decided to quit fighting city hall. But three years later I decided to write a book about this case and I moved to New York City. I began a search for a literary agent and as the testimony has showed I contacted Howard Heiss in early 1993. I believed he was going to begin a legitimate investigation. When that didn't take place, as we know I contacted Walter Jossen believing this strategy would work.

I also was contacting various people who I believed would benefit from the problem. I contacted Mayor Dinkins' campaign people. Remember he was running for mayor of New York City against Rudy Giuliani. I showed them Shays' letters and the letter from Giuliani's office signed by Bruce Baird to prove that Giuliani protected COMEX instead of prosecuting them while he was the United States Attorney. The men I met with believed I had dynamite, which would guarantee Dinkins reelection. They said they'd be back in touch with me in a week. They chickened out. People are really afraid of the feds.

I tried to find work for which I was told I was over qualified. I might have been getting black balled for certain jobs. I did get hired to work for Everlast the company in the Bronx that makes boxing equipment. Now I really wish I had taken that job and dropped this determination to force this case into court.

For 27 months in New York I had many fascinating experiences until I was arrested.

Q.   Did you intend when you sent the 2 faxes to Mr. Moore to extort money from him?

A.   No.

Q.   When you had the letter delivered to Richard Jossen, was it your intent to extort money from him?

A.   No.

Q.   What was your intent?

A.   My intent was to create a resolution to the situation that everybody here in this jury I hope is well aware of by this time.

    MR. REEVE: Thank you I have nothing further.

    THE COURT: Mr. Appleton?

CROSS EXAMINATION BY MR. APPLETON

Q.   Briefly your honor. Sir, you don't deny you sent the letter to Walter Jossen on August 26, 1993, do you?

A.   No.

Q.   You don't deny that you had the 2 individuals deliver the letter to Jossen's house on December 5th, 1994, do you?

A.   No.

Q.   And you don't deny that you made the calls that the jury heard in this case, correct?

A.   No.

Q.   When you had the letter delivered to Richard Jossen, was it your intent to extort money from Mr. Jossen?

A.   No.

Q.   What was your intent?

A.   My intent was to create a resolution to the situation that everybody here in this jury I hope is well aware of by this time.

Q.   You don't deny that you asked Jossen to wire transfer $6,000,000 to your account do you?

A.   I don't deny that.

Q.   You don't deny that you fully expected Jossen to pay you the $6,000,000 so you could turn it over to whom you claimed you were going to turn it over to?

A.   I intended to mail my check to Howard Heiss as soon as I learned if the money had been wired into my account. Whatever that amount might have been.

    MR. APPLETON: No further questions.

    THE COURT: You're excused Mr. Miller. All right, this finishes the evidence. The next stage of the trial will be closing arguments, summation by the lawyers. It's customary that I meet with the lawyers to review the instructions on the law so I think what we'll do is suspend for the day. At 9:00 tomorrow morning we'll start with closing arguments.

    (Whereupon the jury left the courtroom at 2:45.)

    The closing arguments by both sides were mediocre at best. I asked Dick to be definitive by telling the jury that COMEX was guilty of the fraud and that the government knew it and the decisions to not report me to law enforcement made it clear. The meeting with Agent Cugell made it clear that law enforcement didn't want to prosecute me because they knew my plan was to expose them.

But Dick refused to argue those points. Instead he went into a fairy tale story which made no sense.

Finally Judge Nevas charged the jury with a 30 page long statement on the law. I point this out now because it will play an important role in the appellate phase of the case.

When the jury was released for their deliberations I was locked up in the holding cell and Dick came back there to keep me company. About 25 minutes later the Marshal announced that the jury had a verdict. I was happy, believing they had acquitted me. If the case was so clear to them it seemed very unlikely that they would find me guilty.

I believed that no jury would find a defendant guilty in 25 minutes unless there was no defense. Not only was there a huge amount of evidence and testimony to consider for the defense, none of it could have been deliberated in 25 minutes. Part of that 25 minute time had to have been used to choose their jury foreman too.

But the minute the Marshall announced a verdict, Dick smiled at me and said, "You're guilty." I was amazed he said that and with a smile too. I just thought to myself, you are going to be surprised.

Well I got the surprise and there were going to be plenty more surprises to come for me during the following 2 year period.

The sentencing date was set for December 4th, 1996, 2 years from the date of my arrest. Instead of walking out the front door of the courthouse, I was on my way back to Wyatt Detention Center until my sentencing date.

The next step would be the Pre-Sentence Investigation for the court. It's called the PSI and every other convict in the system tries to make this report to the court look as good as possible. I told Dick that I wanted no part of it for a couple of reasons. I was sure I would win my appeal. I knew Judge Nevas would hit me as hard as he could regardless of whatever the PSI said. And most of all I didn't want any delay for me to begin my appeal.

I've seen delays of longer than a year during the PSI phase. The faster I got out of Wyatt, and the faster I began to work on my appeal, the better I liked it.

While my trial was in progress I was confident that the stipulation to preserve being prevented by the court to testify about the competency / insanity defense issue would be important for my appeal. In hindsight now I can see that Judge Nevas knew that the Second Circuit Court of Appeals would hold him harmless regarding any prejudicial and unconstitutional decision and ruling he made.

There were three phases that my appellate process took that were designed to prevent any legitimate right I had under the Federal Rules Of Appellate Procedure.

The first phase was to assign a lawyer who intended to wreck my appeal. I overcame that phase by firing that lawyer.

The second phase was to force me to write a brief prior to making legitimate decisions that prevented me from including important deletions from my transcript. I began a process of filing under separate dockets; complaints that dealt with two of these issues.

The third and final phase was to stay my appeal. Once the appeal is denied the defendant is cooked, finito, caputski. Because I was preventing the court from denying my appeal because I had valid arguments that prevented me from filing my brief, the court just said, "screw you."

Judge Nevas had to know that he had nothing to worry about concerning his stipulation to appeal his decision to prevent the competency issue from being heard by the jury. Federal District Court judges have limitless power because the checks and balances written into the Federal Rules of Appellate Procedure is blandly ignored by the circuit courts and the United States Supreme Court.

The reversals that are ordered by the higher courts are just window dressing to make us believe that our system is guided by laws and not unlimited power packed judges who scoff at our wonderful laws. The vast majority of readers of this statement will decide that I must be crazy to say such a thing. People will believe what they want to believe. I might have said the same thing before I lived through this experience too. That is because I was brainwashed by the endless propaganda machine that has our minds controlled.

Our government has the resources to propagandize us on a daily basis. They are in a position to control us and that is what they intend to do. Unless citizens begin to realize that our government is ignoring our Bill of Rights and legal statutes that were written to protect us from tyranny our voting power will continue to be useless.

I welcome any challenge to the facts I have presented in this story because I can substantiate the facts I have presented. The facts are beyond weird. That is not my fault or because I'm cynical or crazy. I always try to be realistic and I only want to learn the truth. Why try to fool myself? How can I gain by fooling myself?

People form beliefs that they can not admit are just wrong. America became great because our ancestors had the guts to fight against tyranny. We are letting all their hard fought gains disappear.

CHAPTER 9
A WILD RIDE TO COURT

The jury had been sent to deliberate at 11:10 AM, they had a verdict at 11:35 AM. Dick had come back to the lock-up to keep me company. When the deputy marshal announced the jury had reached a verdict, Dick smiled at me and said, "You're guilty." I can't prove Dick made that statement and I can't prove I saw him smile at me, but he did. These two things would fit into a bunch of other facts, which are part of the record.

If you know one juror is definitely going to vote guilty, then you know that the verdict must be guilty. I would expect that unless a case had no viable defense whatsoever, that a super quick verdict is going to be not guilty. It is my hunch that 12 jurors would deliberate some of the defense before they convict a defendant. At least some of those 12 people won't pull the trigger on a defendant until some part of the defense is deliberated. These jurors could not have deliberated any testimony from any witness including the government's witnesses. They could not have deliberated any of the exhibits. Was there no reasonable doubt about the intent to extort for these jurors to deliberate?

Court reconvened at 12:00 for the verdict. At 12:02 the jury was polled and they left. Judge Nevas set the sentencing for December 2nd, 1996, at 9:00 A.M. And I was returned to Wyatt Detention Center to wait for my sentencing.

I wanted nothing to delay my sentencing so I could begin my appeal. A convict has 10 days from the day of sentencing to file a **NOTICE OF APPEAL.** If this notice isn't filed in the ten-day limit, an appeal can be held up for years. When I was convicted on Friday, September 13, 1996, I told Dick to file my **NOTICE OF APPEAL** and he did.

On December 2nd I was awakened around 3:30 A.M. for my ride to the Bridgeport court. A Puerto Rican girl was put into the van for an appearance in New Haven. There were women being held at Wyatt Detention also. When we got to the exit on I 95 for downtown New Haven and drove to the courthouse door to drop off the girl a call to the driver was received. The instant the van stopped at the courthouse door, a radio message ordered them to proceed to Bridgeport immediately. The girl was kept in the van even though we were stopped at the door for her hearing. She told me that Appleton was her prosecutor too.

Appleton scheduled her hearing and my sentencing on the same day in two different locations. Do you think this was an accident?

I was brought to the courtroom lock-up in Bridgeport by the Wyatt guards and then they left to take the girl back to New Haven. About fifteen minutes later I was told that my sentencing was postponed and I was taken to the Marshals' lock-up. I have been in the Marshals' office five or six times, and only one person was ever there. This time there were about 8 to 10 people sitting there. I walked through the office and into the lock-up. There was a kid in the next cell who had been arrested that morning. During the next hour we talked a little bit and he told me why he had been arrested.

In the Marshals' office there are monitors for them to watch the inmates in the cells. I was fairly sure that they had assembled this crowd of agents for a purpose. 8 to 10 agents aren't going to sit idly in an office for no purpose.

Some very attractive woman interviewed the kid about making bail. I've never seen the likes of her interview during my years of incarceration. Then, none other than Dick Reeve came in to represent the kid. This is a hell of a coincidence. Dick is scheduled for my sentencing, but he's here to represent this kid. And Appleton is supposed to be in Bridgeport at 9:00 A.M. And he's in New Haven for the Puerto Rican girl's hearing. This is an amazing coincidence.

There's no conspiracy going on here. It's all a coincidence. Any time someone mentions the word "conspiracy" he or she becomes a conspiracy nut. The nuts are the masses who disregard all the coincidences as accidents. Well if there was a plot hatched with Appleton, Reeve, and Nevas; the question should be, what was their purpose?

Finally Dick comes to my cell and decides to tell me that he's going to ask Judge Nevas to reschedule my sentencing as soon as possible.

Now this is nothing but a charade, which they believed, (I am speculating) would get me very angry because they know I was concerned about getting this sentencing finished. They have assembled 8 to 10 witnesses who are probably agents, watching me on their monitor because they suspect I will become very angry and uncontrolled. Judge

Nevas would love to have about 10 agents file a report, which would substantiate a mental health disorder. I have never displayed out of control behavior regardless of whether I was angry or not.

So I was my friendly, courteous self with Dick while he was giving me the bad news. Dick told me that he would push hard to have me brought back for sentencing as soon as possible. I could only hope that Judge Nevas would comply.

Luckily 4 days later I was back in Bridgeport to hear my sentence. Nevas gave me the top of the guidelines, 108 months, and 3 years of supervised release. He also recommended to the BOP (Bureau of Prisons) that I needed mental health care. So in early January 1997, I began my trip back to FCI Butner. I was classified to be in a medium security facility and adjacent to the 3 units of the mental health facility were 5 general population units.

Dick had prepared a dynamic performance for my sentencing. His primary point was that genuine mob guys who had been sentenced for "heartland extortion cases" received 2 to 3 years. Dick mentioned one case against Vincent Gigante along with other specific mob cases. These guys had the power to order people murdered or hurt for refusing to pay for protection. Their victims usually paid protection to the mob for long periods of time before law enforcement finally brought indictments against the mob bosses Dick had sited to the court as a comparison to my case. I suspect Dick's speech was a charade to add credibility to his fake defense.

When I arrived at FCI Butner I decided to be as sure as possible that I wouldn't be forced medicated. So when I was asked for my religious preference I chose Christian Science. If you don't know, Christian Scientists are not allowed to take any medication or be involved with doctors or medical staff. I contacted a local Christian Science church and they sent me their brochures. When I was told to have my blood pressure taken, I explained that I couldn't and I'd hand them a brochure. I was assigned to Dr. Berger again. I was assigned to a cell with a very crazy child molester.

My plan was to obey all the rules, get a job, and be very quiet. I met the clerk in the landscape shop and he got me a job there. He would be getting released in a few months and I would be in line for his job. The foreman of the landscape shop, George Barnes, was a real good guy who knew a lot about landscaping. About a week later my counselor came to me and told me I had been fired. I said why, I don't know anything about that. I went to ask George Barnes to ask why he had fired me. George said I didn't fire you. I then explained that I had been told that by my counselor. George told me to go back to my counselor and tell him that he didn't know what he was talking about.

What had happened was that some BOP staff person who I suspected was the ISM (Inmate Systems Monitor) changed the roster to put me in a different shop. The computer didn't change my job assignment by itself. When I had failed to report to the other shop for a week, I was fired. I straightened it out because I had a copy of the (cop out) signed by my counselor and George Barnes. George never bothered to check the roster and didn't know that I wasn't on it. In the BOP everything is requested in writing on a form called a cop-out. So my cop out was signed by George Barnes and my counselor to work in the landscape shop and I was out of trouble.

I needed to be on my best behavior with everyone to get moved into general population. During my first team meeting I noticed that my religious preference had been changed to "no preference". I made a point of this to the team. The team was comprised of the Unit Manager, Case Manager, Counselor, and psychologist assigned to me. They recommended to have the prison chaplain confirm my religious preference.

My religious preference was changed for one reason. They intended to medicate me. The prison staff would have no reason to change any person's religious preference. FCI Butner is the only joint that ever asked inmates to indicate a religious preference.

I went to the chaplain with a cop-out to reinstate my religious preference as Christian Science. He told me to put Protestant instead of Christian Science. I responded by telling him that I wasn't Baptist, Catholic, Muslim, Jewish, or anything other than Christian Science. He finally reluctantly authorized my preference.

A few months went by and I got the clerk's job which took me about 20 minutes a week to do. The nice thing was that I had a desk and an electric typewriter to do my appeal. My team finally also recommended that I be moved to general population. Part of my maneuver was to have conversations with the guards, they call officers. Inmates call the guards cops or hacks.

I wanted the cops to know that I was a normal person and didn't have mental defects. I suspected that eventually the prison administration didn't want their employees to recognize that it was obvious that I was housed in a psych unit because the government intended to make me appear crazy because I tried to expose its conspiracy.

My wild ride to the Nevas court had a long way before it ended. The prison administration isn't performing this way with other inmates. If Nevas had just sentenced me as a normal convict none of this would happen in the prison system. As time goes on I will have incidents with the psych staff in every joint I enter. In every case I will also be successful by putting a stop to the incidents.

CHAPTER 10
THE APPEAL GETS UNDERWAY

As soon as I was sentenced Dick filed my **NOTICE OF APPEAL** and he filed his motion to withdraw. I was assigned Ms. Henriette Hoffman, the boss of the Manhattan Public Pretenders Office (Public Defenders). I wrote to her and stated that I didn't want her to file anything for me until she sent it to me to read first. She claimed that she didn't have time for that. So I asked her to please withdraw.

She withdrew and I was assigned a private lawyer that the Second Circuit appointed for me. His name was David Windley from Brooklyn. In our first phone conversation David offered to visit me in North Carolina and promised to send me a copy of my transcript. Lawyers like most people try to create a good impression from the beginning of the relationship. Many people do this in a genuine manner, I think. I have had poor relations with every lawyer who ever represented me, so I am doubtful anytime I need to hire a lawyer.

I could write an entire chapter on my list of lawyers. To get a feel for my experience I'll just use one example.

In 1982, I had a wonderful romance with Candy Farricielli who was divorced from the father of her beautiful 3 daughters, Christy, Donna, and the coolest kid on earth, Robin. Tony, Candy's ex continued to work for Candy's dad as the manager of Farricielli Oldsmobile. Tony worked long hours until 9:00 PM. But Tony wanted custody of the kids. What Tony really wanted was to eliminate paying child support.

Tony hired a vicious lawyer to represent him in his custody battle.

Candy and I planned to take a two week trip. We made arrangements for the kids to stay with Tony and before Tony came home each night Candy's Mom, Josephine took care of the kids when they came home from school to Tony's house.

The night before Candy and I were scheduled to return home we learned from Josephine that Tony had gotten into court and the judge decided to change custody of the kids. I got a copy of the transcript and learned that Tony had lied to the judge. Tony claimed that Candy had abandoned the kids, left town, and disappeared. Tony's lawyer had gotten him into court knowing that Candy didn't disappear.

I decided to hire a lawyer to get custody returned to Candy. What had happened was that Candy's lawyer of record, Tony Grazioso, had received notice of the impending hearing and he failed to contact Candy's father who Grazioso knew personally in order to learn why he was unable to contact Candy. Grazioso would have learned about the short trip Candy had taken by contacting her father and then Grazioso should have contacted the court to have the hearing delayed for a week. This was basic common sense.

The first lawyer I contacted took a $700 fee and then told me he couldn't represent me because of his relationship with Tony Grazioso. The second lawyer was a cousin of mine, named Eddie Cantor. My mother was a cousin of Eddie's mother Sophie. I called Eddie to explain that I needed to hire him. Eddie told me that he couldn't take the case because he had been a school mate of Tony Grazioso at Hopkins Grammar an exclusive private school in New Haven, then Yale undergraduate, and finally at Yale law school.

About 10 minutes after we hung up, Eddie called back to explain that he had a lawyer in his office who would take the case. We went to their office and I paid a $2,000 legal fee. Eddie said she was a tiger.

While this is happening the 3 kids are having to stay at a day care center and wait until Tony returns home from work at 9:30 PM every work day evening to eat a hamburger dinner from MacDonald's. This is instead of being at home with their mother from school and having wonderful dinners, playing, and doing their home work.

On the morning of the hearing we rode up to court on the elevator and the tiger told Candy, "Don't say anything against Tony Grazioso." I'm thinking, this is the tiger worrying about Tony Grazioso, completely ignoring the kids at the day care center watching the other kids eating dinner.

We walked out of that hearing after the judge dismissed the proceeding. The tiger never explained to the judge why he had been mislead. Unless the judge learned that Tony had lied to him and that Tony Grazioso should have asked for the case to be continued until Candy returned the following week, the judge had no reason to believe that he had made a mistake. The judge had no choice because the tiger made no sense.

Later that day I got a call from Eddie. He told me that he knew that I was unhappy with his lawyer associate but that he would return to court himself and fix the problem. On the next hearing Eddie failed. Eddie told me not to come to court. I came to pick Candy up after the hearing ended and Eddie accused me of coming to court. I only was downstairs in the lobby and never went to the court room. Eddie failed because he was so worried about Tony Grazioso. In the mean time the weeks went by and the kids lived in a horrendous condition compared to the comfort of their home.

I then called attorney Sig Miller in Bridgeport. He invited Candy and me to his home where I explained the case and gave Sig $2500. Sig got custody restored to Candy but the judge decided to have Tony pay $5.00 a week extra to compensate for the support payments he squirmed out of paying during the 2 months he had custody of the kids. When a hearing was scheduled to modify the ridiculous $5.00 per week payment, Tony's lawyer failed to show and never had the decency to contact Sig to not waste a trip to the New Haven court. That meant that Sig wasted hours coming to court in New Haven and he wanted me to pay extra for that time. I told Sig that Tony's lawyer had an ethical responsibility to have called him or he needed to oppose the delay and proceed with the hearing without her presence. Should I pay extra or should Sig charge Tony's lawyer for wasting his time?

This is just one of many lawyer debacles for me.

After weeks of telling me that he (David Windley) forgot to have the transcript copied, I suggested that his forgetfulness was becoming annoying and that I needed my copy right away so I could assist with my appeal. On the next call to David, he told me, "go fuck yourself." I was so happy because this is monitored on tape by the BOP. I began to write to the Second Circuit telling the court that I wanted to be pro se, my lawyer Mr. Windley refused to withdraw, I needed a copy of my transcript, and that Mr. Windley had told me to fuck myself. Each time I wrote a pro se motion, they would write back telling me because I had counsel, they weren't allowed to rule on any motion I filed.

I was in a Catch 22, but finally the chief judge of the circuit told me I could write a supplemental brief. I refused. I told them that I didn't want David Windley to have anything to do with my case. I wasn't afraid anymore about the competence issue. And finally Mr. Windley was told to withdraw and he finally filed a motion to withdraw.

Windley sent my transcript and I began to read it carefully. The first thing I looked for was the opening statement by Appleton. It wasn't in the transcript. So it appeared that neither side had made an opening statement.

I had no idea about how to proceed on this fabulous appellate issue. I began to spend a lot of time in the law library researching the best remedy to take advantage of this wonderful opportunity. The opening statement issue had mushroomed into a false transcript issue directed by the unscrupulous, devious, tyrannical Judge Nevas.

I was under a deadline to file a brief. So I needed to move as fast as possible. I learned a number of things. First of all I learned about filing a **JUDICIAL MISCONDUCT COMPLAINT.** The circuit court does not like to see this complaint for a number of reasons. First of all it must be answered by the chief judge and not the panel. Second of all it must be answered quickly. And thirdly it can be reviewed by four more judges in the circuit.

The transcript is considered to be prima facie evidence. It is certified to be true and accurate by the court reporter, so it can't be disputed very easily. I was positive that Susan Catucci would not know to delete the opening statement on her own. She had to be told by only the judge to do that. The court reporter works directly for the judge and is bound by the **COURT REPORTER ACT.**

I needed to make my complaint clean, tight, and hard with evidence. I had evidence because Appleton had written his opening statement and had filed it. It said instructions to the jury. The instructions weren't smoke signals, they had to be spoken to the jurors, and I distinctly recall listening to Appleton while I read the document he had filed to the court. This document proved my complaint. I also had the motion on the docket sheet for an opening statement, which Nevas had denied. The issue was clearly on the record. And I also wrote a letter to Susan Catucci, directly accusing her of deleting Appleton's opening statement. I stated that she had an obligation to contact the chief judge in the District of Connecticut to report Judge Nevas for intimidating her. I also told her to deny my allegation if she was innocent, but that if she failed to answer me she effectively was admitting her guilt.

Susan Catucci failed to respond. Three months later I wrote her once more and emphasized her failure to respond. I also motioned my three judge panel at the 2nd Circuit court to allow me to depose her. They denied my motion and told me to write my brief. Their denial of my motion to depose the court reporter on this critical issue of falsifying my transcript at the very least showed that they did not want my allegation put into their faces.

Each time the court demanded me to write my brief, I responded by stating my transcript had been falsified and that prevented me from writing my brief. If the court refused to investigate to learn if the prosecution's opening statement had been deleted from the trial record it showed that they had no intention of protecting my right to a fair trial. It would then be useless to file the brief.

Susan Catucci was a witness to her own transcript. If the court wanted to learn the truth of this serious matter it would have investigated it by talking to her or letting me depose her. There is no question that Susan Catucci deleted the opening statement Appleton had written and then read to the jury. The only question is did she do it on her own or was she ordered to do it by Judge Nevas. Here again she fails to report Judge Nevas to the Chief Judge for the District Of Connecticut. I am certain they knew that Judge Nevas was the culprit who forced her to delete the statement and they wanted to protect Nevas. The theory that America is a country of laws and not a country of people is plain old fashion hypocrisy.

I found a very important case, **SELVA v. U.S.** as a precedent case for my argument. This is what law is supposed to be about. The rulings in similar cases are to be followed by the courts. In real life though this only works when the courts feel like it. In fact there are many cases, which are unpublished because the courts don't want to reveal their unconstitutional decisions.

SELVA was reversed and remanded because the transcript was deleted by accident. The Supreme Court decided that because part of the record was missing, if there had been a prejudicial finding it couldn't have been found for Selva's appeal. There was no allegation that anything prejudicial existed in the deleted section. The deletion resulted from an honest error after the court reporter got sick and became unable to work, the recorder was relied upon but it broke.

In my case the deletion wasn't accidental and the deletion masked an incredibly prejudicial decision by the court. There was no question that Nevas had denied Reeve the right to make an opening statement because he denied the motion.

A Judicial Misconduct Complaint under the Federal Rules Of Appellate Procedure (**FRAP**) cannot be dismissed by the Chief Judge unless it is frivolous. The Chief Judge is only empowered to appoint a Special Committee to investigate the complaint.

What Chief Judge Ralph K. Winter did was not just an outright lie but a very stupid lie to boot. He wrote his disposition to dismiss the complaint because he claimed that Judge Nevas had **CHARGED THE JURY** and it was 30 pages long in the transcript. The issue raised in the Judicial Misconduct Complaint never indicated anything about the judge's charge to the jury it was only about the prosecutor's opening statement.

Judge Winter's disposition was incoherent. It gave me no chance to lose my next step for the 4 judge panel review unless each judge was willing to conspire by condoning the incoherent disposition to dismiss my complaint. I was positively confident that 4 federal judges would never conspire on the record. How wrong can I be?

In legal terms a great big lie by a judge is called plain error. When you find plain error you can't lose. I was confident that my PETITION to the 4 judge **REVIEW PANEL** would set me free. Federal judges know the difference between an opening statement and a charge to the jury. The charge to the jury is at the end of the trial and the opening statement is at the beginning before the first witness takes the stand.

To dismiss a serious complaint based upon an issue, which is nonexistent in that complaint is the height of absurdity. But it didn't matter. The 4 judge REVIEW PANEL remained mute. They never agreed or disagreed. They made no statement which allowed Judge Winter's incoherent disposition to stand. I was dumbfounded. How can this happen in America?

I had another big issue, but it was going to be my ace in the hole. I wanted to play this one out so I could learn as much as possible before I used my ace.

I had filed motions to my panel along the same lines concerning the false transcript. I believed that if I couldn't get justice under FRAP I had no chance with my brief anyway. Each time they denied a motion they would demand that I should file my brief. If I filed my brief with a false transcript, I believed I capitulated the issue. Finally I threatened to file a **PETITION FOR A WRIT OF MANDAMUS** to the United States Supreme Court to force the Second Circuit to investigate my complaint.

After the Second Circuit saw my petition to the Supreme Court it ordered Judge Nevas to fix the transcript. When they ordered him to fix the transcript that was an admission from them that they believed there was something to fix. I still wanted a definitive ruling that the government's opening statement had been deleted before I filed my brief because until that issue was clear I believed it would go down the drain and be lost. When you are fighting the courts, you must be patient. They have all the time in the world and they know that. The judges aren't sitting in jail they are going home to their families and living in comfort.

When I wrote my petition to the United States Supreme Court I had five appendices from all the motions, the complaint and the petition, which I should have won. I had no doubt that I would win because the reasons used to deny every pleading were lies that ignored the issue on the table, or they were not responsive at all.

I was absolutely unprepared to imagine, let alone believe, that all nine Supreme Court Justices would condone the behavior of all 12 United States 2nd Circuit, Appellate Judges who took part in my case. I was positive that they would draw the line somewhere. Instead it finally sunk into my brain that there is no line. The deception goes beyond any boundaries, and it is cloaked in grandeur and majesty for us citizens to applaud and worship.

Where an absolute right to performance of a particular duty is conferred by statute, the writ of mandamus is the last resort available to enforce said absolute right. Beginning in July 1997, the appellant filed seven separate requests to the respondents citing evidence that concluded the record on appeal had been deliberately deleted to eliminate prejudicial portions of the criminal proceedings had in open court, which the appellant deemed would reverse judgment in this case.

The Judicial Misconduct complaint was filed on July 9, 1997. August 19, 1997, Chief Judge Ralph K. Winter dismissed the Complaint stating, "The Judge's charge to the jury is recorded in more than 30 pages of transcript on the last day of trial." The last day of trial is not the issue of the complaint. The chief judge's statement is simply unresponsive to the issues concerned in the complaint. The issue raised in the complaint was only about the deletion of the six and one half page opening statement on the first day of trial September 11, 1996, not the last day of trial, September 13, 1996.

A Petition For Review was filed September 19, 1997 to the respondents chosen to independently review the petition. On October 22, 1997, each respondent dismissed the petition for review without any reason concerning any point that addressed incoherent, plain errors on the record.

While this was in the mill, Judge Nevas was ignoring his order to fix the transcript. He never responded to the 2nd circuit court's order for nine months until I questioned my appellate panel. After I raised the issue Judge Nevas responded claiming that there was nothing for him to fix. By this time the Supreme Court had denied my petition.

CHAPTER 11
MY ACE IN THE HOLE

Now I began working on my ace in the hole. When I first read my transcript I read the voir dire and learned that Kent Moller's wife Maggie worked for my brother in law's law firm, Cohen & Wolf in Bridgeport. Now some of the pieces began to fit. I understood why the McCarroll group was seated at my defense table to distract me. I understood why Dick Reeve refused to ask Nevas to have them move elsewhere so I could listen better. And I understood why Dick smiled at me and said, "You're guilty." when he heard there was a verdict. He knew Moller guaranteed one guilty verdict, so the verdict had to be guilty.

Putting Kent Moller on my jury had no benefit unless Kent was going to be approached to guarantee one conviction vote. It would have made a lot of sense for Judge Nevas to delete or alter the transcript to prevent me from reading that Kent's wife worked for Cohen & Wolf. For Kent Moller to decide to vote guilty before the trial began he would need to be told to do so. How can a juror be approached by the government? Try to imagine being on a federal, criminal case jury and having some government official approach you to tell you to vote guilty in a case before a trial began. What would you do? Would you discuss that with other jurors? Would you report it to the judge by telling a deputy marshal? Would you just go along with it possibly fearing that a serious problem might affect your life in the future?

It is a certainty that no one just went up to Kent Moller and said, "Vote guilty in this case." A conversation would begin to feel out Mr. Moller and his wife's job at Cohen & Wolf. An opening would be sought by the agent involved before any overt statement hit the nail on the head. The agent probably never identified himself until the proper time. It would all depend upon how the conversation was proceeding. The conversation was probably very short.

If Moller opposed the plan, who could he report the incident to? No one in law enforcement would question Judge Nevas. One thing for sure is that this type of incident is probably unique. Seating the McCarroll circus at my defense table is also unique, so its being unique doesn't make it impossible. The McCarroll incident in and of itself should reverse the judgment in this case.

To put my theory into context with how the proceedings were conducted by the court to determine whether any jurors in the pool might be prejudiced before the trial began due directly to a specific association with prosecution or defense participants I need to use the verbatim dialogue on record. My contention that Judge Nevas directed jury tampering could be farfetched baloney, but it isn't.

When AUSA Appleton addressed the jury pool for the purpose to learn if any of the potential jurors had conflicts of interest because:

1) some of these people might know a lawyer who worked for the United States Attorney's office,

2) the public defender's office,

3) law enforcement officials,

4) experienced being a victim of a crime,

5) had been convicted of a crime, or

6) other issues that might affect his verdict.

The court omitted asking about a certainty it knew was a conflict of interest. That conflict was the financial relationship juror #74 had with the brother-in-law of the defendant. Money went directly into the pocket of Maggie Moller and Kent Moller from Cohen & Wolf. The prosecutor isn't going to want a juror who is receiving a steady paycheck from the defendant's brother-in-law unless that juror has committed a verdict of guilty. How simple can this get?

APPLETON: My name is Robert Appleton and I'm an Assistant United States Attorney here in the District of Connecticut. And I represent the United States in this criminal case. There are a number of prosecutors in the office in which I work, I'm going to name them right now so if you know anybody or know me please indicate that to the judge after I'm through. And I also will read a list of witnesses and I'd ask you to do the same, indicate to the court if you know any of the people that I name.

(Whereupon at this time Mr. Appleton read off his list.)

APPLETON: Does anybody know any of those individuals? I see no response your honor.

THE COURT: Lady, want to stand and give us your name and number please.

JUROR: One-oh-three, I know a John Moore from New Jersey but I don't know what he does. I don't know if he's the same John Moore, he's a sports producer.

THE COURT: No.

APPLETON: Thank you your honor.

THE COURT: All right thank you, Mr. Reeve?

REEVE: Thank you your honor. My name is Mr. Reeve I represent Stephen Miller who is seated right here next to me at counsel table. I'm an attorney with the Federal Public Defenders Office, and what that means is I represent people who are charged with crimes in federal court who the court has determined cannot afford to retain private counsel. And it is in that capacity that I represent Mr. Miller in this case.

I have a lot less names than the U.S. Attorney's office. I work in New Haven with two other lawyers. Their names are Sarah Chambers and Michael Sheehan. We have an office in Hartford and the three lawyers there are Thomas Dennis, Gary Weinburger, and Terry Ward. If you know any of those individuals or obviously me or Mr. Miller, you should make that known to Judge Nevas.

I see no response your honor.

There are a number of witnesses that might be called as part of the defense in this case and I'd like to give you those names. If you think you know any of them please let the judge know.

William Bowman who resides in Madison, Richard Wisot who I believe resides in Orange, Richard Goodwin who lives in the New York City area, Edward Cugell who is an FBI Agent assigned to White Plains, New York, and Gary Mastronardi who is an attorney here in Bridgeport.

I see no response thank you your honor.

THE COURT: Anyone here or any member of your family or any close friend currently employed by a law enforcement agency or formerly employed by a law enforcement agency? When you stand give us your name and number and I'll recognize you and just tell us who it is. Yes.

JUROR: Juror 61, Carrie Lozyniak, I have a brother-in-law who lives next door, he's on the Westport Police Department and I also have a brother-in-law who is a Bronx detective in the 52nd precinct.

THE COURT: Okay Ms. Lozyniak, if you were selected to sit on this jury, would those relationships affect your judgment in anyway?

JUROR: No.

THE COURT: Could you be fair and objective?

JUROR: Yes.

THE COURT: All right.

JUROR: Sixty three, Richard Lynch. All my wife's cousins are New York City policeman. I don't think it would affect me.

THE COURT: Could you be fair and objective?

JUROR: Yes.

There were six more potential jurors in the 93 person jury pool who had close ties to law enforcement people. People who responded to the court:

THE COURT: With respect to the next question you can answer it as you stand in place but if anyone would feel uncomfortable answering the question publicly, just indicate that you would like to come forward and we'll take your answer at the bench. The question is has anyone here or any member of your family or close friend ever been involved in a criminal matter that concerned you or your family member where you or they have been charged with a crime or you've been a witness or a victim of a crime?

JUROR: Alexander Head, number 39. I got convicted of drunken driving twice.

THE COURT: Mr. Head would that experience with the justice system affect your judgment in anyway if you were selected to sit on this jury?

JUROR: No.

THE COURT: Could you be fair and objective?

JUROR: Yeah.

Four more people mentioned their contacts with the criminal justice system. All of them told the court that they could be fair. Then the court made the following statement:

THE COURT: Let me just indicate ladies and gentlemen, that as I said to you, Mr. Miller is charged with a crime. He's presumed to be innocent. It's the government's burden to prove his guilt beyond a reasonable doubt, and he's entitle to be judged by a jury of his people who would not prejudge the case, who will be fair and objective and listen to this case and listen to the evidence and make a determination of guilt or innocence based on the evidence they hear in the courtroom. Not based on any prejudices or biases or preconceived ideas. He's entitled to be judged by that kind of a jury, just as any of you who if you were charged with a crime would want the same kind of jury to judge you. So if there's any doubt or hesitation in your mind and you don't think you could be fair, say so.

Then 4 more people declared their issues and all of them stated that they would be fair if they became jurors. The court is being careful not to ask juror #74, Kent Moller, if he can be fair and objective based upon the evidence he will hear in the courtroom in lieu of his wife's paycheck from Cohen & Wolf.

The way I analyze these verbatim questions and answers into context with how the court questioned jurors to learn if any juror **except Kent Moller** had a conflict of interest with either side (prosecution or defense) is that Judge Nevas , Bob Appleton, and Dick Reeve all know that my brother-in-law, Irv Kern is a lawyer and partner with Cohen & Wolf in Bridgeport. They not only know that no attorney from Cohen & Wolf is representing my defense, they know that there is very bad blood between Irv and me.

It is fair to presume that when Kent Moller testified that his wife worked for Cohen & Wolf that statement had been heard by Nevas, Appleton, and possibly Reeve too. There is no question that Susan Catucci heard Moller's statement about his wife's employer because Ms. Catucci, the court reporter wrote the transcript. Moller's wife's paycheck directly links him to a financial interest in my case. It isn't certain that Moller was ever told that his wife worked for my brother-in-law, its ~~possible that he was never told. But what is certain is that McCarroll was~~ seated at my defense table, that he and his party continued to discuss his case (that never existed) at the direction of the court.

The McCarroll circus distracted me throughout the proceedings and Dick Reeve knows that because I kept complaining to him about that. For him to refuse to request that the court remove the distraction at our defense table is too great a factor not to recognize that the distraction was created for a purpose.

We know for a fact that the jury selected Kent Moller to be its jury foreman. Moller had to have influenced the other 11 jurors that he was their leader to be selected their foreman in a few minutes. Then only about 20 minutes was left for them to deliberate the evidence and arguments they heard. The jurors all voted with no concern for any evidence or testimony they all had heard and that they all voted guilty with absolutely no deliberation of any single point. Jurors have that right but that would completely exclude any deliberation by any of them. The letters written by Congressman Shays to Attorney General Thornburgh and Controller General Bowsher were irrelevant to the jurors in their deliberations because Judge Nevas prevented that evidence from being read to the jurors. Although Judge Nevas stated that the jury could read Shays' letters, they failed to take the time and effort to read that powerful evidence.

The jurors may have felt comfortable being in complete agreement with an instant unanimous vote but if they were asked to share their thoughts about what they thought was the defense for the intent of the defendant's actions they might not be so comfortable. I hesitate to ask this question by calling jurors now because I doubt I would get any answer much less an honest answer.

If the court expected such an easy case it would not have created the psychiatric ruse it forbade to be exposed to the jury during the trial.

When Dick smiled at me and said, "You're guilty" he could not know that the verdict would be guilty unless he knew that there was a guaranteed guilty vote. Putting this into context with the McCarroll incident and the care by Judge Nevas to learn of potential affiliations with jurors and their friends and experiences that might form prejudicial factors, that level of care fails to square with knowing that Moller's wife worked for Cohen & Wolf.

It didn't matter how well Dick performed in front of that jury because the best I could have done was to get a hung jury. I wasn't going to walk out of that courtroom on September 13th, 1996, because Kent Moller had been placed there to prevent that. But if Dick had made the same opening statement to the jury that he had made to Judge Nevas and when he stated his closing arguments with the fact that COMEX officials had rigged the copper market for the past ten years, there might have been a hung jury.

Now what I needed to learn was, did my brother in law know about being involved in the jury tampering by Judge Nevas. My brother in law, Irv Kern, was supposed to be a genius. He had gotten straight "A"'s in school. In 1986, I was ostracized by him, my sister Andrea and my Mother who orchestrated it. I had never had any bad relations with Andrea and Irv about anything. But now in 1997 it was 11 years had passed without having any communication with them. I had to factor that into the possibility that he might be a willing part of this Kent Moller, jury tampering.

I also considered the possibility that Nevas decided to go behind Irv's back. And I hoped that that's what happened. I hoped that Irv wouldn't want any part of a nefarious criminal act because if that got around, it might not be good for his reputation. So I placed a call to Irv and began to ask him some questions. We had a few long conversations. The first thing I asked him was, does Maggie Moller work for you? He said yes. Then I asked him if he knew that her husband Kent was on my jury? He replied, "No I didn't, but no harm no foul."

Hey, Kent Moller is my ticket out of prison. Kent Moller has a financial interest in my case. His wife draws a paycheck each week from Cohen & Wolf. I don't think its possible to lose this argument. Let's consider all the possibilities of what happened and what didn't happen. First of all there was no way for Nevas to know if I would happen to hear the name Cohen & Wolf mentioned by Kent Moller. Its very possible that I might have heard him say that his wife worked for Cohen & Wolf and then I would have removed him from the names in the pool.

There were 93 people in the pool. Both sides can remove a certain amount of them. Then the rest of the names are put into a drum and chosen at random.

After Kent Moller agreed to guarantee a guilty verdict his name could not be put into the drum with the other 92 potential jurors, minus the names that had been eliminated by both sides, let's guess 80 names were left because I can't remember now. There will be 67 names left in the drum after 13 jurors had been extracted by chance. Nevas, Appleton, and Reeve aren't going to take a chance on Moller unless his name is firmly in the hand of Judge Nevas before he starts drawing the other names.

Kent Moller's name never went into the drum. Moller had to have agreed to the deal before the voir dire hearing had begun. Judge Nevas had to know that Moller was on board before he decided to use the McCarroll circus to try to distract me from hearing Moller state that his wife worked for Cohen & Wolf. Reeve isn't going to sit there next to me while I keep asking him to ask Judge Nevas to remove the McCarroll circus if he isn't bound by the scheme to seat Moller on the jury.

Because Appleton and Reeve both know that Irv Kern is a partner with Cohen & Wolf, they both know he is my brother in law too. They both know Irv nor any lawyer with Cohen & Wolf is representing me, and they both know I tried hard to find another lawyer in Bridgeport, and they both know that there is bad blood between Kern and me. Both Appleton and Reeve had the same reason to remove Moller to prevent an appellate reversal when they both heard Moller state that his wife worked for Cohen & Wolf.

Suppose I was acquitted. Appleton could have filed an appeal to overturn the acquittal claiming I had a juror with a financial interest who became the jury foreman and influenced the jury to acquit because his wife's job was on the line. There would have been an investigation.

At the end of the voir dire process both Appleton and Reeve asked the jury pool if any of them know any of the lawyers in their offices. If they want to learn if any of the jury pool knows any of the lawyers in their offices, they should definitely want to learn if any of the jury pool knows any of the lawyers at Cohen & Wolf, the defendant's brother-in-law's law firm.

If Kern and I were on good terms, does Kent Moller and his wife Maggie want to be part of the reason that Kern's brother in law is in prison? Even if I was guilty it might cause hard feelings. In most families it would especially when the family was aware of the motives by their relative, their brother who had been ripped off with the blessing of senior government officials. In my family my brother lost money in his account because copper prices were rigged. Could I try harder to get my brother's money returned than I tried? Ask my brother Mike why he's angry at me and has refused to speak to me since 1989.

Now I'm trying to learn by talking to Irv and Andrea if Irv was in the plot, or maybe Appleton had someone approach Kent Moller and explain that it would be good for Maggie's career at Cohen & Wolf. If Kent helps put the disliked brother in law away, maybe Maggie gets a raise. Moller gives a wink and Irv Kern never finds out about how Appleton used him to win this case. If Maggie never gets her raise, so what? What can Moller do, ask Kern about his own involvement to convict his brother-in-law?

Irv tells me "You're guilty so there's no harm, no foul". I ask him how would he know I'm guilty? He tells me because he read the story in the paper. I told him, then all they needed to do was give the jury the paper and they wouldn't need to hear any testimony or see any evidence. I kept exploring because I needed to be absolutely positive before I began to use this for my appeal.

I was still hoping that the Supreme Court would force an investigation into the false transcript. A mandamus is a special writ which asks the higher authority to force a lower authority to do a job its mandated by law. At that time I still believed that Supreme Court Justices take their oath of office to protect and uphold the United States Constitution as a solemn oath. I trusted this and believed this as strongly as any person in our great country. If I didn't believe in the sanctity of the United States Supreme Court I would never have engaged in the court's process.

I filed my Petition to the Supreme Court and I decided to not write my brief yet to the Second Circuit. I decided to write my second JUDICIAL MISCONDUCT COMPLAINT concerning the jury tampering by Judge Nevas and I tried to use special care to benefit from my prior JUDICIAL MISCONDUCT COMPLAINT.

Finally to make absolutely sure that I knew that Irv was in the plot or not, I wrote a letter to Kent Moller. I wrote the letter in care of his wife, and I mailed the letter in an envelope directly to Irv at Cohen & Wolf. That way I know that the envelope would be opened by Irv's secretary.

In the letter I stated that I wanted Irv to read the letter first, and then pass it to Maggie to learn from her if she knows that Kent was the jury foreman on his brother in law's trial in federal court. When I called Irv he told me he wasn't going to pass the letter to Maggie. I told him that he didn't have to find out from Maggie if he knew from the beginning and she knew from the beginning that Kent was placed on my jury to guarantee at least one guilty verdict because he knew the answer without asking her the question.

Since Nevas had no qualms about deleting the opening statement by the prosecutor written in the transcript, I would think he would have also deleted the part when he's talking to McCarroll, his lawyer, and his prosecutor while they sat at my defense table too. A purposeful distraction during any part of a trial orchestrated by the trial judge is not only bizarre but grounds for a reversal in the judgment.

To be logical, it made no sense distorting any part of the transcript knowing that no appellate issue would be reversed.

What I have learned by my experience in the criminal justice system is that American federal justice is a hoax. The courts have certain cases, which they use to bamboozle the public by seeming to bend over backwards on very fine points. There is no way for any average citizen to see this avalanche of propaganda as a brain washing tool.

My second JUDICIAL MISCONDUCT COMPLAINT was dismissed and again the reason by Chief Judge Ralph K. Winter was something having nothing to do with the complaint. He stated that if I had a problem with my attorney that I needed to bring it to the proper authorities. Sure, I mentioned that Reeve refused to respond each time when I asked him to ask Nevas to move the McCarroll distraction. But Reeve was a witness to the act directed by Nevas. The complaint was against Nevas. Reeve had his role in it but Reeve didn't control the court. Reeve had no power to move McCarroll from the defense table. Normally Reeve would have made the request because he would know that I would have raised my hand to speak to the court.

I had no intentions of taking a chance to be returned to Butner for life because Judge Nevas decided that I had caused an outburst in his court. Also, why ruin a great appellate issue, presuming the appeal will be legitimate.

We saw during the trial that Reeve could be forceful. He knew that the McCarroll distraction was in play and he didn't want to go on the record by objecting to Nevas.

I was completely confident that the Second Circuit Court of Appeals would reverse the judgment and remand the case for a retrial. I also was confident that the government would not want to put me on trial again. I had a lot to learn. The 108 month sentence imposed by Judge Nevas was meaningless to me then because I was so confident that the judgment would be reversed.

My first pro se motion was to change venue. I had been put on trial in the wrong jurisdiction. This case was in the Eastern District of New York. I was not a fugitive from Connecticut and the government was wrong to have extradited me to Connecticut. When a motion goes to the Second Circuit it must be submitted with 5 copies and a form, the T1080 form. If this format is not precisely correct the motion will be returned by the clerk. I was told that I had failed to file the T1080 form with the motion. This was not true. Five forms had been stapled to all five copies of the motion. Five T1080 forms didn't all fly away by themselves.

I wrote to the Chief Judge to complain that the clerk tore off my T1080 forms, which had been stapled to each copy of the motion and then the clerk was falsely claiming that my submission was defective. I was told that the clerk was too busy to tear off the T1080 forms. How long would it take to tear off the forms? These people don't just lie, they use stupid lies. Finally it was agreed that I needed to send one copy of the T1080 form to the Clerk of the Court and he would make copies and attach them to the motion.

What purpose would the Clerk of the Court have to purposely make it appear that a motion was defective? Is this type of maneuver done under the scrutiny of the judges or would the clerk take it upon himself to pull this type of scheme? One thing became clear, the judges condoned what was done.

THE LIST OF SECOND CIRCUIT JUDGES

1) Jack B. Weinstein
   District Judge

   replaced by the second panel
   SDNY

2) Amalya Kearse
   2nd Circuit

   replaced by the second panel

3) John M. Walker, Jr.
   2nd Circuit

   On the panel
   Review Panel for #97-8522

4) Guido Calabresi
   2nd Circuit

   on the panel
   Review Panel for #98-8500

5) Ralph K. Winter
   Chief Judge

   on the panel
   2nd Circuit

6) Denis Jacobs
   2nd Circuit

   Review Panel for #97-8522

7) Peter Dorsey
   Chief Judge

   Review Panel for #97-8522
   District of Connecticut

8) David Larimer
   Chief Judge

   Review Panel for #97-8522
   NDNY

9) Joseph M. McLaughlin
   District Judge

   Review Panel for #98-8500
   WDNY

10) Thomas Griesa
    District Judge

    Review Panel for #98-8500
    SDNY

11) Thomas McAvoy
    District Judge

    Review Panel for #98-8500
    NDNY

SUPREME COURT JUSTICES

12)	Anthony M. Kennedy
13)	Sandra Day O'Connor
14)	Antonin Scalia
15)	Clarence Thomas
16)	William H. Rehnquist Chief Justice
17)	Stephen G. Breyer
18)	David H. Souter
19)	Ruth Bader Ginsburg
20)	John Paul Stevens

UNITED STATES SUPREME COURT

***

Do I expect too much for believing that our government should obey the Constitution, The Bill of Rights, and the laws it writes? Why would Judges Jack Weinstein and Amalya Kearse be replaced from my panel by Judges Guido Calabresi and Ralph K. Winter the Chief Circuit Judge? Am I paranoid for suspecting that Weinstein and Kearse couldn't stomach the deceit that they watched and when they were opposing it to their colleague John M. Walker, Jr. (President George W. Bush's uncle) Judge Walker reported the problem to Judge Winter who then replaced them?

When you think about this, their replacement on my panel removed the oversight from the appellate process. In other words, Judges Weinstein and Kearse caved into pressure instead of standing up for justice. The solemn oath to protect and uphold the constitution was transgressed. What other possible reason might there be for the two judge switch? Were judges Weinstein and Kearse incapable of being the judges for my special case that only Chief Judge Winter and Judge Calabresi had some unique judicial insight. Let's keep in mind Chief Judge Winter's wacko disposition for the opening statement issue that Winter claimed was a judge's charge issue.

When you hear Senators and Judges claim that America is a nation governed by laws and not by people, that is a statement of pure crap. They use laws when it suits their purpose and when laws don't suit their purpose they do whatever they want. After I had studied the BILL OF RIGHTS and various statutes along with precedent cases I began to notice that contradictions were the rule, not the exception. I also learned that federal prosecutors would site cases which were supposed to substantiate their argument but most of the time the cases they had chosen were contradictions or irrelevant to their argument.

Keep in mind that I filed two other cases for myself and I helped many inmates with their legal matters. In addition there are real street lawyers in prison. I got good advice from some of them and I argued issues and strategies with them also. There is plenty for anybody to learn about the law and about the system, but in the nine years I spent in prison I learned plenty. Much of what I learned will never be taught in any American law school. That is not to assume that law professors and legal text book writers don't know the truth about our system, it is to assume that the ocean of hypocrisy is deep and knowledgeable people who are part of the system want to be a part of the hypocrisy.

Susan Catucci, the court reporter had typed the transcript which made her a witness. Court reporters work for the federal judges. THE COURT REPORTER ACT is the legal guideline, which determines their obligations and regulations. They are accountable and if the COURT REPORTER ACT were followed, the court reporter is a check and balance for preventing the tampering of the official record.

In my case I was positive that Susan Catucci would not know to delete the OPENING STATEMENT by the government on her own. She had to be told to falsify the court record and Judge Nevas is the only suspect in this crime. Susan Catucci should have contacted the Chief Judge Peter Dorsey in the District of Connecticut to report Judge Nevas for intimidating her to break the law. She is obligated by the COURT REPORTER ACT to do that when the judge she works for decides to intimidate her to perform an illegal act.

I suspect that Susan Catucci was concerned with her future career as a court reporter and decided not to start trouble, which would most likely put herself out of business. By so doing she followed her orders and became a witness and conspirator of a criminal act. I wrote Susan Catucci a letter to put her on the spot and create evidence for the Chief Judge of the Second Circuit and the Chief Judge of Connecticut to consider. I explained to her that I understood her problem and that I didn't blame her. She had a gun to her head. In my eyes she committed no crime because reporting Judge Nevas to Judge Dorsey would have ended her career.

I made an accusation to her and about her; also stating that if she failed to respond to my accusation that she would be making a de facto agreement to my allegation. She chose not to reply to this letter and to its follow up allegation. I believe that an honest person would conclude that if she had been innocent, that her certification claiming that the transcript was complete and accurate, she would have felt free to deny my allegation.

I also filed a MOTION TO DEPOSE THE COURT REPORTER to my panel. They denied my motion. I had the wagons circled but I was firing blanks. Put another way, my ammo couldn't pierce the armor plating which Judicial Officers are given when they are appointed by the President and confirmed by the United States Senate.

When I filed my JUDICIAL MISCONDUCT COMPLAINT in July 1997, it was a masterpiece. The reason I can say this is because the disposition by Chief Judge Winter was a crazy lie that was laughable. If my complaint had a flaw, the law clerks working for the chief judge of the Second Circuit would have had an argument that made sense.

The law clerks chosen to work for federal judges are supposed to be the most brilliant lawyers with the highest law school grades in America. The law clerks who are chosen by the Chief Judge in New York City, the home of the Second Circuit are the most superior.

The complaint addressed two separate issues. The primary issue was that the trial record deleted the OPENING STATEMENT made by the government prior to the first witness. The secondary issue was added to show the Court that Judge Nevas was unethical to the core. This was evidenced by his decision to have his lie published by THE CONNECTICUT POST that claimed he committed me for a competency evaluation because I wanted to make an **opening statement** in April 1995, after my first jury had been chosen. This argument was substantiated by Reeve's motion time stamped after Judge Nevas had filed his own order to force me to be evaluated. The lie published by THE CONNECTICUT POST was never addressed by Judge Winter.

Finally my panel ordered Judge Nevas to fix the transcript. They stated in their order, a motion having been filed by appellant pro se 'for investigation to verify [a] false transcript.' It is ordered that the motion be and hereby is construed as a motion to modify or correct the record pursuant to Federal Rules of Appellate Procedure 10(e), and transferred to the district court for consideration in the first instance. Any further proceedings in this case appeal are stayed pending resolution of the Rule 10(e) motion in the district court. Within 30 days of entry of a district court decision on the Rule 10(e) motion, either party may move to vacate the stay and a new scheduling order will be issued."

Nothing happened. Judge Nevas ignored this order to correct the record. My appeal is stayed until the district court decision. When 9 months went by, I got a feeling that Judge Nevas decided to ignore the order to correct the record indefinitely, thereby defying the order by the Second Circuit. You might imagine that the higher court would not be pleased when the lower court is in contempt of its orders. In real life

I have seen this approach many times by the lower court and the higher court just disregards what appears to me to be contempt. The Judicial Branch of government is a charade. The public is not in any position to see these things.

I have seen many inmates in the system win their appeal for re-sentencing. When they return from the District Court expecting to get good news, the District Court often ignores the order from the Circuit Court sending them back to prison to file another appeal.

There are a huge number of appellate cases that have been published, there are also a huge number of cases that are not published. It is impossible to know what the unpublished cases are about unless you have filed one of them. I have an unpublished appeal from my first case in 1992, and I know why the Circuit Court doesn't want it published. In this case my charges were dismissed even though my appeal was denied. On September 10, 1992, I walked out of prison a free man. This story is enmeshed with my present extortion case because it focused upon the COMEX copper fraud but it will need to wait until after this book is published to be able to gauge the interest and reaction to this story.

When I began to research cases that had appealed deleted portions of the transcript, I located Selva v. United States. In Selva the court reporter became ill and was unable to perform. The court decided to use a recording device. The recording device broke down and a large part of the trial was omitted from the record. Selva was reversed by the Supreme Court because it decided that if there had been any prejudicial factors at trial, counsel failed to have the opportunity to find and use prejudice on appeal. No prejudice was alleged by the appellant, but his case was reversed.

Because I also believed that the rulings on all my pleadings were crazy lies I would be stupid to rely upon my brief to get fair treatment. After the appellant files his brief, his appeal ends. An appellant can't keep filing appeals after it is denied.

My last motion to the Second Circuit was to lift the stay on the grounds that the district court had failed to comply with the order from the Second Circuit. Their response was that Judge Nevas did comply with their order.

Because I never got a copy of Judge Nevas's response I asked to see it. When I received the response it was time stamped after my motion had been filed. Judge Nevas claimed that nothing was wrong and therefore he had nothing to fix. He never served his answer to me because he never filed it until after I raised the issue that he ignored the Court's order.

Judges don't care about the lies they put on the record because nothing can be done about it. Our American Judicial Branch stinks to high heaven. America got a taste of this alarming situation when the Supreme Court decided to select George W. Bush to be President. The Democrat Party could have tried to have hearings in the Senate and the House Judicial Committees. These Committees have oversight powers that can recommend impeachment. The reader can speculate as to why the Democrats dropped this issue.

I will speculate that it is because our elected officials want voters to believe our government is honest. These officials draw the line when an honest decision is going to destroy this image. I used to be curious as to why the Kennedys' failed to defy the Warren Commission cover-up of the greatest conspiracy of all time, the assassination of JFK. It finally dawned on me that its more important to them to prevent the unvarnished truth because the Kennedys' are prominent government officials.

Only complete fools who spent time studying the JFK assassination believe that Lee Harvey Oswald was the lone assassin who fired the magic bullet. I studied this case by reading every book ever published that I could find on this story. I did this to try to learn how far our government will go to cover-up extremely serious matters. After I had given serious consideration to the conventional belief that the Mafia (Carlos Marcello, Santo Traficante, and Sam Giancana) masterminded the JFK assassination I came to the conclusion that the mob had no way to influence the pathologists who performed the autopsy, create the Warren Commission, etc. I then concluded that Kennedy was assassinated by LBJ and his Texas friends who intended and did profiteer by the Viet Nam war. LBJ gained by his succession to the Presidency and created the Warren Commission to officially deceive the country with the help of FBI Director J. Edgar Hoover.

Americans can't learn by history unless history is accurate. President George W. Bush started his war against Iraq so his big contributors can profiteer again. Our soldiers are being sent to be maimed and die for the money that is being contributed to President Bush by Haliburton, Enron, Bechtel, and the other companies who are in Iraq to profiteer from the American Treasury. The media goes on and on debating the issues of why President Bush claims he started the Iraq war. American voters didn't learn by the bad experience of Viet Nam and won't learn from the Iraq war either.

You can say that I am vitriolic. I'm interested in the truth. I didn't get due process. I got nothing close to a defendant's rights under the BILL OF RIGHTS. My criminal conviction can not stand in the light of day but there is nothing I can do except to write this book and hope that I can expose the American government to our citizens who read

my story. I wish voters would open their minds to learn the truth, but I fear that the constant propaganda being used to deceive voters will prevent us from being objective and searching for the truth for our own interest.

I listen to the voters who call in on the C-span shows to voice their opinions. I hear many people who really know the score, but those voters are a very small minority of total voters. The only elected officials who I like in America is the Independent Congressman from Vermont, Bernie Sanders. Bernie tries to educate people on C-span but his voice is drowned out by the media. The other one is Congressman Dennis Kucinich, who was such a fantastic choice for President, but the media convinced voters that Dennis was unelectable.

The best candidate was deemed to be unelectable. John Kerry who was running very low in the polls far behind Howard Dean became the darling of the media, and Kerry emerged the nominee. A small group of people called into C-Span to make this accurate claim. I wasn't the only person able to recognize this obvious manipulation.

There are many people these days in 2004 who are very disgusted with being screwed by the American economic system being run for the benefit of the billionaires by their elected officials. We could correct this problem by electing a third party, but it will not happen because American voters will vote against their own self-interest. Is that irrational?

I filed my JUDICIAL MISCONDUCT COMPLAINT to expose the seating of Kent Moller by Judge Nevas. I believed I had learned the ropes before I wrote this complaint. I still expected justice. Another dumb bet by me. Chief Judge Winter dismissed this complaint by blaming my attorney for the problem. He suggested I take the matter to the jurisdiction which would deal with counsel, Dick Reeve.

When I filed my petition to the Review Panel, I made it plain that it was Judge Nevas who seated the commotion at my defense table. I complained that Dick refused to respond to Judge Nevas each time I asked him to request that the distraction be moved. Dick refused because he knew that Judge Nevas did not want to hear Dick try to eliminate the distraction at the defense table. While Dick was a part of the plot to seat Moller, Dick did not run the courtroom.

Before I wrote the misconduct complaint I wrote a letter to Dick asking him to verify that I had asked him more than several times to request JudgeNevas to remove the McCarroll distraction. I used the same technique on Dick that I had used on Susan Catucci. I wrote that if he failed to respond that he effectively agreed with my point. Dick failed to acknowledge my letter. He either had to lie on paper, or lie by omission.

[246] Stephen A. Miller

CHAPTER 12
FAMILY, FRIENDS, and ENEMIES

This has been a very strange story to be sure. I have lived a fairly abnormal life because I was born a curious person. I can remember funny things I did as a young kid. Most of the things I have done were pretty harmless and some of them resulted with benefits for me and others. I have always had a good sense of humor and enjoyed some good times with my friends.

While I was in prison for a total of 9 years and 2 months I became friendly with some of the administration. In general the prison system has two distinctly separate groups of people, the prisoners who were very boring, untrustworthy, and obnoxious, and the correction officers and staff who were normal working people. There were exceptions in both groups as there always tends to be exceptions. A few incidents serve to frame the positive interaction I had during these years.

But first to get an idea about the criminal mind, when I met Mario Gallo in Wyatt Detention Center in 1996, he was bragging that the mob guys in the Brooklyn, Metropolitan Detention Center were getting shipments of brand name alcohol and the finest deli and other delicious food. They were paying some of the hacks to bring it to them. Shortly after I learned this, a story got published that the hacks got busted. Obviously the bragging got back to more senior officials who had to enforce the contraband rules.

The staff of any prison is not there to fraternize with inmates but they are there to work with them. I developed a friendly relationship with the Captain at FCI McKean, Robert Reich. While I was typing this manuscript on an old typewriter in my room, I was using white out to correct mistakes. I had obtained a correction paper type of white out from the prison librarian a Ms. Fantaskey. When I ran out and tried to get some more, she had given out her supply. I asked her for liquid white out, but she told me that liquid white out was contraband.

In the law library there was liquid white out that was not contraband.

At all FCI's there are staff people at lunch who are there to discuss issues with inmates. After lunch one day I approached Captain Reich, to ask him why liquid white out was contraband in the units but not in the law library. The Captain was standing next to Associate Warden Belfonti, and Lieutenant Morales.

Captain Reich said, "Miller, how long have you been in prison?" I replied, "About 7 years." He said, "And you don't know?" I said, "I don't have a clue."

Then the AW (Associate Warden) began telling me that inmates can alter documents with white out and that there is a chemical in the liquid white out that can cut through metal. I said, "You mean cut through the bars?"

I found this to be comical and in my sarcastic manner I began telling them that I was in enough trouble as it is and because the files are in computers now, that altering a document was not likely to allow any inmate to escape. Also I told them that if inmates are able to alter documents in their cells with liquid white out, they can either do it in the law library, or take the bottle of white out from the law library to their cells. I began to really laugh at the notion that a chemical in the liquid white out can cut through the bars of a cell. The Lieutenant said, "Miller, do you see that door?" I said, "Sure." He said, " Hit it."

The next day when I passed the Captain, I said, "You know I was just kidding." He laughed.

That night I was telling this story to the Unit CO because I knew he would report it back to the Lieutenants and the Captain. My purpose was to make a joke out of it and at the same time use a little pressure to get some white out for my writing. The Unit CO's are all trained to convey messages concerning the security of the prison back to the senior staff. A day later, I got called down to the library and Ms. Fantaskey handed me a sheet of the paper white out. I am positive that she only did that because Captain Reich told her to try to get Miller some white out.

Captain Reich gave me a break because he appreciated my friendly and respectful manner I had with him. I didn't go around bragging to any inmates that I got the paper white out. I didn't get the white-out because I ratted on people.

In FCI Butner I got to know the Warden, Warden Harley Lappin fairly well. Warden Lappin was later transferred to USP Terre Haute, that is where death row is located. When McVeigh was executed it was Warden Lappin who was the B.O.P., spokesperson before the CNN cameras. Harley Lappin is now the Director of the B.O.P. I found Warden Lappin to be a pleasant, fairly young gentleman. He seemed fairly reasonable although he tried to back his staff even when he was certain they had over stepped their bounds. I always suspected that there would be a limit that would be tolerated and my suspicions proved correct.

After a really crazy incident at Butner, I was put into the hole. Warden Lappin made the rounds of the hole every day. Most wardens only come to the hole once a week or once a month. When Warden Lappin came to the hole, I asked him if he knew why I was there. When he said, "No" I began to explain the incident. He had me released in about two hours, which is faster than light speed in prison.

I had mentioned to the Warden's lawyer, Ms. Fuzzymore, that it was a very bad idea to have had the "crazy guy" from the super max in Marion, IL., put into FCI Butner because they anticipated he would do something crazy because that would then justify the increased security that had been installed. Butner was going from being like a college campus (pure club fed) to being a real prison. No one wanted to be transferred to a low security joint from the Butner medium before they were changing it. The food was excellent, cells were unlocked all the time because there were no toilets in the cells, and it was a pleasant place generally.

They started putting up fences and razor wire to make it look like a prison. They took out the wooden borders of all the gardens because the wood could be used as a battering ram or weapon. The biggest change came in 1996 when civilian clothes had to be shipped home. Prisoners all had to be dressed in BOP issued clothes.

The "crazy guy" held a nurse hostage with a shank for a short time before he was restrained and returned back to Marion, the super max. No sane person is going to mess up his being held at Butner medium when he knows he's going back to a super max for the rest of his miserable life.

A few days before he took the nurse hostage, he had come to my cell to start a conversation. He was housed in my unit. He began to tell me that he knew John Gotti at Marion and bragged that Gotti liked him. Being associated with Gotti in prison was like claiming you knew the President or some very powerful person in the real world. The "crazy guy" left my cell on a note that he wanted me to feel we could be friendly. He had bragged about murdering people that had gotten him the distinction of being housed in the super max.

The B.O.P. had to know that this guy was so crazy that it was a guarantee that he would pull something. In reality, that nurse stood a good chance of being murdered while he held her hostage, and the B.O.P. knew that. My comment to Ms. Fuzzymore was meant for her and Warden Lappin's consideration only. Instead Ms. Fuzzymore decided to tell the lieutenants.

About half an hour later I was summoned to the lieutenants' office and questioned about my remarks to inmates. I denied ever making any remarks to inmates. The lieutenant was trying to make it appear that I was inciting trouble among the inmates. I was then told to wait outside. Captain Zuercher finally entered the lieutenants office and I was summoned back. Captain Jerome Zuercher decided to put me into the hole and suggested that I was a potential conspirator with the "crazy guy". The Captain knew I had nothing to do with the "crazy guy" so he finally told me to reflect upon my criticism. B.O.P. Warden Lappin saw it differently because he knew me fairly well.

I could write an entire book full of interesting incidents that I encountered personally while I was in prison, but my point is that I am a friendly person albeit in an abrasive, sarcastic manner sometimes. I have had a wide variety of friendships or acquaintances because I am versatile and curious to understand people from different walks of life. I have had some great memories throughout the years but there have been some very bad memories too.

I had a big problem in my home when I was a child. It's hard to say bad things about your own mother because people don't like to hear bad memories about mothers. We all expect our judges and our mothers to be nice people, and most mothers I know are very nice people. My mother, Charlotte, was different than all my friends' mothers who were very nice. Its also hard to make sense out of the part of this story which involved the jury selection of Kent Moller unless there is information which describes the associations I had with my sister Andrea and her husband Irv, the lawyer. These associations all tie together with my nasty, hostile relationship I had with my mother throughout my life.

It will be difficult for many readers to believe my allegation that my own brother in law would be involved in jury tampering unless I explain the important background information, which puts our relationship into perspective. I wanted to believe that Irv knew nothing about Kent Moller being placed by Judge Nevas on my jury. It was a real slap in the face to learn that your own brother in law would agree to be involved in the unmitigated injustice of fixing a criminal conviction.

My legal strategy was to try to get Cohen & Wolf on my side. I hoped that the principles at Cohen & Wolf might recognize that their own ethics would destroy their reputation with the legal community. Attorneys who practiced in the Nevas court against Cohen & Wolf were at a severe disadvantage because Judge Nevas owed Irv Kern a favor. If

Judge Nevas jeopardized the reputation of Cohen & Wolf without them knowing and agreeing to become involved in my case, Cohen & Wolf might see it in their own interest to suggest to Judge Nevas that it would prefer being removed. The only way to remove Cohen & Wolf from this case would be for Judge Nevas to reverse his judgment against me.

Irv Kern and my sister Andrea had been aloof since 1986, with me, a ten-year span of time prior to my trial. There had been no argument, no financial relationship gone bad, or anything in the open to cause this condition. Prior to 1986, we were never close friends but we had a friendly relationship. When I spoke to Irv in 1997, 11 solid years had elapsed with not a word. I think it would be fair to assume that Irv Kern and my sister Andrea had some reason in their minds for me to suspect that they didn't like me.

When I brought this subject into our conversation Irv denied that there was any reason to justify their desire to leave me out of their ~~family gatherings. He denied that he had any reason. I told him directly~~ that his denial was ludicrous. Its one thing to tell a lie and another thing to tell a ludicrous lie. When your own brother and brother in law is told not to visit, not to come for Thanksgiving dinner every year, you must have some reason in your mind.

If my reason for my own aloof behavior toward my sister is my own character flaw, then I too would not state that reason either. I have never been close to my sister Andrea. She was a nice kid and a nice person too. I was five years older than she. When I was the baby sitter, she would tell on me and get me into trouble claiming that I mistreated her. I hardly remember any specific incidents but I remember there were many of them.

One incident that I remember was when I was supposed to drive Andrea to my Uncle Mike's for a medical check up. I brought along a girl, Nancy Wolf, who I wanted to date. When Andrea told my parents that I had this girl with us, my parents were really angry. They believed that I intended to ignore Andrea. The argument became so horrific that I returned to Staten Island being very upset. I had been living with my Grandmother on State Island for about eight months because I had such a constantly miserable relationship with my mother.

I had a terrible relationship with my mother but in my family people liked to make believe problems didn't exist. My mother and I were oil and water. Nothing ever changed that because it just existed. My mother was extremely controlling, and I am impossible to control. My mother was never affectionate and I never loved her. I loved my father and I loved my grandmother so I experienced love for family members. I also had close relations with uncles, aunts, and cousins during my first

30 years of life. Our family had done the urban to suburban American move and wound up in various places.

While I spoke to Irv in 1997, from prison I also told Irv that I wanted him to ask my sister to give me permission to call her at home. Irv told me that Andrea was upset with me because I had bad feelings about our mother. But in lieu of that Andrea agreed to have me call her. I then engaged Andrea in about five long conversations. I made it clear to Andrea that my intention was to learn if Irv had been involved with the seating of Kent Moller on my jury.

We talked a lot about our family going way back into our childhood. I had had a much closer relationship with our relatives than Andrea did. As a child, Andrea had no close relationships with our cousins, aunts, uncles, and grand parents, but I did. My dad was popular with everyone in our family and people all said that I looked like him. I had fun with all my relatives who were characters in their own right.

When I began to inform Andrea that Judge Nevas had tried to prevent me from going to trial by claiming that I was incompetent, Andrea refused to question this tactic by Nevas. I found this to be amazing. Andrea had lived with me and knew me as a well educated, hard working, well informed person. I engaged people in conversation with a sense of humor. For my sister to tell me that she could believe that Nevas was legitimate when he used the incompetence tactic that was hard evidence. I asked her if she knew what the legal criteria was to establish competence, and she knew exactly.

As our conversations continued Andrea and Irv were convincing me that they would lie about anything and that any punishment inflicted by the government to hurt me was fine with both of them.

I began to believe that my mother still had power from her grave to cause me trouble. I have asked the few relatives who would still talk to me if they knew what had been created to make them ostracize me, but none of them would identify their purpose. My closest aunt was my Father's sister, Lil Farr. My mother's sister, Sally, we all called her Auntie, was the only relative that stuck with me from the beginning of the case. Auntie told me that Lil wanted to speak to me but she thought I didn't want to speak to her. I then told Auntie that I'd be happy to speak to Lil. I called Lil and we had some good laughs. I was surprised that at the age of 90 Lil was very sharp and remembered everything well.

I had developed many friendships as I grew up in the 1950's. I was born on October 1, 1942, in Staten Island, N.Y. where my dad's family lived. World War II was in full bloom and my father served in the Merchant Marine during the war. My grandparents owned a little tavern on Bay Street where they had made a comfortable living in Staten Island serving the Irish neighborhood of longshoremen and seafaring men a good time. My grandparents were both characters so it wasn't just booze which attracted their business. My grandfather, Nate was a gambler and their bar always had action. Late at night when the place closed, there was often a card game running well into the morning.

There were many comical stories about my grandmother who would raid the games and take my grandfather home. They would post a look out (who usually passed out drunk) to watch for my grandmother's raids. Most gambling joints were concerned for the cops, not the owner's wife. When Nana busted in, she would flip the table over. The cards and money would scatter and she'd haul Nate back home. It was all good natured fun when we looked back, the stories were hilarious.

My dad was a character and a good natured guy who was loved by everybody. Well not quite everybody. My mother relentlessly taunted and badgered my dad. There was no love shown there at any time.

While I lived in Staten Island with Nana in 1962, she told me a story I'll never forget. Nana and Nate dropped by my parents home in New Dorp, Staten Island to visit. Nana said she walked into their home and my Dad was sitting there alone. He told Nana and Grandpa that Charlotte had left with me. Nana told Dad, "Let her go Dave." That's a quote that sticks in my mind. "Let her go Dave."

That was a great piece of advice. It's a terrible shame that Dad didn't listen to his mother.

Charlotte, moved to Manhattan into the neighborhood called Washington Heights up near the George Washington Bridge. She shared an apartment with her sister Sally who we called Auntie, and my maternal grandmother Anna. Shortly after my father returned from the war my family moved to Stratford, CT. in 1947, where I grew up and went to school.

Our plan to move to Stratford began when Charlotte's brother Bert, who had returned from the Army, and dad decided to buy an old laundry in Bridgeport. We moved into a new housing development with very nice neighbors and kids to play with. From outward appearances everything seemed wonderful. But inside my home there was constant hostility, and aggression. It was impossible for my father to please my mother. Charlotte had a number of traits, which made my life miserable at home. She was constantly verbally abusive to my dad and to me, which also led to physical abuse. She didn't want to be pleased, she wanted oppressive domination. My parents would make plans to join another couple for a social event such as a New Years Eve celebration, then always at the last moment Charlotte would complain about washing dishes, or cleaning the house, and that they couldn't go out because she needed to do a chore. It was a constant pattern, which turned a potential good time into a fight.

The arguments were relentless. She used anything for an excuse to complain. To her, my father was useless and never made enough money. In a way she had a point because my father was a poor business man and loved to play. He was either playing cards for small stakes, playing golf, or playing paddle ball at the Bridgeport YMCA. He just wasn't a businessman. He should have stayed in the Merchant Marine and eventually wound up going back to sea in 1968. He finally retired at the age of 70 with a small union pension and his social security. The MEBA, (Marine Engineers Beneficial Association) had a rule, that after 65, nothing was vested into the member's pension. So 23 years that went by from WWII in 1945, until Dad went back to sea at 53 years of age reduced his pension considerably.

For years as a child I would be attacked at the Sunday dinner table every week. Charlotte would cook a roast, rare. When I ate rare beef, I would feel ill and therefore I refused to eat the meat. Years later I learned that I was allergic to rare meat. Sometimes I chose to hide the meat, excuse myself to go to the bathroom and then flush it down the toilet. The next step was that both dad and Charlotte would demand that I go to my room because I refused to eat the meat. I had 2 choices. Either I had to pass my father, which always meant a very hard whack. My father was incredibly powerful. His hit was more painful than any pain I ever experienced in my life. Or I could go the other way, brushing Charlotte out of my way to run out the back door. Then my Sunday afternoon was spent finding one of my friends in the neighborhood to kill the day until it was safe to return. Neither Andrea nor Mike, my brother, ever was hit and I can't remember them ever being accused of anything wrong and were never disciplined.

Maybe Dad was happy to have Charlotte going after me because that kept her off him. She would get him to spank me for something and then when it got too rough, she would come to my rescue. But in my mind, she started it, so I blamed her more than I blamed him. My dad let Charlotte lead him around by the nose.

I never counted these physical attacks but if they were once a week for five years, that's 260. Once at the age of 16 or 17, I came into the house at about 3:00 AM and Dad threw a punch at me that knocked out my front tooth. I don't blame him for being angry because I told him I was just going to the diner for a while getting permission to use his car. Instead, my friends and I decided to go to Manhattan to the Peppermint Lounge. Dad always got up to go to the bathroom and since the car wasn't back, he was rightfully worried.

I grew up in the greatest rock 'n roll era of all times and I loved the girls, the dancing, and the music. Hitting the clubs meant drinking alcohol to loosen up, driving drunk, and a few bar room brawls too.

But I always stayed out of trouble. None of my crowd ever considered committing criminal acts, it was just a lot of fun.

I was 5 years older than Andrea and 7 years older than Michael, so I didn't play with them. We grew up with a distant relationship. As I made friends with kids my own age, I spent as little time as possible at home. I grew up with my friends' families, especially my friend John DelVecchio. I loved being around John's family because they were fun to be with. I met John in our mechanical drawing class in junior high school. John had moved from Bridgeport's east side to Stratford and I found him to be fascinating from a different world. The east side of Bridgeport was an old Italian neighborhood and everybody there knew Johnny DelVecchio. John's mom Nancy and dad, Mario, were wonderful people and wonderful parents who encouraged John's friends to hang around their home, the complete opposite of my home. As the years went along I grew closer and closer to the DelVecchio family. I even moved into their home for a while when things got very bad at my home, and I wish I could have stayed as a foster child.

There was a mafia influence on the east side, which intrigued me. Being a close friend of John DelVecchio gave me a close view of this mafia influence. John had no criminal ties to mob guys but he was very well received by all of them.

I had a completely different set of friends too. These friends were good students and good athletes. In that respect I was very well rounded because I got along very well with a very diverse set of friends.

Charlotte found fault with every friend I had and most of my friends were very nice kids who wound up getting well educated and becoming successful. But to her nobody was any good. She wanted to isolate me to keep me from all these kids she decided were no good. She wanted complete control of Dad, Andrea, Michael, and me. I am fairly difficult to control as you may have noticed by now. They knuckled under and I didn't.

Most of my time was indulged in playing sports. Football in the fall after school, ice-skating, and basketball in the winter, and baseball and then golf in the summer. Stratford had 4 little league baseball teams and I was able to make the Raybestos team. The kids would ride their bikes to the game but Charlotte wanted to drive me to the game. Of course I wanted to ride my bike with the rest of the kids but Charlotte would insist upon driving me. I had to do what Charlotte ordered so I would wait for her ride. But she would always be late. Finally I would jump on my bike and start for the field. Before I got to the end of the block Charlotte would drive up and tell me to get into the car. I had to return my bike to the house and get into the car, which would make me very unhappy before every game. She would drive me to the field and leave. She never stayed to watch a game or socialize with other parents who came to watch their kids play baseball.

She thrived on taking the fun out of everything in life. These stories are endless. She was an antisocial person who was never normal, but she knew how to keep up appearances for outsiders. In fact, she could be sickeningly sweet to certain people who then thought the world of her. It's possible to assume that Mom is trying to help her son by driving him to the ball park for the game and her son doesn't appreciate Mom's help. She may have even believed that she was being helpful when she offered to drive me. But she forced me to be late and that made me angry. I didn't want special treatment that my friends and team mates didn't get, I wanted to be with my friends.

Andrea was her favorite because she would do everything Charlotte expected from her. One of those expectations was to marry Irv Kern the lawyer. Irv was a nice guy who was also a very good student. He became the apple of Charlotte's eye.

My life at home became so bad for me that finally I moved to live in Staten Island with my grandmother the year I left the University of Bridgeport at the end of the fall semester in 1961. It was my Uncle Mike who had the idea for me to move. I looked up to Uncle Mike because he was very successful and he was the toughest guy I've ever met. I would go to him for advice but before he gave me advice he would grill me. Uncle Mike was training me to think clearly and to examine all sides of a situation under a pressure packed grilling. But Uncle Mike had a great sense of humor too, as did all of my dad's side of the family.

I remember once when Uncle Mike came into Nana's bar. He was a doctor, so one of the customers tried to ask him for some medical advice. Mike told him, "You look well preserved in my mother's alcohol."

Charlotte had problems, which were kept secret by our family. Most of my relatives were financially successful. Charlotte borrowed money from each of them, but never paid back a dime to any of them. In my case she never bothered to ask to borrow my money, she just took it. From the time I was 11 years old I always worked to earn and save money. I caddied and mowed lawns in summer and I shoveled snow in winter. As I accumulated $50 (which could be a week's wage in the 1950's) I would give it to Charlotte to bank for me. As it turned out over the years, Charlotte stole this money. For years she kept telling me that the money was in a bank account. When I asked to see the bank book, she answered that the bank book was in a lock box in a different bank. One day, years later when we drove past the other bank, I asked her to stop to get the bank book so I could see it. There was no bank book, my money had been stolen. It was a secret loss. I didn't think to tell relatives or anybody else about it. When I learned that my mother was a thief and a liar it was too embarrassing for me to tell other people.

My relatives were seldom around Charlotte and when they were it was for short visits. I on the other hand lived with her. I couldn't dismiss her tyrannical behavior. I recognized that she took advantage of our relatives mostly because she knew she would get away with it. I resented her relentless finding fault with everyone because I could see her faults. Instead of loving my own mother I disliked her.

I have a natural tendency to fight back. As you can see that tendency resulted in a long prison term. I became disrespectful of my mother in front of my sister Andrea and this bothered Andrea much more than I ever imagined. Andrea is a natural hypocrite and she is not interested in the truth especially about her own mother. Furthermore, Charlotte was very nice to Andrea and she adored Irv Kern.

I suspect this was a very influential factor, which prompted Irv to decide to get involved with Judge Nevas in the rigging of my jury. Judge Nevas would have dismissed my case if his only option was a legitimate trial. He proved that on April 13, 1995.

Until Judge Nevas decided to rig my jury the only two other options were to dismiss the case, or commit me as dangerous. I can only thank God that Nevas decided to rig my jury. In the end Judge Nevas chose to create this bizarre, unconstitutional case rather than dismiss the case.

As I was growing up, my best friend was my cousin Richard Farr. His mother Lil was Dad's oldest sister and she was a lot of fun too. Richard was the funniest, most comical kid I ever knew. He was also very daring and a great prankster. When we visited each other funny things would always happen. At night we would talk for hours before we went to sleep. One night Richard told me that he had shit in his pajamas. It was very quiet on Ocean Terrace on Staten Island while the light of the moon shown into the bedroom. He got out of bed and he had a bulge in his pajamas visible by the moon-light. Then he said he was going to throw it at me. He threw the socks against the wall, which made me start to vomit on the floor. Aunt Lil came in to see what was going on, with me vomiting and Richard laughing. He had thrown socks at the wall and it was so quiet I had heard them softly hit making me imagine shit hitting the wall.

One time the Farrs came to our house in Stratford for a visit. I decided I would stow away and go back to Staten Island with them. I hid in the back seat of Lil's car and she drove away not knowing I had stowed away. Before we got to the end of the block Richard, my cousin Susan, and I began laughing. Aunt Lil went along with it and we drove to Westchester before she decided to call to let my parents know I was going for a visit to Staten Island. Charlotte got angry and told Lil to leave me there and she would pick me up. Lil told her she wasn't going to leave me there and we continued to their home. Finally Charlotte became really nasty to Aunt Lil and Lil drove me back to the Staten Island ferry for my late trip back to Stratford.

Richard graduated from the Wharton School of Finance and then earned a law degree. He made a career of the Air Force and retired a full Colonel and he's still comical. After I got arrested in 1994, Richard refused to speak to me too. And he won't give me any reason either. I spoke to Aunt Lil and to Susan. When I brought up wanting to speak with Richard they told me that he is too busy. My favorite cousin has been too busy to talk to me for ten years, since I got arrested in 1994. That is a great disappointment. I miss being friends with Richard because we always had great fun, laughs, and fascinating conversations.

While I was in the Navy, my uncle Louie died and left me $1,000 in his estate. Charlotte forged that check too. None of my relatives nor I were about to recoup our money from Charlotte and nobody ever addressed her behavior. We were all too ashamed.

The only person who ever got their money returned from Charlotte was Auntie. Auntie had a lien on our house at 22 Lobdell Drive so she forced a foreclosure to get her money. We then moved up to 834 Freeman Avenue in Stratford and I gave dad enough money to pay the movers. For some reason my parents were always broke. I never understood why they were always broke. Dad wanted people to believe that he had money so he always treated people to dinners and drinks. It seemed like he spent money frivolously. His gambling was for very small bets on golf matches and gin rummy games. Dad enjoyed eating at very good restaurants and he always picked up the tab.

Charlotte passed her real estate exam and began to work for Scott Realty in Stratford, She sold one piece of property and somehow got hold of the deposit. She ripped off the guy's deposit but it was hushed up. She would have gotten prosecuted for this one but I think the deposit got returned and that ended Charlotte's real estate career. Charlotte was simply a thief and a pathological liar on top of being a relentless, nasty nag.

The benefit to me of all this unpleasantness was that I moved to my grandmother's whom we all called Nana. Nana was a wonderful person who was not formally educated but who was very intelligent. She also had a terrific sense of humor and was fun for me to be around. From 1962 when I moved to Nana's until she died in 1978, I became very close to Nana and acquired some of her great qualities. Nana was very observant and very direct but I never heard her say anything bad about anyone including Charlotte.

In September 1962 I joined the Navy and served a 4-year enlistment.

I returned to live in Staten Island in 1966 with Nana. I went back to college at Wagner and got my first job working for E.F. Hutton & Co. The Navy had been a good experience because now I knew it was time for me to work hard to accomplish what I wanted in life. I intended to make my mark on Wall Street and I had a great beginning with Hutton. Besides learning the business from the best Wall Street minds on the street, I made good friendships with the top people at Hutton. In 1968, I became a registered broker and worked hard to build my business. At the end of '68 I got the luckiest brake of my life. I met a beautiful woman who I fell in love with immediately.

Nancy Hale had lived one flight up in my building on East 84th Street. I had never laid eyes on her until one morning we both came out of our apartments to go to work at the same time. I caught a glimpse of her legs, which are the most beautiful legs I've ever seen. I walked out the front door and delayed my walk to the subway by stopping to speak to the super (New York for superintendent of the building).

She came out of the building and started toward the subway. I caught up to her and asked if she was going to the subway. I told her I'd walk to the subway with her. We got on the downtown train and had a great conversation. I got off at Wall Street and was in love. We married 3 months later on March 1st 1969, in Sarasota, Florida. Nancy had a wonderful family, which was a huge bonus for me. I not only had a wonderful wife who I loved passionately, but I had a great family too. Nancy and I both worked in White Plains, N.Y. where Nana had moved into my Uncle Mike's nursing home. Nana and Nancy became fond of each other. Nana loved Nancy and her folks too. These were the best years of my life. Each night I came home from work, Nancy would be resting upstairs and she would always say, "Stevie wonder boy, your bunny rabbit is waiting for you." I would run upstairs just like it was our first date.

Shortly after we returned from our honeymoon we received some documents from my father-in-law, J.T. Hale. The documents contained a cash value insurance policy, a post card, and a school paper. The post card was a picture of a Chinese Restaurant in China Town. For our first date we watched the 1969 Super Bowl when the Jets upset the Colts.

The morning of the game I decided to call Nancy to ask if she wanted to watch it. When she said yes I told her that I would come up to her apartment. She then explained her TV had been stolen. A burglar had also stolen my TV while he had hit 5 apartments in our building. Therefore I decided to call a friend who lived close by to ask if he wanted company to watch the game. That led us to my friend's apartment to watch the game and after the game he suggested a ride to China Town for dinner at his favorite restaurant. The post card was a picture of the same Chinese Restaurant that we enjoyed during our first dinner and date. Coincidentally the post card had been sent by Nancy when she had visited New York City on a school trip about 10 years earlier. Why her dad had kept only this post card and no other post cards in his lock box during all these years I believe was divine intervention. I make this assessment because it was coupled with one additional coincidence.

Keep in mind that if the burglar hadn't stolen each TV, hers and mine, we would not have gone to my friend's home to watch the game and never had dinner at the special Chinese restaurant, The Canton House. These circumstances make destiny unquestionable.

We had taken our honeymoon on a ship called the Homeric. The school paper J.T. had kept in his lock box with the insurance policy and the postcard had a list of words all beginning with letter h. The first word on the page was Homeric. Homeric was the only proper noun on the list of words. This paper was written when Nancy was in grammar school probably in the third grade. I will always believe that these were signs of destiny. But by the same token, if god almighty destined our union in 1969, I must also wonder why it only lasted until 1973.

This past year I began to study the Bible with Bible scholars. I finally recognized the reason God dissolved our divine marriage. I had failed to thank God for his blessing. Even though my in-laws attended a Christian Church in Mayfield, KY, Nancy and I never worshipped God or prayed to God. Although we were never atheists we used to kid by claiming that we were upstanding atheists.

Charlotte decided to have a bridal shower for Nancy soon after our marriage. Charlotte also decided to not invite Nancy's mom, Sarah, to the shower. When I heard that Sarah had not been invited, I asked Charlotte to invite her. She refused; claiming it would cost Sarah too much money to travel from Kentucky to Stratford. I pleaded with Charlotte to let Sarah decide if she wanted to spend the money for the trip or not. It was another nasty act by Charlotte to cause bad feelings. Nobody ever said another word about it, it was so embarrassing.

In 1970, Nancy and I moved to Memphis, Tennessee to be closer to the Hales and had many wonderful visits to Mayfield, Kentucky. I loved going there more than Nancy did because I got to hang out with J.T. We both enjoyed golf and the stock market, and he was the neatest guy I ever met. Nancy's Mom Sarah was a great person too. Her brother Ted was a golf pro who had won the Kentucky Amateur Championship, went to the University of Houston on a golf scholarship, a terrific person married to a beautiful Kentucky filly.

In 1977, I moved back to Connecticut and worked for Smith Barney until I quit the brokerage business. It was November 1979, when I got hired by Echlin to create and manage the risk management of copper, silver, and interest rate costs. At this point I tried to renew my family ties. I would visit Dad and when he left and returned to his ship I would drive him to the pier and pick him up at the pier. I enjoyed visiting the ship and I've always had fun listening to Dad's stories about his merchant marine adventures. I was glad for him that it took him away from Charlotte's relentless berating.

In the early 1980's I convened a meeting with Andrea and Mike to discuss providing funds for dad's retirement. After that meeting it appeared that they had no interest in this problem. So I went to dad and explained that he needed to begin saving money to supplement his pension and social security. Dad's merchant marine pension was only $250 per month because he quit going to sea for more than 20 years after the war when he owned the laundry and worked as a salesman. Even though Charlotte made money as a legal secretary and dad earned a good living sailing as a second assistant engineer, they saved nothing.

The plan was to open an account to deposit money after each voyage. I was going to manage the investments in that account. When I saw he had opened a joint account with Charlotte I refused to be involved unless he closed that account and opened an account just for himself. During the next three years dad saved about $20,000. By 1984 my management of these funds increased the account value to $106,000.

At the end of 1983, my girl friend Candy Farricielli and I decided to visit friends in Cairo. Candy's daughters were left with Candy's parents and their father for the holidays. Our dog a beautiful Springer Spaniel I named Brophy (after Arnold Brophy who rented a room in Nana's house) was left with Dad.

Brophy worked on the Staten Island Ferry piers. He had been an old hobo who traveled the rails of America and told me many fascinating stories while we both lived at Nana's.

When Candy and I returned from Cairo it was late at night and we had been traveling all day. We first stopped to pick up Brophy and learned that Josephine, Candy's Mom had called my parents to explain that our home had been destroyed because the pipes had broken in a freeze and water had ruined the house. We decided that I would drive Candy to stay at her parents and to be with the kids. I returned to spend the night at my parents.

When I returned to my parents' home, Charlotte said, "When are you leaving?" I looked at Dad who stood there saying nothing. I'm thinking, hey your account is now worth $106,000; you have nothing to say? So I said I'm leaving now. I took my dog and went to my brother Mike's house to sleep on the couch for the night. I was a millionaire and I should have just gone to a hotel.

My feelings were hurt again. Charlotte had done her thing again and Dad had done his thing again. The next day I found a furnished apartment in a house in Shelton. I wanted to stay away from my own family because they caused me too much grief for too long.

I had decided to break up with Candy before our trip to Cairo and hoped maybe a fun trip would change that plan but it didn't. I was very angry with dad and my personal life was now poor. I had plenty of money and was not enjoying it. I decided to liquidate all my investment positions and hold cash. I did the same thing for dad and never made another transaction in his account.

While all this was going on, I had a friendly relationship with Andrea and Irv. That is I was always invited to their home for holiday dinners. Apparently to me we had a congenial relationship. We never socialized outside of their home except for one time when they came to spend the day on my boat in 1983. But we had a peaceful, pleasant relationship. I never had any disagreement with them about anything. But then in 1986, I was told by Charlotte to never visit Andrea without an invitation. I never got another invitation.

In 1987, I moved into a house with my brother Mike who had just gotten divorced. Mike sometimes would visit Andrea but nothing was ever discussed about that. Finally I invited Andrea to visit me at the house I shared with Mike. We discussed things including Charlotte. This conversation probably lasted less than 15 minutes before Andrea began to cry and left. Andrea didn't want to hear the truth about her mother.

This was the last time I saw Andrea. In the mean time, one day Mike left a letter he received from Charlotte advising him to kick me out of the house. At that time I had been approved by RICOH for a dealership and I was getting my dealership business off the ground. By the fall of 1987 I was also working on my problem against COMEX and Mike was my partner in the account with the 4 copper contracts. I also had puts on Texas Instruments, which I sold at a nice profit when the stock market crashed on October 19th. The account at AG Edwards had more than a $12,000 profit on the day after the crash, which turned into a loss because COMEX widened the backwardation copper spreads by rigging those spreads.

Mike was working for Norden, a division of United Technology, which was closing Norden, and Mike got laid off. By this time I had the RICOH dealership doing well so I hired Mike. I was selling a phone switch which needed to be installed to the phone lines, to allow the RICOH fax machines to function without a separate, dedicated phone line. Mike would make the installations and I hoped he would sell some equipment too. After each installation Mike made I was called because the product failed to work. He needed to return to fix each installation. I suggested for him to call the manufacturer to learn how to make the installation properly the first time, but he never got one right until he returned to fix his mistake. It seemed strange that each job got fouled up and that Mike was finished for the day.

Something was bothering him. Naturally he was not happy about the money lost in the copper account but he never made an issue about it. Then a very crazy thing happened. I can't remember what set Mike off, but we had some disagreement. He went into his room and I heard the slide of his automatic pistol cock. I was on the couch in my bare feet. I decided to get out of the house quickly because I thought Mike might shoot me. I took off with only pocket change and bare feet. I began walking down the street and decided to walk to the nearest phone. It was a fair distance in bare feet to the closest shopping center where I could find a phone. Coincidentally I passed Irv's parents in the shopping center and I said hello, feeling weird because I looked strange walking in bare feet. I didn't want to tell them that Mike might have been on the verge of shooting me, which made my bare feet more understandable, so I passed them by quickly and found a phone.

I called my old friend, John DelVecchio to ask him to drive to the store to pick me up and take me back to his house. John came to help me and I explained the problem to him. After a few hours I called Mike to ask him if he was okay and could I return home safely, which I did. This story is going to reemerge later in this chapter which is the reason I included it now.

Mike knew that I was pressing the government as hard as I could to recover his money. People ask me all the time, how much money did you lose? The amount of money I lost was completely irrelevant to me. What mattered was that this simple, obvious crime was taking place, which generated more than $9,000,000,000 annually, while law enforcement knew it. I really wanted to get Mike's money back and I kept telling him that I would. I told him that because I believed it.

If I made the money back because of this book I would have gladly returned his lost money. But now I wouldn't give Mike a dime even if this book made me $10,000,000 because of what he did later in this story.

On October 1, 1989, I sold my business in Fairfield, Ct. and moved back to Memphis, TN. This was a birthday present to myself. I had a new mission and I completely dropped the COMEX crusade.

In September of 1993, I returned to NYC to resume my COMEX mission, which focused on writing this book. I moved to Auntie's apartment in Manhattan for a few months before finding my apartment in Brooklyn. While I lived with Auntie she would tell me that Andrea didn't want anything to do with me. On Thanksgiving Auntie was invited to Andrea's and I was invited not to come. The next Thanksgiving, 1994, right before I got arrested, I called Andrea for the first time in 8 years and tried to talk to her. I let her know that she hurt my feelings and I wondered why she was so angry. She refused to tell me.

When I got locked up in the Bridgeport jail I asked John DelVecchio to contact Andrea to ask her to visit me. She told John that she wouldn't and then sent him a card with $100 for him. I read the card. John didn't ask her for money and neither did I. So why did she send him $100? For the entire time I was in prison my only relative who stayed in touch with me was Auntie, and she helped me a lot. During these years I would ask Auntie to tell Mike and Andrea that I wanted to talk to them and I hoped they would visit me. That never happened and they would never explain why.

It wasn't until 1997 when I read my trial transcript that I learned that Juror #74, Kent Moller's wife Maggie worked for Cohen & Wolf. It was then that I learned my trial had been fixed by Judge Nevas and I suspected that Irv Kern might have been involved. I waited until the fall after my first JUDICIAL MISCONDUCT COMPLAINT had failed until I called Irv Kern to investigate his possible involvement.

I had never had any hostile or unfriendly words with Irv. When I called his office he was pleasant and so was I. I told him that I wanted to speak with Andrea and I wanted for him to explain that to her. As we spoke the only thing he mentioned about Andrea was that she was upset because of my poor relationship with my mother. I explained that my mother was dead and we could go on from this point in time without discussing that sore point.

Andrea agreed to speak with me. I made a number of long calls to Andrea and we talked openly about the jury issue. My purpose was to persuade Irv to contact Judge Nevas to explain that Kent Moller's role as the jury foreman in my trial was not a good thing for him, for his family, and for his status in the legal profession. It would be a problem and it needed to be fixed by the court. I believed that this mess had to reverse the court's judgment because Irv was involved by his firm's employment of Maggie Moller. I believed that the government wouldn't put me on trial again if the judgment was reversed. The case would be dismissed and my conviction would be eliminated.

When I spoke to Andrea about the competency issue, I was amazed that she had no doubt that Judge Nevas had legitimate reasons to stop me from trial for incompetence. This told me that the truth didn't matter to Andrea. I told her that she had known me all these years and she had to know that I was competent for trial. Of course she knew, but she could lie shamelessly. I asked her repeatedly to explain why she wanted to ostracize me, but she refused to give me any reason.

As time went by I had long conversations with Irv and Andrea. I became convinced that Irv was a willing participant with Judge Nevas in helping me get convicted and making sure I couldn't get a fair trial. I tried as hard as I could to give Irv an escape hatch even if he was guilty, but he refused to budge. Finally it was time to file my JUDICIAL MISCONDUCT COMPLAINT and include Irv as a participant.

I don't know how Charlotte did it but she made some powerful arrangements for me before she died. One day Auntie told me that Aunt Lil had asked about me and she didn't think that I wanted to speak with her. I told Auntie that I'd be happy to speak with her. I had no reason not to. I called Lil and had a lot of laughs. We talked about the old days on Staten Island. When Lil brought up my guilt as a criminal, I told her that I wanted her to know that there were many circumstances she didn't know about. My cousin Richard is a lawyer too and a retired Air Force Colonel. I told Lil that I wanted to send information to Richard and I wanted to talk to him too. Lil kept telling me that Richard was very busy and he traveled. Richard is retired, how busy could he be now. Even though he worked, I thought he could fit in a conversation with his cousin.

Then I suggested to Aunt Lil that I call Susan, Richard's sister. This was agreed and I called. After Susan and I spoke I then sent documents to her to forward to Richard. I wanted to expose Irv and Andrea to my family. I had been much closer to my cousins than Andrea had ever been. Andrea had always been distant to Richard because Charlotte hated Richard too. I began having long conversations with Susan and finally Susan said, could I ask you something? I said sure, ask me anything, I have nothing to hide.

Susan asked me if it was true that I had held a gun to my brother Mike's head. I couldn't believe it; my sister Andrea had turned the story upside down and backwards. I said listen, "Not only didn't I hold a gun to Mike's head, but I was forced to run out of the house when I heard Mike cock his automatic. Please call my friend John DelVecchio because he can confirm the truth." I wanted Susan to call right away so I couldn't call John and tell him to lie to Susan. I begged her to call him.

I waited and then I called John to learn if Susan had called him. She didn't. Since then they recanted that lie to me. Even though Susan learned that Andrea had ruined her own credibility by cooking up this lie about me, Susan began to make insulting statements to me. She decided to end our long friendship and retain her minimal friendship with Andrea.

These conversations got me stirred up to retaliate against Irv Kern and Andrea. I wanted even more to expose him and to try to correct his reputation for the person he really is. I see my sister Andrea as being a dupe by Charlotte and then by her husband. They are not proud of what he has done and their denial of his decisions are based on statements of nonsense. Irv's denial of the jury rigging incident includes his question which asks if Judge Nevas and Bob Appleton would do something like rig my jury. He infers that Judge Nevas and Bob Appleton are men of integrity who would never use such an extreme criminal act to rig a jury. All of the coincidences, which put Kent Moller onto my jury and elected him jury foreman were innocent. You have read about the series of incidents controlled by Judge Nevas. Do you judge this person to be a man of integrity?

Federal judges are invincible and it can be very dangerous to try to expose any federal judge. I have learned that powerful organizations always try to protect any individual of their group because they naturally believe that tarnishing one of them in turn tarnishes all members of their group. I have written this book intending to tarnish all 22 judges who have made decisions in my case. If Irv Kern gets tarnished too, that will be fine with me.

I believe it is logical for a group to punish severely any member of their group who causes them embarrassment, but life does not work logically. A great example of this irrational behavior are the sex scandals which have exposed the Catholic Church. Instead of throwing the priests out of the Church and wanting them prosecuted for their crimes, the highest authorities of the Church deliberately have done the opposite. Now they have been exposed for who they are. I can't think of a better example to explain the decisions made by the twenty appellate judges in my case. If I just made all the Catholics angry at me too, its not a secret revelation.

I am not against Catholic people but the Pope and the Cardinals who decided to cover up the child molester priests have now been exposed and it shows that the human inclination by the rulers of society is irrational. It is contrary to law and to common sense. It would have been rational for the Cardinals to contact law enforcement to prosecute the priests rather than to hide and protect them.

In September 1999, I decided to try to expose Irv Kern to the top partners of Cohen & Wolf and to the legal community in Bridgeport, CT. I wrote the following letter to begin my campaign.

September 9, 1999
Mr. Stuart A. Epstein
Attorney At Law
Cohen & Wolf, PC

1115 Broad Street
Bridgeport, CT 06604
Dear Mr. Epstein:

As you may or may not know, I am the brother of Andrea Kern. I was put on trial in the federal district court, by U.S.D.J. Alan H. Nevas. Your employee, Ms. Maggie Moller's husband, Kent Moller (Juror #74) became the jury foreman for my case.

I would like to learn if you are aware of this impropriety involving your law partner, Mr. Kern and your employee, Ms. Moller?

A series of events, as follows, conclusively prove that Mr. Kern violated my right to a fair trial by his criminal activity to tamper with Mr. Moller's participation on my jury. The potential injury to your firm's reputation by Mr. Kern's involvement in this criminal act should influence your decision to act appropriately after you investigate the facts contained in the record.

1)   Some time around 1986, I was told not to contact the Kern family. Respecting this admonition, I have had no contact with Mr. Kern until after I read the transcript of the voir dire for my trial sometime in 1997. The voir dire was held on 9/4/96.

2)   A separate defendant in a different case, his attorney, and the AUSA on his case were seated by the Court at my defense table by Judge Nevas for the entire time during my voir dire They were instructed by the Court to negotiate a plea agreement. As you can imagine, their negotiation created a distraction, which impaired my ability to hear some of what the jury pool was saying.

3)   I asked my defense counsel repeatedly to request the Court to seat this party elsewhere. My defense counsel refused to act on my behalf. At times, this party was speaking so loudly that the Court told them to be more quiet. These remarks by the Court are contained in the official Court record.

4)   U.S.D.J. Nevas, A.U.S.A. Appleton, and my counsel Richard Reeve all know that Irv Kern is a partner of Cohen & Wolf, that he is my brother in law, and that we have a hostile family relationship going back to 1986.

5)   My jury only deliberated for about 25 minutes before they reached a verdict in this case which presented many exhibits, conflicting and erratic testimony by witnesses which verified the defense, and chose Kent Moller as jury foreman. At the moment that the Marshal announced a verdict was reached, counsel was talking to me in the court lock up. Mr. Reeve smiled at me and said, "You're guilty." After I completed my investigation into this matter, Reeve's smile and comment indicated that he knew that the verdict had to be guilty because he knew that Moller guaranteed one guilty verdict.

6)   The government had gone to unusual lengths to prevent me from my right to trial. Prior to my eventual trial in September 1996, a trial had begun in April 1995 until the government aborted it after my jury had been selected. This event was captured in the official court record during the government's hearing on its motion, April 13, 1995. During the following 17 months the Court falsely claimed I was incompetent for trial. This false claim was not used because the Court believed a jury would fail to deliberate anything and then find me guilty in 25 minutes.

I have carefully analyzed the pattern of events and the facts contained in the official record. I wondered whether or not Irving Kern had joined the conspiracy, or whether Kent Moller had been mislead by the government without Irv's knowledge. I hoped the latter would be the truth because I suspected that it would be to my advantage if Irv's objective would be to confront the Court to remove him from this foul play.

Irv had the power to reverse my judgment on the basis that Kent Moller had a financial interest in the verdict because he believed that his wife might benefit if Irv Kern wanted to help Judge Nevas convict Kern's brother in law.

To investigate this matter, seeking the truth, I made a series of calls to both Irv and Andrea to hear what they had to say. They both agreed that they were satisfied with my conviction regardless of the circumstance, which included Cohen & Wolf employee Maggie Moller, her husband Kent, and Irv.

I will call your office shortly to learn if you decide to investigate your law partner, Irv Kern, and his decisions to involve your firm for further unethical behavior. I hope you intend to respond in a dignified, professional manner to protect the reputation of Cohen & Wolf.

Yours truly,

Stephen A. Miller

Here is the response I received:

COHEN AND WOLF, P.C.

ATTORNEYS AT LAW

September 14, 1999

Mr. Stephen A. Miller

Reg. No. 12367-074

P.O. Box 8000

Bradford, PA 16701-0900

Dear Mr. Miller

Your letter of September 9, 1999 addressed to Stuart A. Epstein has been turned over to me for response, since Mr. Epstein is no longer associated with our firm.

I have reviewed with Mr. Kern the various allegations in your letter. As a result of that review, I am convinced that Mr. Kern is totally without responsibility or liability for the situation in which you find yourself.

Very truly yours,

Austin K. Wolf

Then after contacting family members and lawyers in Bridgeport which kept getting back to Irv and Andrea, I received this letter from Irv on a blank piece of paper with his signature on it.

June 19, 2000

Dear Steve:

For the record, I am going to tell you one more time and for the last time, I did not know until you advised me that Kent Moller was a member of your jury. I have never discussed your case with Kent Moller. I have never discussed your case with his wife. I have never discussed your case with Judge Nevas. Why you think that I did or that for some reason, I tried to set you up, I don't know. But, it just isn't true. You can obviously believe what you want, and I can't change that. But the truth is what it is, and I have no problem standing by the truth.

Irv

It is what Irv Kern did not say that is most important. It is most likely that Mr. Wolf preferred not to know what happened concerning the problem that I presented. His glib brush-off would be expedient unless this problem surfaced to many of the Cohen & Wolf clients who might wonder how the close connection to Judge Nevas might help or hurt them in future litigation.

June 26, 2000

Mr. Austin K. Wolf

Senior Partner

Cohen & Wolf, P.C.

1115 Broad Street

Bridgeport, CT 06604

Dear Mr. Wolf:

Your decision to not question your employee Ms. Maggie Moller, concerning her knowledge of her husband's position as the jury foreman in my criminal trial in the federal court on 9/4/96, 9/11, 9/12. And 9/13, is extremely meaningful in light of the following facts:

1)   Maggie Moller has a financial interest in my case because she receives a salary paid by Cohen & Wolf, and her husband was the jury foreman.

2)   Irv's secretary, Nancy, also told me that she did not know that I was Irv's brother in law until I asked her in 1998. Do you have phantom brother in laws too, Mr. Wolf?

3)   The strategy by Judge Nevas to place 3 people facing me at my

defense table to discuss their plea agreement (an obvious distraction), while I was simultaneously forced to choose a <u>fair and impartial jury</u>, resulted in the seating of Kent Moller as the jury foreman.

<u>Would the litigators of Cohen & Wolf</u> permit a continuous distraction placed at their table throughout the entire jury selection process?

Would any criminal prosecutor fail to oppose a juror who had a financial interest to the defendant he (or she) was prosecuting and a business relationship with the defendant's brother in law?

Your glib denial in the wake of these and other points I have raised is more convincing that Irv Kern has a lot to hide. Your decision to dismiss the questions and facts I have posed instead of an ethical search for the truth indicates your denial is flawed.

Yours truly,
Stephen A. Miller

***

I was born into a family of intelligent and educated people. I have no poor relatives. They all live in nice homes and have the financial means to support a comfortable life style. Many families quarrel and have disagreements amongst themselves too. But I know what I would have done if I had been Irv Kern and my sister Andrea.

People naturally love to have close ties with their families, I know I do. When I was still excluded in 1993 and '94, my feelings were hurt and I called to try to speak with Andrea on the Thanksgiving morning of 1994. If I had been in her position and believed I was correct for behaving in this manner, I would have stated my reason. She refused to do that.

I can speculate what might be on Andrea's mind but I'm not a mind reader. I now know that Andrea is under psychiatric care because she is deeply disturbed. I suspect that she knows that the jury was rigged and it bothers her. If her therapy is designed to block out the truth about the jury-rigging incident or that the incident will never surface, that therapy might never work.

Not inviting a brother to your home is a sign of problems. Andrea and Irv refuse to admit that any problem ever existed. The jury issue is on a different level and, it is a significant part of this story. Jury rigging by a Federal Judge may be unique. If I chose to exclude the background information about my family history that was critical for my hypothesis the reader would be correct to assume that I am paranoid and delusional.

The infamous Joel Steinberg child abuse case is a completely different league than the mild (by comparison) child abuse I experienced. There was an unhappy union formed when my Dad married my mother.

Auntie came to my rescue and I am very grateful for her help throughout the past 10 years of my life. She is pretty old now and her health is deteriorating. I wish there was something I could do to help her and make her life better. But she is very content living on the upper east side of Manhattan where she goes to the senior center to visit her friends.

I am content to be in contact with some of my old friends from school in Stratford and other friends I made in life. One great friend in particular is Dave Korponai. Dave was a terrific athlete and is a tremendous person. He lives in Kiev, Ukraine while he works for U.S. Aid but he makes his home in La Paz. We keep in contact on the internet where he reviews my work and helps me to stay on point.

Larry Lanni is a wonderful person I met when I attended the University of Bridgeport. Larry was a tremendous football player and the captain of our team. From that time in 1961, we have enjoyed some uniquely enjoyable and humorous experiences. Larry is a person of great integrity, also from a wonderful family that warmly welcomed me in their home in Port Chester, NY.

In September 2004, I entered a Christian mission called the Bridgeport Rescue Mission. There I studied the Bible under Bible scholars and learned the truth about our savior Jesus Christ. One of my school friends and a Deacon in the Catholic Church, Frank Masso learned of my being born again and contacted me. This was an act of true Christian fellowship and I am grateful to Frank and his lovely wife Sandy for their hospitality. I joined a Pentacostal Church pastured by Vincent Provenzano, a wonderful pastor.

I had been a Deist before I became educated about God's word. I learned that I enjoy the fruits of the Holy Spirit as a born again Christian.

There have been a lot of Italian names of people in this story. There are hundreds more Italians who I know that are not in this story. I have always been fascinated and admire the Italian culture, Italian food, the Italian language, the Italian sense of humor, the brilliant society, products, architecture and government of Italy. I have been to Italy three times and I have considered retiring in Italy. If I make enough money on this book or in some other way I probably would retire in Italy.

When I was a kid I spent a lot of time at John DelVecchio's home, my girl friend Diane Crocco's home, and Larry Lanni's home. I knew their parents very well and enjoyed the hospitality in their homes. I wished I had an Italian mother too.

If I left America I would miss many things about our country but watching America changing for the worse is one reason I would consider leaving most of what I love about life here in America. At some point in time I suppose Americans might wake up to the erosion of our standard of living. We just watch the elite continue to bribe our government that continues to shift the wealth of the middle class to the super rich. Our pension funds protected by the ERISA laws have been raided and wrecked in other ways. The latest news now in May 2005 is that pensioners who had worked for United Airlines will not receive payments from its pension fund.

I have written about reality and my perception of reality. Its not a popular viewpoint.

EPILOGUE

2004, the ex-Secretary of the Treasury, Paul O'Neill who worked for President George W. Bush at the beginning of Bush's term that began in January 2001, wrote a book that many people felt betrayed Bush. This book went quickly to the #1 Best Seller on the New York Times Best Seller List. On the weekend before O'Neill's book went on sale he appeared on 60 Minutes.

The primary point I want to make is that the American culture has reacted in a very negative way to what O'Neill has done. In my perspective O'Neill has exposed Bush for betraying America and its citizens. O'Neill is a super straight shooter. He is educated, has had a very successful career as the CEO for Alcoa and yet he is being discredited. He is being ridiculed for having sour grapes because Bush fired him.

More books are being published by credible writers such as Bob Woodward who have claimed that our government has been deceitful. We all can observe the manner in which the media reports these incidents, and by listening to the call-ins on C-Span we can observe the disparity of citizens' points of view.

The war on Iraq has been a terrible mistake. In many ways it is the repeat of the war on Viet Nam. Both wars were started solely to profiteer. JFK got into the way of the profiteers from Texas that developed into the most spectacular conspiracy ever. The political issues to stop a Communist takeover in Viet Nam, and now to stop terrorism in Iraq are similar too; fruitless nonsense.

There are huge risks for Americans to keep believing that we are always right. No one is always right. I learned a lot by this experience.

I used my time in prison to read informative books that I feel gave me a better insight than I would have ever gained if I hadn't gone to prison. The future will tell if I will capitalize on my thoughts, ideas, and knowledge. I am more ready to rebuild my life. There is little time left for me now, so there is more urgency to work as hard as possible.

INDEX

[276] Stephen A. Miller

[278] Stephen A. Miller

www.ingramcontent.com/pod-product-compliance
Lightning Source LLC
Chambersburg PA
CBHW071401170526
45165CB00001B/133